T0072550

Also by James W. Finegan

Blasted Heaths and Blessed Greens:
A Golfer's Pilgrimage to the Courses of Scotland

Emerald Fairways and Foam-Flecked Seas:
A Golfer's Pilgrimage to the Courses of Ireland

A Centennial Tribute to Golf in Philadelphia:
The Champions and the Championships,
The Clubs and the Courses

Pine Valley Golf Club:
A Unique Haven of the Game

All Courses Great _and_ Small

A Golfer's Pilgrimage
to England and Wales

James W. Finegan

SIMON & SCHUSTER
New York London Toronto Sydney Singapore

SIMON & SCHUSTER
Rockefeller Center
1230 Avenue of the Americas
New York, NY 10020

SIMON & SCHUSTER and colophon are registered
trademarks of Simon & Schuster, Inc.

For information about special discounts for bulk purchases,
please contact Simon & Schuster Special Sales:
1-800-456-6798 or business@simonandschuster.com

Designed by Bonni Leon-Berman
Maps by Amy Hill

Manufactured in the United States of America

2   4   6   8   10   9   7   5   3   1

Library of Congress Cataloging-in-Publication Data
Finegan, James W.
All courses great and small : a golfer's pilgrimage to England and Wales / James Finegan.
p.   cm.
1. Golf courses—England—Guidebooks. 2. Golf Courses—Wales—Guidebooks.
3. England—Guidebooks. 4. Wales—Guidebooks. I. Title.
GV984.F54 2003
796.352'06'842—dc21   2002044795
ISBN 978-1-4165-6797-4

For Jim, John, and Megwin,
whose affection for the game is, mercifully,
a little less obsessive than their father's

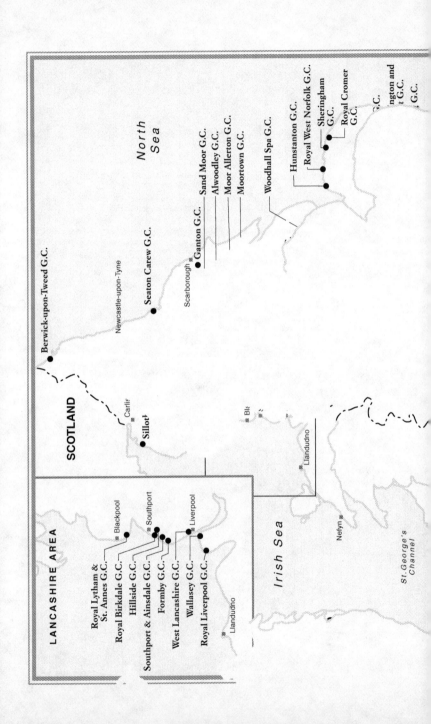

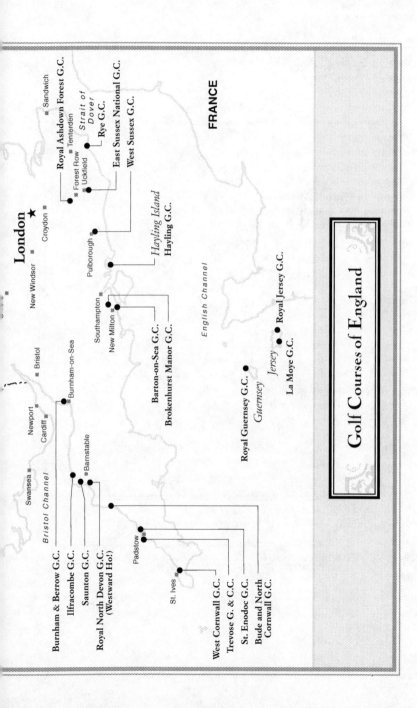

Golf Courses of England

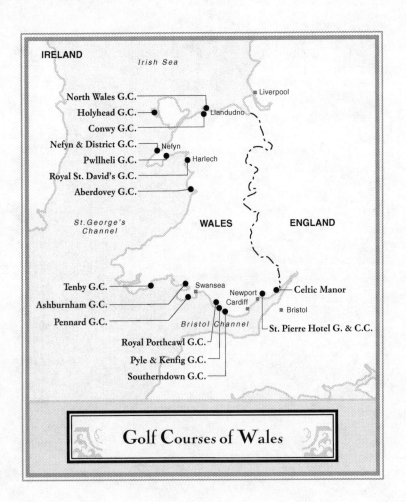

IRELAND

Irish Sea

North Wales G.C.
Holyhead G.C.
Conwy G.C.
Llandudno

Liverpool

Nefyn & District G.C.
Nefyn
Pwllheli G.C.
Royal St. David's G.C.
Harlech
Aberdovey G.C.

St. George's Channel

WALES

ENGLAND

Tenby G.C.
Swansea
Ashburnham G.C.
Newport
Cardiff
Celtic Manor
Pennard G.C.
Bristol
Bristol Channel
St. Pierre Hotel G. & C.C.
Royal Porthcawl G.C.
Pyle & Kenfig G.C.
Southerndown G.C.

Golf Courses of Wales

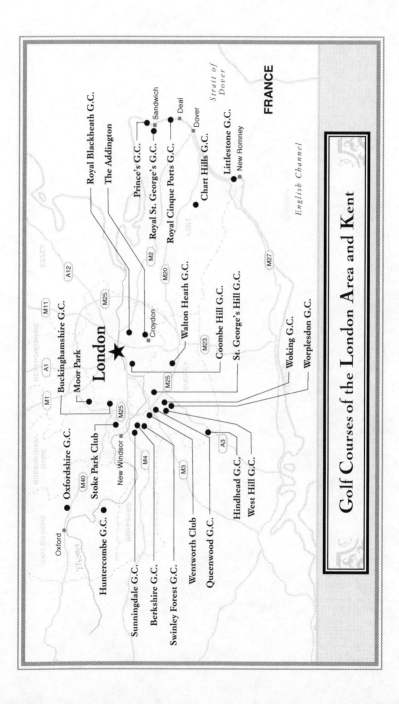

Golf Courses of the London Area and Kent

Royal Blackheath G.C.

The Addington

Prince's G.C.

Royal St. George's G.C.

Royal Cinque Ports G.C.

Chart Hills G.C.

Littlestone G.C.

Sandwich

Deal

Dover

New Romney

FRANCE

Strait of Dover

English Channel

Buckinghamshire G.C.

Moor Park

London

Croydon

Walton Heath G.C.

Coombe Hill G.C.

St. George's Hill G.C.

Woking G.C.

Worplesdon G.C.

Oxfordshire G.C.

Huntercombe G.C.

Stoke Park Club

New Windsor

Sunningdale G.C.

Berkshire G.C.

Swinley Forest G.C.

Wentworth Club

Queenwood G.C.

Hindhead G.C.

West Hill G.C.

Oxford

ESSEX

KENT

SURREY

BERKSHIRE

BUCKINGHAMSHIRE

M1

M11

M25

M2

M20

M23

M25

M27

M40

M4

M3

A1

A12

A3

CONTENTS

INTRODUCTION   1

ONE: **In the Dunelands of Northern England**   9
Berwick-upon-Tweed (Goswick) G.C. ·
Seaton Carew G.C. · Seascale G.C. ·
Silloth-on-Solway G.C.

TWO: **Yorkshire: Alister Mackenzie, Front and Center**   22
Alwoodley G.C. · Moortown G.C. · Sand Moor G.C. ·
Moor Allerton G.C. · Ganton G.C.

THREE: **Robin Hood, a Ryder Cup, and Inland Glory**   35
Lindrick G.C. · Notts G.C. (Hollinwell) · Woodhall Spa G.C.

FOUR: **Links, Clifftop, Heathland, Parkland:**
An East Anglian Smorgasbord   45
Hunstanton G.C. · Royal West Norfolk G.C. (Brancaster) ·
Sheringham G.C. · Royal Cromer G.C. · Thetford G.C. ·
Royal Worlington and New Market G.C. · Gog Magog G.C.

FIVE: **Old and New—North and West of London**   60
Huntercombe G.C. · Stoke Park Club (Stoke Poges) ·
Moor Park · Buckinghamshire G.C. · Oxfordshire G.C.

SIX: **Harry Colt in Berkshire and Surrey**   73
Sunningdale G.C. · Berkshire G.C. · Wentworth Club ·
Swinley Forest G.C. · Queenwood G.C.

Contents

SEVEN: **Ten More London Courses—
Three of Them Great**   **94**
*Walton Heath G.C. · Woking G.C. · West Hill G.C. ·
Worplesdon G.C. · Coombe Hill G.C. · Hindhead G.C. ·
Royal Blackheath G.C. · The Addington · St. George's Hill G.C.*

EIGHT: **Kent and England's Greatest Course**   **116**
*Chart Hills G.C. · Littlestone G.C. · Royal Cinque Ports G.C.
(Deal) · Prince's G.C. · Royal St. George's G.C. (Sandwich)*

NINE: **The Channel Islands**   **136**
*La Moye G.C. · Royal Jersey G.C. ·
Royal Guernsey G.C. (L'Ancresse)*

TEN: **Is Rye the Toughest Course in England?**   **147**
*Royal Ashdown Forest G.C. · West Sussex G.C. (Pulborough) ·
East Sussex National G.C. · Rye G.C.*

ELEVEN: **Hampshire: An Unknown Links
and a Well-Known Hotel**   **161**
*Hayling G.C. · Barton-on-Sea G.C. ·
Brokenhurst Manor G.C.*

TWELVE: **Cornwall, Starring the One and
Only St. Enodoc Links**   **169**
*Trevose G. & C.C. · West Cornwall G.C. ·
Bude and North Cornwall G.C. · St. Enodoc G.C.*

THIRTEEN: **Turning Back the Clock at Westward Ho!**   **179**
*Saunton G.C. · Royal North Devon G.C. (Westward Ho!) ·
Ilfracombe G.C. · Burnham & Berrow G.C.*

Contents

FOURTEEN: **Three Courses at The Belfry,
Plus Six You've Never Heard of**   193
*The Belfry · Little Aston G.C. · Beau Desert G.C. ·
Stapleford Park G.C. · Woburn G. & C.C.*

FIFTEEN: **Lancashire: Three Royals,
Five Uncommon Commoners**   208
*Royal Lytham & St. Annes G.C. · Royal Birkdale G.C. ·
Royal Liverpool G.C. (Hoylake) · Wallasey G.C. ·
West Lancashire G.C. · Formby G.C. · Hillside G.C. ·
Southport & Ainsdale G.C.*

SIXTEEN: **North Wales: Seven at the Sea**   230
*North Wales G.C. · Conwy G.C. · Holyhead G.C. ·
Nefyn & District G.C. · Pwllheli G.C. · Royal St. David's G.C.
(Harlech) · Aberdovey G.C.*

SEVENTEEN: **South Wales: One of the World's
Great Golf Destinations**   247
*Celtic Manor · St. Pierre Hotel G. & C.C. ·
Royal Porthcawl G.C. · Pyle & Kenfig G.C. ·
Southerndown G.C. · Ashburnham G.C. · Tenby G.C. ·
Pennard G.C.*

APPENDIX A   273

APPENDIX B   283

INTRODUCTION

IT IS SEVEN YEARS since the publication of my books on Scotland and Ireland, in 1996. During that period I have from time to time considered writing a book on the courses of England and Wales. It would personally be quite satisfying to be able to point to a trilogy that covers the entire golfing world of Britain and Ireland. On the other hand, I had to admit that Americans have yet to demonstrate much enthusiasm for golf in England or Wales—nor, in truth, have they been encouraged to. Oh, they are aware of a trio of links courses where the Open Championship is played (Royal Birkdale, Royal Lytham & St. Annes, and Royal St. George's), as well as a trio of inland courses (Sunningdale, Wentworth, and The Belfry's Brabazon eighteen) where important competitions also pop up with some regularity. But having acknowledged this half-dozen, they might be at a loss to name three or four more. And that is regrettable. For the six just mentioned constitute only the proverbial tip of the iceberg.

Perhaps a few figures are in order. If you take the number of outstanding courses in Scotland (shrines plus the other worthies), some fifty-five to sixty, and add to it the number of outstanding courses in Ireland, about fifty, why, lo and behold, that total, 105 to 110, is very like the total of outstanding courses in England (ninety) and Wales (fifteen).

A few more figures serve to explain why this circumstance should not be surprising. Scotland has 5.2 million people and 550 golf courses. Ireland has 3.5 million people and 400 courses. But England and Wales, with *50 million people* (47 million in England), have more than 2,000 courses (1,900 in England). Is it any wonder, then, that there should be nearly a hundred outstanding venues in England alone? Indeed, the law of averages would see to it.

It should be noted that the game in England, though no less royal than that in Scotland, is considerably less ancient. The initial wave of interest here in golf occurred between 1880 and 1900. For the first 450 years of its existence, the game was confined solely to Scotland; only in the latter part of the nineteenth century did it invade England, Wales, Ireland, Canada, and the United States.

The Lure of Seaside Golf

Golf on true linksland, seaside and sea level, where the play along the rumpled ground is as critical as the play through the air, is a rather rare experience. Among the more than 32,000 golf courses on the planet, fewer than 160 of them are authentic links, the great majority of which are in the UK and Ireland. This book takes a look at forty-three links courses, thirty-one of them English, a dozen of them Welsh. They are laid out on the sand-based soil that serves as the buffer between the sea and the fertile stretches at a remove from the salt water.

Over tens of thousands of years this linksland evolved as the sea receded, leaving behind sandy wastes that the winds fashioned into dunes, knolls, hollows, and gullies. Gradually grass, fertilized by the droppings of the gulls, began to grow in the hollows. Since nature did not endow the links with trees, encroaching limbs and claustrophobic foliage are not encountered. There is an enticing spaciousness, an exhilarating sense of openness and freedom about seaside courses that is rarely found in inland golf. The beauty here is severe, sometimes stark.

Mindful of the fact that the British Open is contested only on a true links, we will, of course, be looking closely at Royal Birkdale, Royal Lytham & St. Annes, Royal Liverpool, Royal St. George's, Royal Cinque Ports, and Prince's, the latter two having hosted this greatest of all championships more than seventy years ago. It was on these six links that many of the game's storied figures—Harry Vardon, J. H. Taylor, Bobby Jones, Walter Hagen, Gene Sarazen, Henry Cotton, Bobby Locke, Peter Thomson, Arnold Palmer, Gary Player, Lee Trevino, Tom Watson, and Seve Ballesteros—scored some of their most notable triumphs.

But I suspect that this book may be of more value—possibly even of more interest—when we play courses that readers may have heard about but have only a hazy notion of (Woodhall Spa and Ganton, for instance, or Walton Heath, Royal West Norfolk, and Rye). And maybe most intriguing of all are the truly unheralded gems, some of them just around the corner (The Addington is in suburban London), some of them in the shadow of renowned courses (Southport & Ainsdale is not ten minutes from Royal Birkdale), still others far off the beaten track (you have to take a plane or a boat to get to Royal Jersey, in the English Channel and just twenty miles off the coast of France).

But whether celebrated or unsung, they all (well, *almost* all—

there are a few courses here that I am not a fan of but that I think you might want to be acquainted with) promise a round of golf that could turn out, for you, to be at least thoroughly enjoyable and just possibly the golfing experience of a lifetime.

If you believe that man doth not live by golf alone (for some, a wholly untenable precept) and that hotels, dining, and sight-seeing also have to be first-class, I'm optimistic that you will value the information provided on these subjects. Some fifty different accommodations—everything from a restaurant with rooms such as The Seafood Restaurant, in Cornwall, to palatial Danesfield House, high above the Thames in Bucking-hamshire—are described. We dearly love that British/Irish insti-tution the country-house hotel, and I'm delighted to have the opportunity to bring to your attention a number of these gra-cious inns, among which are seventeenth-century Devonshire Arms, in the Yorkshire Dales, and nineteenth-century Horsted Place, an East Sussex estate where the Royal Family occasion-ally spent long weekends. I should mention that the cooking in places such as these, not to mention many of the less opulent inns we've patronized in England and Wales since I first started playing golf there in 1973, is of a consistently high standard. So much so, in fact, that we rarely find ourselves going out to a restaurant; we almost always dine right where we are spending the night. You'll hardly go wrong doing the same.

Some Practical Advice

This book is intended to be useful in three ways. First, the arm-chair traveler with an interest in knowing more about golf clubs and courses in England and Wales will enjoy it. In addition to touching on the British Opens and the Ryder Cup Matches contested at the courses covered here, I identify the course architects. They are golf's new royalty, its crown princes if you will; so in the instance of the most eminent and most prolific of them—James Braid, Harry Colt, Alister Mackenzie, Robert Trent Jones—I've offered a word or two about their background and achievements. Second, and rather more important, this book can serve as a planning guide for the player who wants to put together his or her own golf holiday itinerary. And lastly, it can be a traveling companion, portable enough to pop into a suitcase and have at hand for ready reference throughout your trip.

There are two appendices, one for golf clubs and courses, the other for hotels. In each instance, addresses, phone numbers, and fax numbers are listed. This information will be helpful for those who intend to make their own reservations for rooms and starting times.

From April into mid-November (since England is a bit milder than Scotland, the season is a bit longer), tee times can actually be more difficult to pin down than hotel rooms. This is particularly true in the case of the best-known courses. With so many clubs now employing starting times seven days a week, I suggest you make a phone call, generally to the pro shop, to learn whether the date and time you have in mind are available or if you should change your plans accordingly. You also have the opportunity in this conversation to find out the green fee, the deposit that may be required, the availability of caddies and/or carts (golf carts, which the Brits call "buggies," are becoming more common every day), and any restrictions on women's play.

James W. Finegan

The broad accessibility of English golf courses may come as a surprise to some Americans. After all, as readers of this book are well aware, it's simply not that way in this country. You don't just drop in at Augusta National or Pine Valley or Seminole because you've a mind to. Without a member at your side, you cannot play at these private clubs. Not so in England and Wales. With only a handful of exceptions (Oxfordshire, Rye, The London Club, Swinley Forest, Queenwood), clubs there welcome the visiting stranger. And this is as true of the royal clubs as of the "commoners," though in a number of instances neither open their doors on weekends to visitors.

The green fees paid by outsiders constitute a major source of club revenue, sometimes *the* major source. It is these tariffs, now steadily climbing, that make the members' dues so modest—rarely twenty-five percent of what Americans pay annually to belong to a golf or country club. As this book is published in 2003, green fees can range from £23 ($37) at, say, Holyhead, in Wales, to £215 ($333) at England's Wentworth Club. Clearly, there is a lot of room in between, but equally clearly, there are very few eye-popping bargains today.

To give you some idea of what you will pay for accommodations, let me say that a room for two in season and generally with full English breakfast, service and taxes included, can cost in 2003 anywhere from about £70 ($112) per night (the Dormy House at Royal Porthcawl) to £410 ($656) at Chewton Glen (dinner included here). Between these two extremes are hotels such as the Hoste Arms, £95 ($152); Saunton Sands, £125 ($200); and New Hall, £220 ($352).

One final note: At a few English and Welsh courses, visitors may be required to show a current handicap card or a letter of introduction with handicap confirmation from their club professional. Only rarely is a golfer asked to produce either, but it is prudent to have one or the other with you.

In Praise of the White Markers

For very like forty years I was what is generally considered a good club player. My handicap moved between 1 and 4, and I won five club championships and a couple of senior club championships. I was always a short hitter, and today my Sunday punch delivers a drive of no more than 200 yards, on the flat and in the calm. My handicap has escalated to 9 as I cling, however precariously, to a last vestige of single digitism. I play only on days that end in a "y." Surely George Bernard Shaw had someone like me in mind when he wrote, "To that man, age brought only golf instead of wisdom."

I mention these things so that you'll know whose hands you're in as you roam through England and Wales. With me, you play from the white tees. Too often, it seems, descriptions of golf holes find the author back on the blues, tackling a course that measures more than 7,000 yards and boasts six or seven two-shotters over 435 yards, plus a couple of par fives in the 590 neighborhood. I'm inclined to believe that many readers of this book will enjoy the round a lot more when they are swinging from the regular markers, where the course's overall length averages 6,300–6,400 yards. Besides, it is difficult for a visitor to get permission to use the back tees (often called the medal tees) in England and Wales; they are reserved for members in competitions.

James W. Finegan

The Simple Scheme of It

I've organized this book as though you and I had the luxury of carving three or four months out of our lives to play these one hundred and five courses one after another. Each chapter finds us traveling onward to a new territory, which may have only three courses or could have as many as eleven. We take them as they fall on the map, with little regard for their pedigree. In the end, we will have seen much of England and Wales, played their finest courses, learned something about the men who laid them out and about those who gained a measure of fame playing them, taken in the more noteworthy sights, stayed in attractive lodgings, and made the acquaintance of some interesting people.

Our grand tour commences in the north of England and concludes in the south of Wales. It's high time, you must be thinking, that we set out on this 2,000-mile pilgrimage.

—*James W. Finegan*
September 2002

CHAPTER ONE

In the Dunelands of Northern England

IN ALL THE ROUNDS I've played in Britain and Ireland—very like a thousand—the game at Goswick in the summer of 2001 marked the only time I'd ever had as my companion a man who had first been captain of the club (equivalent to club president here at home) and then, not too long after his term of office, a worker on the grounds crew. But the Berwick-upon-Tweed (Goswick) Golf Club is a very egalitarian institution, to say nothing of a warmly welcoming one, so perhaps I should not have been surprised.

The club, founded in 1889, is located about eight miles south of town in a remote spot on the seaward side of the A1, on the far northeastern coast of England. For the most part, the holes are laid out along the flanks of the sandhills. The classic linksland fairways are undulating, rumpled, even tumbling, the legacy of the receding seas over tens of thousands of years. A number of golfers of national and international repute had a hand in shaping the holes we play here today, including James Braid, the Scot who won the Open Championship five times at the beginning of the twentieth century; Frank Pennink, 1937 and 1938 English Amateur champion and a Walker Cupper; and very recently, English-born Dave Thomas, a four-time Ryder Cupper best known for designing, with Peter Alliss, The Belfry's Brabazon Course, site of four Ryder Cup Matches (Chapter 14).

The club secretary introduced me to Jim Manuel, whom he described as a longtime member, a past captain, and a single-digit handicapper who would be pleased to play with me. And off the two of us went on a pretty summer day, high cumulus clouds in a predominantly blue sky, with a mild breeze that would not prove destructive to my all-too-fragile golf swing.

The opening hole at Goswick, 388 yards long, aims toward the sea, with bunkers on the right of the tee-shot landing area, where the hole bends emphatically around a spinney of fir trees and climbs steeply to a sloping and sand-defended shelf of green in the dunes. The 2nd, a shortish par three over a deep, grassy chasm, is followed by a fine 404-yarder from a high tee in the sandhills. Then come a short par five (good birdie chance) and a superb 410-yarder that bends smoothly left as it rises into the prevailing wind. Bunkers right, left, and short render the dramatic bi-level green elusive.

On the tee of this exacting hole, Jim, a husky man in his mid-sixties with a good head of silver hair, directed my gaze deeper into the dunes, where a derelict old white-washed stone cottage squatted. "That's a fishermen's shiel," he said. "Been there as long as this course, maybe longer, maybe a lot longer. The fishermen would stay there overnight, to be close to their work when it was time to go out before dawn. The beach is just on the other side of that dune ridge."

A 6-handicapper, Jim had muscular forearms and, with a following breeze, would hit his 7-iron 170 yards. He clearly loved the game, playing five or six days a week, and he loved this links. At the par-four 7th he said to me as we stood in the fairway while he chose his iron, "Those trees beyond the green, they're Mediterranean pines. I brought the seedlings back from France about eight years ago and planted them."

Goswick measures 6,294 yards from the regular markers. Par is 72. On the inbound nine, both par fives are short (485 and 480 yards), and there are two short par fours, one of which, the 18th, 263 yards, has been driven more than once from its tee high in the dunes. Still, make no mistake about it, there is a lot of sport on the second half, particularly on a four-hole stretch beginning with the 12th. Testing and charming us are two comprehensively bunkered one-shotters, played from elevated tees on opposite sides of the central dune ridge; the 13th has lovely views out to sea, and the 15th commands the pleasant inland aspect with its pastures and croplands and low hills on the horizon. On both holes, the wind plays havoc with the shot. Equally appealing are two par fours, the 384-yard 14th, its green tucked around to the right in the dunes, and the quirky 12th, 325 yards. Here the second shot rises over an abrupt rough bank, then falls to a completely hidden green, just on the other side, that slopes away from the shot. A number of members have long thought it unfair, so a decision has been made to move the green back forty yards, out of the lee of the hill. It is doubtless fair now, and less endearing.

As we moved into the final holes, Jim explained that he had worked for more than thirty years on the local newspaper. "I was what we called a paste-up man. Then—this was about ten years ago—management decided to go to computer to put the paper together. I was made redundant. That was not long after my year here at Goswick as captain. When the greenkeeper was looking to add a man to his crew, I took the job and stayed on it for six years, working on the links."

I asked about his family. He hesitated, then said, "My wife died four years ago today. Lung cancer. And she wasn't a smoker. She had had a fine job—she was head of the Scottish Power office here in town—really a very good position. We had our son living with us. He was twenty-seven when she died. Nearly a year later, he moved out. He couldn't bear to stay in the house any longer because it's so filled with memories of his mother. He got a flat not half a mile away."

There was no self-pity in Jim's recital—not about being made redundant nor about his wife's death nor about his son's decision. I asked him whether his son was a golfer and this brought a smile to his face.

"He used to be, when he was a boy, and then he stopped playing—I don't remember why. But a couple of weeks ago—now mind you, he hadn't played in fourteen years—he decided to come out with me one evening. It was as though he'd never been away from the game. He's strong. He was hitting the ball enormous distances, thirty, forty, fifty yards beyond me off the tee. He made the course look easy. He finished with 78. I think there's a good chance he'll come back to the game now."

When we had holed out on the 18th and were heading toward the clubhouse, Jim took me on a slight detour, over to the 1st tee. It was bordered on the side nearest the clubhouse with a dazzling bed of impatiens—red, blue, pink, purple, gold, a starburst of color. "I'm the head gardener these days," he said, laughing as he added, "All right, the *only* gardener. I try to brighten things up around the clubhouse. Keeps me busy and I don't have to pay the annual subscription [£260: $380]. A few of us are talking about getting over to France for a week's golf this fall."

"Who knows?" I said. "You might even bring back some more seedlings."

"I might," he replied. "I might at that. But we don't want this links to start looking like a parkland course." Now we both laughed, then headed into the modest clubhouse of this democratic organization, where a man can go from captain to grounds crew in a matter of months and be no less highly regarded for all of that. Both roles are at the heart of the game. And at Goswick, it is the game that counts.

The town of Berwick-upon-Tweed can't be more than three miles from the Scotland border. An ancient seaport established where the Tweed River enters the North Sea, it was alternatively English and Scottish over the centuries and was finally surrendered to England in 1482. My wife, Harriet, and I spent the night at the Kings Arms, an eighteenth-century inn with comfortable but scarcely stylish guest rooms, two restaurants (one of them Italian), and a fetching walled garden.

We now head south on the A1 for nearly two hours, then turn left onto the A689 to Seaton Carew, at the mouth of the Tees River. Prior to reaching the club parking lot, we drive through two of the tawdriest blocks on the entire east coast of England: video arcades, bingo games, souvenir shops, pizza parlors, and amusement rides, all the accoutrements of a down-at-heels seaside holiday spot. And that's the good part. The links itself, while bounded on the east by the North Sea, is otherwise bordered by a nightmarish industrial wasteland whose chemical processing plants send flames perpetually skyward from menacing towers. Not to mention the sewage treatment facility, largely masked by a high hedge, that almost abuts the 18th green.

The links, however, triumphs over its surroundings, which prove to be the ignorable (if ignitable) backdrop for a superlative course.

The club was founded in 1874 by a transplanted Scot, Duncan McCraig, M.D., who judged the linksland along the Tees estuary to be, well, exactly what the doctor ordered. In 1925 Seaton Carew brought in another doctor, Alister Mackenzie, who was well on his way to establishing himself as one of the seminal figures in golf course architecture (Cypress Point, Augusta National, Royal Melbourne, Crystal Downs, and other notable courses); he changed a number of holes and created four new ones on land nearer the sea.

In the summer of 2001 I played a course that measures 6,207 yards from the regular markers against a par of 71. My companion was Peter Wilson, the club's honorary secretary and, like Jim Manuel, a former captain.

"My wife, Diane," Peter told me, "is the ladies' secretary. She was ladies' captain twice and she won the club championship a couple of times. I play off 13, she's a 9. She has to give me three strokes—three-quarters of the difference. *If* I'll take them." He chuckled at this and I smiled, comfortingly.

A man of medium height and build, with a slightly ruddy complexion and thinning gray hair, Peter was a retired grade-school teacher who finished his career as a deputy headmaster. It was easy to envision him at the head of a classroom, where a sense of humor is invaluable. His 13 looked highly suspect to me as he produced a dozen pars in the round we played. He holed four ten-to-twelve footers, protesting each time that he almost never makes a putt, that this was a round like no other, and that I must have brought him good luck all the way from America.

As it happened, the United States had been prominent at Seaton Carew less than a week before I got there, when the club hosted the British Mid-Amateur Championship.

"This was not the first time the R&A brought one of its competitions here," said Peter. "In 1986 we had the British Boys Championship. But this time there was a big American contingent. Thirty of your countrymen came over. They all play off 2 or better. They may have been a little uneasy when they pulled up—with all the chimneys and cooling towers and what not—but once they got a taste of the club's hospitality and then of the links itself, well, they loved the place, they loved it. And they were so polite and so grateful for anything we did for them. They represented their country splendidly, and we hope they'll come back."

Out of deference to my weak legs, Peter and I rode in a golf cart. This enabled him to pack in a full supply of small cigars and chocolate bars. Apparently feeling no need to apologize for the cigars, he did say with a twinkle as he unwrapped a KitKat early in the round, "I do enjoy a bit of sweets."

There is very little elevation change on this narrow strip of linksland. Hills are no prerequisite of first-rate links golf. What we look for are rippling sand-based fairways, greens that are both naturally and strikingly sited, straight-faced bunkers that thwart the gambling recovery, penal rough, and even, to spice up the stew, an occasional blind or semiblind shot. We get all of this at Seaton Carew, especially the perfectly sited greens. We find them tucked a bit right, a bit left, a bit up, a bit down, perhaps in a cleft in the sandhills (the 4th and 5th) or in a dell of dunes (the 11th) or on a plateau (the 3rd) or framed by low mounds right and left (the 1st).

This links is studded with superb holes, like the exposed 3rd, 161 yards, knob to knob, with a steep falloff at the left; the 165-yard 6th, played from a raised tee down to a semiblind green (we can see the flag, not the putting surface) in an amphitheater of rough-cloaked mounds; the 371-yard 12th, heading straight toward the sea, the fairway narrowing as it rises gently to a generous, dune-framed green; and the celebrated 17th. It is an Alister Mackenzie design, it is called "Snag," it measures 397 yards, and it bends almost imperceptibly right. We must drive to the right of a spine of hillocks if we are to get a good look at the small, fan-shaped green. Bunkered tightly left and right, it is mildly elevated but at varying levels. A mound at the left front of it is an additional complication. Standing there in the fairway, perhaps 170 yards to go, we actually find ourselves wondering if it is possible to hit and hold this green.

At lunch in the spiffy and spacious clubhouse, Peter told me that he and Diane, in their camper, were driving up to St. Andrews in September. She was to partner with a Seaton Carew member, who belongs to the R&A, in a mixed competition on the Old Course. He seemed quietly pleased to be the spouse on what was a rather prestigious occasion.

About half an hour from Seaton Carew, in pretty County Durham countryside, is the Hall Garth Hotel, a cluster of stone buildings dating to the sixteenth century. Ask for Room #5, "Rosedale"—spacious, comfortable, tasteful, and with a fireplace (albeit nonworking). Be sure to dine in romantic Hugo's, where the food is top-notch.

All Courses Great and Small

The other two courses in this chapter, Seascale and Silloth-on-Solway, though also in northern England, are on the opposite coast. As the crow flies, Seascale is some ninety miles due west of Seaton Carew, but the drive, partly through the beautiful Lake District and the Cumbrian Mountains, could well take three and a half hours.

The town of Seascale, with a population of about 2,500, is not picturesque, but its setting, on high ground above a golden beach of the Irish Sea, is undeniably attractive. The Seascale Golf Club was founded in 1893. At the far end of the links, on a hill above the 11th green, stands the Sellafield Power Station, the local electric utility's nuclear power plant, complete with the obligatory giant cooling towers. It would be going too far to call this facility a blot on the landscape, but it is certainly a powerful—for some players, an ominous—presence.

Against a par of 71, the course measures 6,416 yards from the back tees, 6,103 yards from the regular markers. A couple of short par fours—one steeply uphill, the other level—open the round. They are not promising. The 3rd, however, is distinctly reassuring: From a high tee with a magnificent view over the links to the sea, this 407-yarder spills downhill, bends around the corner of a pasture, then ripples along to a green partially blocked by a sandhill at the left front. It is a hole full of ginger and fascination. And no hole that follows lets us down.

At Seascale we seem ever to be changing levels, whether negotiating humps or hollows or little falloffs, perhaps climbing or descending moderate slopes or tackling bona fide hills. This is not mountain-goat country, understand; nor are the stances and lies awkward. It's simply that the terrain is always in motion, giving the holes added interest. And the vistas, whether inland over the Lakeland hills that prompted some of Wordsworth's poetry or out to sea, are captivating. The majestic 9th, 387 yards, finds us driving from a high platform straight at the Isle of Man, some twenty miles across the Irish Sea. It is essential to keep the tee shot left, where it will finish on a plateau fairway 165 yards from a smallish green sitting far below. The second shot is unnerving: A hillock covered with tangled grass defends the left front of the green, subtly urging our iron shot right, and right into the sliver of stream along the edge of the putting surface. There is no strategy involved here, just the need for very precise ball-striking.

The final four holes, all two-shotters, are wonderfully diverse, starting with the 312-yard 15th on an elevated tee beside the railway line, where our drive must be fired over the 14th green (the links is a bit squeezed here). Sixteen, the hardest hole on the course and one of the best, is ferocious: a 473-yard par four, often playing more like 523, much of it over a tumultuous fairway on the lower ground, then steeply up to a blind punchbowl green sealed off by a bold and rugged embankment. The charming 17th brings us back to the railway line—and a pretty view over the beach beside it—for a drive so abruptly uphill as to be almost vertical, but this leaves only an 8- or 9-iron to a receptive green with a pair of pot bunkers on each side. As for the home hole, 353 yards, it's an eccentric delight with a deep hollow defending the green in front—the large putting surface slopes *away* from the shot—and three hidden bunkers lurking in the back.

Rarely has so much satisfying links golf been packed into so few acres, surely less than a hundred. This is marvelous stuff.

Ten miles north, on the coast road, is the Blackbeck Inn: OK for a night—small, simple rooms (but comfortable enough) and basic cooking (but large portions).

In 1983 the then-secretary at Hunstanton Golf Club (Chapter 4) said to me, "I believe that the finest little-known course in the country is up in Cumbria, on the Solway Firth. It's called Silloth-on-Solway." It took me eighteen years to follow up on this tip. I could only berate myself for not having come much sooner. For Silloth is a great course.

The drive due north from Seascale on the coast road, A595, takes an hour and a quarter. There is no difficulty in finding the golf club, which is squarely in town, at the bottom of the main street. And overlooking the village green, two blocks up the street, is the Golf Hotel, a cozy inn with acceptable meals in both the dining room and the bar, which, for hotel guests, has "flexible hours."

Silloth-on-Solway Golf Club was founded in 1892. In their landmark *The Architects of Golf,* Geoffrey Cornish and Ron Whitten say that the course is the collaborative effort of Willie Park (four-time Open Championship winner, between 1860 and 1875; designer of Gullane #1, among others) and Willie Park, Jr. (Open champion in 1887 and 1889; designer of the Old Course at Sunningdale and, among others, Formby, Edinburgh's Bruntsfield Links, and the North Course at suburban Chicago's Olympia Fields, venue for the 2003 U.S. Open).

What we find here, miles from anywhere, is that rare combination of great golf holes in a setting of transcendent beauty. From high tees like the 8th, we can take in, across the open water, the coves and beaches and hills of Scotland's southern shores and, to the southwest, the Isle of Man. Due south on the horizon and soaring above 3,000 feet are Lakeland Fells such as Skiddaw.

James W. Finegan

But the borrowed grandeur of Silloth's surroundings is only part of the picture. The links itself is beautiful, a beauty that stems principally from the course's naturalness. How often we find ourselves playing along exquisite dune-framed valleys, heather and gorse and the long golden fescues gladdening the heart (though imperiling the stroke), the target green perhaps nestling in a hidden dell (the 1st) or, teasingly, on a plateau (the 3rd) or starkly against the sky on the crest of a hill (the 13th). It is all the fulfillment of our fondest dreams of links golf, played on sand-based turf over rumpled fairways through mighty sand-hills, the green sites at one with nature, the implacable pot bunkers with their steep, revetted faces imparting tension to a swing that by all rights, on this inviting course, ought to be free and easy.

Silloth has its share of blind shots, the inevitable result on rolling terrain of moving almost no earth to build the course. A hundred and ten years ago, all course designers were minimalists, adhering to a lay-of-the-land philosophy. They had little choice in the matter—there was no bulldozer.

The course measures 6,358 yards from the whites. Par is 72. The layout is lightly bunkered. Most greens are open across the front, with room on this crumpled terrain to execute bump-and-run shots. The course generally plays firm and fast, so it's important to have a feeling for finesse shots. Tee through green, this turf is perhaps unsurpassed at the sea anywhere in England.

The problem with discussing individual holes here is that not one of them, with the possible exception of the 495-yard 17th, itself entirely acceptable, is other than sparkling. So let's look at just one short hole one two-shotter, and one par five.

The 187-yard 6th plays from a high tee down to a green

stoutly defended out front by a pair of low "cartgate" sandhills (the path between them would accommodate a horse-drawn cart). Eating into each of these sandhills is a deep bunker. The hole is simplicity itself—and it is superb.

The 7th, 403 yards long and a gentle dogleg left, begins on a low tee in the dunes. The drive is launched into a fairway full of mounds and humps and hollows, and the second shot, not only blind but likely to be long since we are playing into the prevailing wind, is hit uphill, disappearing over a crest and drifting down to a picturesque punchbowl green framed by charming if inhospitable dunes.

At only 468 yards, the par-five 13th looks on the card to be a birdie opportunity. But it too is played into the prevailing wind and emphatically uphill, with impenetrable gorse lining the left side of the hole virtually all the way. The drive must clear a low ridge. The second shot must clear another ridge and climb steeply to high ground. The bunkerless green, arrestingly set against the sky, is of the pesky crowned variety, inclining to shed the pitch, sending it determinedly toward the falloff right or the falloff left. The delicate little recovery for a one-putt par is, at best, a dicey business.

Over recent years, as the motorways have made Silloth-on-Solway more accessible and people with an eye for outstanding golf holes have found their way here, praises have rained down on this great and inspiring and exhilarating links. I think I'll let the nonpareil Bernard Darwin have the last word: "Never in my life have I seen a more ideal piece of golfing country—there is everything that a golfer's heart can desire."

CHAPTER TWO

Yorkshire:
Alister Mackenzie,
Front and Center

 IF YOU WERE BENT on playing the courses in this book according to the order in which they are presented—a highly dubious undertaking—you would now find yourself driving some thirty miles from Silloth east to Carlisle and the M6, south on the M6 toward Bolton and Manchester, then northeast to Leeds, in Yorkshire, on the M62. The entire run would take at least three and a half hours.

Mention Yorkshire to an American and the response may well be, "Oh, yes, the Yorkshire Dales, James Herriott." Or perhaps, "Isn't that where the Brontë sisters lived, the ones who wrote *Wuthering Heights* and *Jane Eyre?*" What you are unlikely to get is any mention of golf. Yet Yorkshire is where the immortal Alister Mackenzie first made his mark.

Mackenzie was born in Leeds in 1870, the son of Scottish parents. At Cambridge University he earned degrees in medicine, chemistry, and natural science. While serving as a surgeon with the British Army in South Africa during the Boer War, he was much impressed by the Boers' use of camouflage in the open field to disguise their troop positions. He studied their techniques and when he later turned to golf course architecture as his life's work, his emphasis on using the natural features of a course reflected his knowledge of camouflage.

In 1907, now practicing medicine in Leeds, Mackenzie was one of a small group that founded Alwoodley Golf Club. He had never designed a golf course, but in collaboration with Harry Colt, Mackenzie was able to lay out Alwoodley. He then closely supervised the construction of the holes, ensuring that the bunkering and the greens reflected his own thinking in every particular. The net of Mackenzie's energetic participation is a wonderfully natural heathland course that, almost a hundred years later, is virtually unchanged except for the lengthening of holes.

There are four sets of tees at Alwoodley today, the shortest adding up to 5,663 yards, the longest to 6,785 yards. Fairways of springy turf are framed by heather, gorse, straw-colored grasses, low scrub, and at a discreet remove, trees. This is a secluded spot.

Except for modest dips on three or four holes, Alwoodley has little elevation change. But the fairways, far from flat when it comes to setting up at the ball, ripple exuberantly. And the eighty bunkers, of all sizes and shapes and often with shaggy surrounds, incline to be deep and perilous. Stern-forced carries are common from the tee. As for the greens, they are large, imaginatively contoured (an obvious Mackenzie touch), and velvety. A quick-drying course at any time of year, Alwoodley plays especially firm and fast in summer, with a number of holes accommodating bounce-and-run shots or knockdown shots

James W. Finegan

under the breeze. If all this sounds suspiciously like seaside golf, so be it, for Alwoodley can fairly be called an inland links.

A number of holes are superlative. The deceptive and subtly testing 510-yard 3rd, for instance, straightaway and nearly hazard-free (there is just one bunker, to catch a hooked drive) was singled out as one of the top 100 holes in the authoritative volume *The 500 World's Greatest Golf Holes,* by George Peper and the editors of *GOLF Magazine,* published in 2000. This hole strikes us as essentially uneventful. But the green, in the gentlest of hollows, slopes markedly from right to left. So unless the second shot is neatly positioned on the left side of the fairway, enabling us to pitch into the slope and thus hold the green, we may find what had seemed like a birdie possibility turning into a bogey reality.

Another three-shotter, the 489-yard 8th, is perhaps even more testing. It doglegs smoothly left around the woods. The big hitter will take the tight line, skirting the trees to gamble on gaining the sand-guarded green in two. On the other hand, the average hitter, playing safely out to the right from the tee, now looks ahead to a pinched and curving fairway, bunkers tight on either side, heather left, trees left and right. Failure to pull off this exacting long second shot will result, at best, in one dropped stroke.

Down in the far corner of the course lies the 11th, 167 yards. It rises to a sloping green all but islanded in sand and with steep falloffs on its flanks. Long recognized as one of England's best par threes, it is fair and fine—and the very devil to hold in the prevailing right-to-left breeze.

You will want to have lunch or at least a drink at Alwoodley, either on the terrace or inside the beautiful new clubhouse (1995), which, thanks to its turreted roof sections, is vaguely reminiscent of manor houses in the Dordogne. In his autobio-graphical *The Spirit of St. Andrews,* written in 1934 but lost until 1995, Mackenzie wrote, "I do not know any better club in the world to belong to than Alwoodley." And when Ben Crenshaw, paying homage to Mackenzie, played Alwoodley a few years ago, he was so taken with it that he felt compelled to join the club.

In 1909 a group of men who had obtained a lease on land directly opposite Alwoodley, on the other side of the Leeds/Harrowgate Road, approached Mackenzie with a view to his laying out a course there. In *The Spirit of St. Andrews,* Mackenzie tells a charming story about getting the new club, Moortown, off the ground:

> I asked them [the founders] how much money they had raised for the construction of the course and they informed me one hundred pounds.
>
> I told them that they would not be able to make more than one hole for this sum but I thought there was an opportunity of making such a good hole that it would attract new and richer members. They agreed . . . and we made a hole which since then has become world renowned, namely . . . the Gibraltar Hole, as it has come to be known.
>
> The Committee took visitors to see it and told them that this was a sample of what the course was going to be like. They said, "This is wonderful," and asked to be put up as members of the club. In this way, sufficient money was obtained to construct the remainder of the course.

James W. Finegan

It was at Moortown in 1929 that the Ryder Cup was first contested on British soil. Since steel shafts were banned in the United Kingdom, the American squad quickly had to get used to playing with hickory. Still, this team headed by British Open champion Walter Hagen, U.S. Open champion Johnny Farrell, and PGA champion Leo Diegel, to say nothing of Gene Sarazen and Horton Smith, was smugly confident. At the end of the first day—four thirty-six-hole foursomes (alternate stroke) matches—the U.S. led, 2½–1½. The Americans figured to be a shoo-in in the 36-hole singles. Instead, they were shellacked, 5½–2½, surrendering the Cup, 7–5. In the battle of the playing captains, it was the dismantling of the great Hagen, 10 and 8, by George Duncan, that astounded—nay, delighted— the huge crowds, particularly after Hagen had deliberately placed himself opposite Duncan, boasting, "There's a point for our team right there."

Most of us find Moortown's regular markers—6,465 yards, par 72—sufficiently testing. The start is unprepossessing, a couple of short par fives that, if we had warmed up on the practice ground, might have yielded at least one birdie. But the pace quickens on the taskmaster 3rd, the first of six par fours measuring more than 400 yards. As at Alwoodley, the broad fairways are lined with gorse, heather, and trees (half the silver birches in Yorkshire must be here!); the greens are spacious and undulating; and sand is the principal hazard. Unlike Alwoodley, however, Moortown has ditches and streams and, beginning at the 9th, ups and downs, all of which lend much-needed interest and variety.

The 9th is a marvelous two-shotter, 436 yards, elevated tee, the fairway bending around a clump of trees on the right, room at the green if only we can get to it. Then comes Mackenzie's fabled "Gibraltar," 158 yards long and so named because the plateau green is sited on solid rock. It fully lives up to our expectations: slightly rising, fearsome bunkering wherever we look, a large and dangerously sloping green. As Mackenzie points out in his book *Golf Architecture,* "The green is delightfully picturesque. It is extremely visible against a background of fir trees—it stands up and looks at you."

The 540-yard 12th is also strong, with forced carries over heather on both drive and second shot followed by a downhill pitch to a closely bunkered pear-shaped green. But almost certainly it is the 416-yard home hole that is Moortown's best. It rises gently and bends smoothly right. Sand in the crook of the dogleg imperils the drive. Sand right and left at another pear-shaped green puts pressure on the long second shot. Under the very windows of the clubhouse, the green, boldly contoured, is eminently three-puttable.

Perhaps a quarter of a mile from Moortown lies Sand Moor, which opened in 1926. There is serious doubt as to Mackenzie's involvement in the design. In its history, published in 2001, the club is less than forthright, calling him "the major influence in the creation of the course." That is scarcely definitive. Others attribute the layout to Henry Barran, who owned the land.

Most golfers will enjoy Sand Moor immensely regardless of its authorship. It measures 6,429 yards against a par of 71 and boasts dramatic elevation changes. Many fairways undulate in linkslike manner. There may be a few too many blind shots (an inevitable result of the steep hills), but this course is full of classic golf holes that do not require the quirky or eccentric for their character and charm.

James W. Finegan

The round begins with birdie opportunities on the short par-five opener (491 yards) and the very short par-four 2nd (258 yards). So much for encouragement. There is not another easy hole here. More important, beginning with the altogether splendid 8th—186 yards, hillside to hillside, stringent bunkering—we relish an unbroken succession of first-rate golf holes. My instinct is to single out the par threes, so exceptional are they—the sidehill 173-yard 10th, with its plateau green, is perhaps the best of the quartet. Still, at richly scenic Sand Moor, with Eccup Reservoir and with the gorse and the heather and the occasional spinney of fir trees all contributing to the challenge, the par fives and the two-shotters are also excellent. The contrast, for instance, between the captivating 13th (339 yards, downhill, the pitch to a sand-defended green that is sited teasingly right, beyond evergreens) and the killer 14th (another par four, this one 464 yards, rising easily from the tee, then stretching away seemingly forever to a green open across the front and decidedly closed at the sides) could scarcely be more marked. The net of it all is a golf course less heralded than Alwoodley and Moortown—and perhaps owing little or nothing to Alister Mackenzie—that is on no account to be missed.

Less than ten minutes away, and a couple of miles off the Leeds/Harrowgate Road, lies Moor Allerton Golf Club. The original eighteen, laid out a few miles from here in 1923 by Mackenzie, is no longer in existence. The club moved here, to Coal Road, at the edge of the village of Wike, in 1970. Then it was that the new course, designed by none other than Robert Trent Jones, opened for play. Probably the most influential golf architect in history—in truth, the man who almost single-handedly made golf course design a well-respected and well-paid profession—Jones laid out twenty-seven holes here for this, his first assignment in the British Isles. They nicely illustrate his belief that a hole ought to be a hard par and an easy bogey.

All three nines on this 220 acres of hilly and picturesque Yorkshire countryside are quintessential Trent Jones: big, bold, brawny golf holes, replete with his trademark airport-runway tees, generous fairways, spacious and daringly contoured greens, exotically shaped bunkers, and water in play again and again—in short, the modern American look that he created and established.

The par-five 14th—woods tight on the right, a stream and four ponds skirting the left side of the hole and insistently threatening each shot—is a perfect example of the maestro at work. As is the 383-yard 18th, an adventurous and original two-shotter. Here the second shot, often from a downhill lie, is played over a deep swale (at the bottom of it, trees right and a hidden pond left) to an elevated and inexorably bunkered green on the far hillside.

We are not surprised to learn that over the years Moor Allerton has hosted professional tournaments, attracting many of the world's premier players, including Tony Jacklin, Gary Player, Tom Weiskopf, Seve Ballesteros, Nick Faldo, Greg Norman, Nick Price, and Ian Woosnam.

The fifth—and best—of the top Yorkshire courses is neither just across the road nor just around the corner. In fact, Ganton is an hour's brisk drive north of Leeds on the A64.

Except for the seaside shrines, no course in the British Isles has been the scene of such a blue-ribbon list of competitions as has Ganton: the British Amateur, British Mid-Amateur, English Amateur, British Ladies, British Youths (Jose Maria Olazabal winning in 1985), Dunlop Masters, British PGA, Curtis Cup (U.S. victorious in 2000), Walker Cup (2003), and in 1949, the first postwar Ryder Cup Match in Britain.

A nonplaying Ben Hogan, recuperating from that near-fatal collision with a bus seven months earlier, captained an American squad that included Sam Snead, Jimmy Demaret, Lloyd Mangrum, and Dutch Harrison. Colin M. Jarman, in his definitive *The Ryder Cup,* published in 1999, quotes Hogan: "We care about who is selected, but we care more about winning." Ah, some things never change. The U.S. won, 7–5.

The first golf holes at Ganton were laid out in 1891 by two little-known figures, Tom Chisholm, of St. Andrews, and R. Bird, the club's first greenkeeper. Over the next sixty years, however, the roster of those revising or adding holes was a mini-hall of fame of British golf: Harry Vardon, who won three of his six British Opens while serving as the club's professional from 1896 to 1903, Alister Mackenzie, Harry Colt, Herbert Fowler, James Braid, Ted Ray, Harold Hilton, C. K. Hutchison, C. K. Cotton, and Frank Pennink. This has turned out to be one of

All Courses Great and Small

those instances when too many cooks did not spoil the broth. Ganton is a feast.

Like Alwoodley, it is an inland course of seaside character. The turf is sand-based and the ground undulates in linkslike fashion. There are no climbs—the overall elevation change cannot be as much as ten feet. Fairways and greens are firm and fast.

Playing Ganton is a starkly confrontational business. Hole after hole, shot after shot, without so much as a moment's letup, it is golfer versus golf course. Never is there a free swing, where we can open the shoulders, "grip it and rip it." Always, catastrophe lurks in either the sandy caverns or the great stands of gorse. At times we incline to believe that the entire course must have been dredged up out of a sea of gorse, an intractable expanse of potentially unplayable—and literally prickly—lies. As for the bunkers, 123 by actual count—many of them malevolently deep, their banks often gorse-infested, some pits with revetted faces, a few with boarded faces, certain bunkers requiring steps in order to get in and out—these hazards fiercely stare us down at every turn. The pressure on the swing at Ganton is intense and relentless. This is a truly penal course in the tradition of Oakmont and Royal Lytham & St. Annes (Chapter 15).

There are only two par threes (shades of the Old Course and of Elie) and three par fives. Which leaves thirteen two-shotters and a par of 73 (6,474 yards from the regular markers). This collection of par fours is one of the finest in the world. Their remarkable diversity is illustrated by the first four holes. The 373-yard opener is straightforward and uncompromising—bunkers on both sides of the tee-shot landing area and on both sides of the green. On the much longer 2nd, 418 yards, the drive over a modest crest leaves a gently downhill second shot to another green forcefully defended by sand, this one very difficult to hold because it slopes away from the player. The 3rd, a mere 334 yards, is a birdie opportunity only if we gamble successfully on slotting our drive into the neck of an hourglass-shaped fairway. The 406-yard 4th is one of the chosen in *The 500 World's Greatest Golf Holes*. On this dogleg right, it is the second shot that is harshly demanding, a 180-yarder that must clear a shallow (and sometimes wet) diagonal gully and come to rest on a low plateau green with a steep falloff at the left and a single, artfully placed bunker at the right. Alignment is almost as difficult a problem as making a good swing.

There are, of course, a lot more where these four came from, including the mighty 429-yard 16th. First we must carry a colossal crossbunker—vast, deep, intimidating—and then launch a long, gently falling shot to a green framed by gorse and sand and pines.

The graceful red-brick clubhouse is a welcome haven after the rigors of the round. The lounges afford grand views over the course toward the escarpment of the Yorkshire Wolds. What's more, the famously tasty Ganton Cake, made from a secret recipe, is as celebrated in British golfing circles as the snapper soup at Pine Valley is in America's.

Yorkshire forces us to make some hard choices when it comes to spending time away from the golf course. Among the numerous attractions are York itself (majestic cathedral here); the old fishing port of Whitby, with its cliff-framed harbor; stately houses such as Castle Howard, one of the dozen most opulent dwellings in England; ancient abbeys like Rievaulx (moody ruins in the valley of the river Rue); and the Dales—stone fences, sheep-dotted meadows, quaint villages.

All Courses Great and Small

Over the years we've stayed at four places in Yorkshire, all of them recommendable. In Scarborough, fifteen minutes from Ganton, is traditional Holbeck Hall, which has many guest rooms with sea views. On the outskirts of Leeds is nineteenth-century Oulton Hall—luxurious public spaces, cheerful guest rooms that incline to be ordinary, and, on the other hand, spacious and nicely appointed guest suites that can be an excellent value. In the Dales near Skipton and half an hour from the Leeds courses is seventeenth-century Devonshire Arms Country House Hotel, on the river Wharfe. Log fires, sofas you sink into, antiques, old paintings, sophisticated cooking—in sum, an inn to cherish. And finally, also in the Dales but not at all convenient to any of the courses, is the atmospheric Kings Arms Hotel (in tiny Askrigg), where the pub scenes in the BBC-TV series *All Creatures Great and Small* were shot.

Not too far down the road from the Kings Arms is Hardraw Force, said to be the highest unbroken waterfall in all of England. My wife and I had looked forward to seeing this marvel of nature. I recall stopping our rental car just beyond the hamlet of Hardraw and saying to a hiker, "Can you tell us where the waterfall is?"

"Through the Green Dragon," he replied, pointing back down the road.

"The pub?" I asked. "The Green Dragon pub?"

"Aye. Not that they own Hardraw Force. But they own the right to visit it. You pay fifty pence at the bar. You'll find the Force just up the glen. That is, if it's flowing. Sometimes, when we've had little rain, there's no water, which means no waterfall."

Harriet and I entered the Green Dragon and I placed a one-pound note on the bar but did not take my hand off it. "The waterfall," I said tentatively to the bar maid, "is it . . . uh . . . is it flowing today?"

She fixed me with a steely gaze, smoothly picking up the one-pound note as she replied, "The Force has *never* run dry."

I felt properly chastened.

We proceeded through the pub and out the back door, then along a shady path beside a stream. We heard the Force before we saw it, the muffled sound of water falling onto rock. And then suddenly we were in its presence, in a cul-de-sac of limestone. Just how tall is this thrilling cascade? Ninety-eight feet. And how broad is this sheer torrent? Well, you can't quite get your arms about it, but almost. The knowledge that Blondin, the nineteenth-century daredevil who risked his life crossing Niagara Falls on a tightrope, had done the same death-defying stunt here struck us as hilarious. Realistically, however, we were forced to conclude that, at fifty pence, the Force was fairly priced.

CHAPTER THREE

Robin Hood,
a Ryder Cup,
and Inland Glory

 WE'RE DRIVING SOUTH NOW for very like three hours, from one Ryder Cup venue, Ganton, to another, Lindrick, which is located at Worksop, in Nottinghamshire. The club was founded in 1891, and Tom Dunn, the most prolific course designer in the last decade of the nineteenth century, laid out nine holes. A second nine was added three years later. Fred W. Hawtree effected certain revisions after World War II.

In addition to the Ryder Cup, Lindrick has been the venue for the 1960 Curtis Cup as well as for many professional events, including the Dunlop Masters, the Martini International, and the Women's British Open.

The U.S. team for the 1957 Ryder Cup Match was notice-ably lacking in gate appeal. Sam Snead and Ben Hogan had decided not to travel to England, and the PGA chose not to invite Cary Middlecoff and Julius Boros after they bypassed the PGA Championship. The depleted American squad, led by

Tommy Bolt, Dow Finsterwald, and Doug Ford, lost, 7½–4½, to a British and Irish side that included Max Faulkner, Christy O'Connor, Sr., and Dai Rees. It was the only American defeat between 1933 and 1985. The opening singles, Bolt versus Scotsman Eric Brown, was marked by a singularly ill-tempered denouement, with the players refusing to shake hands. Bolt insisted that he had not enjoyed the match, and Brown responded, "I don't suppose you did . . . because even you knew when the games were drawn that you never had an earthly hope of beating me."

Lindrick measures 6,270 yards from the regular tees; par is 71. This is a beautiful and impeccably conditioned moorland course, imaginatively routed, each hole in its avenue of trees. Fairways are broad, regularly forty yards wide; greens are natural, diverse, lovely; the rough is largely tall, beige-colored fescues. Gorse is often a threat. But it is sand, plentifully and artfully deployed greenside, moderately used at the tee-shot landing area, that is the principal defense for par. The shots to the green are extremely demanding at Lindrick.

The two par threes on the outbound nine, the 165-yard 3rd and the 140-yard 6th, while challenging enough in view of all the sand, are rather too cousinly. And the 370-yard 10th, rising smoothly, is somewhat ordinary. But these shortcomings are soon forgotten in our enjoyment of a number of outstanding holes.

Lindrick's most famous hole is encountered early on. The 478-yard 4th, a very short par five, is pure fun, both in the playing and in its highly colorful past. It drifts downhill from the tee and then plunges blindly to a hidden green far below in a hollow framed by trees, beyond which the peaceful river Ryton flows. Long ago this green was actually the setting for cockfights. The boundaries of Yorkshire, Derbyshire, and Nottinghamshire used to come together here. This convenient circumstance made it easy to shift the arena into an adjacent county at a moment's notice if the law suddenly showed up from any one (or even two) of the three counties.

The second nine has several particularly strong holes, including the 13th, 433 yards, bending left, falling, then climbing steeply. A pair of bunkers in the crook of the dogleg at the bottom of the hill await the pulled drive. At the green, high above us and silhouetted against the sky, two bunkers on each side defy us to hit a 5-metal solidly enough and straight enough to gain the putting surface in two. By any standards, a great two-shotter.

No down and up on the 391-yard 17th. It moves steadily downhill from tee to green, curving left, gorse imperiling the drive right and left, a trio of bunkers out in the fairway thirty to seventy yards short of the green making judgment of this falling second shot trickier than it would otherwise be. In the 1982 Martini International, Greg Norman took a 14 here—don't ask!

The 210-yard 18th is very good indeed, even better than that in the eyes of the editors of *The 500 World's Greatest Golf Holes.* A level hole, it is bunkered greenside right and left but with plenty of room across the front to run the ball onto what is a very slightly raised putting surface, this subtle touch putting a desirable sting in the tail of an excellent course.

Perhaps fifteen minutes from Lindrick, on the outskirts of the village of Blyth, itself most agreeable, is the thirty-four-room Charnwood Hotel, with modest-size guest rooms and, overlooking a lagoon, a dining room much favored by the locals, who appreciate good food and service.

Staying within the confines of Nottinghamshire, we now

drive south for less than an hour to the Notts Golf Club, at Hollinwell, the name by which the club is better known. The course, on 550 acres, sprawls across a vast bowl, with wooded hills on two of its flanks. The seclusion is total.

The club was founded in 1887 by Scottish-born John Harris and the Rt. Rev. A. Hamilton Baynes, a clergyman convinced, perhaps erroneously, that this new game must be more heavenly than hellish. Thirteen years later, with the club now at its third (and present) site, Willie Park, Jr., laid out eighteen holes. Many important tournaments have been contested here, including the English Amateur Strokeplay Championship (Sandy Lyle the winner), the British Ladies, English Ladies, Dunlop Masters, and the Tournament Players Championship (Nick Faldo the winner). There can be no doubt about the championship quality of Hollinwell, nor, in fact, about its greatness.

I played here on a Sunday in late August of 2001. My companion, Ian Symington, the club secretary, and I were two of only twenty-four or so who were abroad on these outstanding golf holes that day. I judged Ian to be in his late thirties. A shade over six feet tall, he has dark hair and a warm smile. He struck me as quietly capable, and I imagine the members hold much the same view of him.

By British standards, Hollinwell is an extremely long course, 7,100 yards from the tips. From the forward markers, it measures a hefty 6,623 yards. Ian and I played from the white tees, a debilitating (for me) 6,905 yards, par 72. Though graced with thousands of trees (oak, silver birch, pine, et al.), Hollinwell is often open in aspect. But heather, gorse, and bracken are to be avoided like the proverbial plague. There is only one water hole, the 8th (more about it later). Crossbunkers that have to be cleared on five holes bring sand boldly to the fore.

The opener, 366 yards, is level, pleasant, thoroughly undistinguished. On the other hand, the 2nd, also level, is a great hole: 428 yards, bending strongly left around a steep and high hill crowding the fairway and, for drives left of center, concealing the green on the long second shot. A kidney-shaped bunker in the fairway thirty yards short of the putting surface is disturbingly in play. The green is backdropped by a high rock formation. Pointing toward the top of it, Ian said, "That's called Robin Hood's Chair. The myth has it that he sat there, waiting for Maid Marian." As you would expect, Robin Hood is made much of here in Nottinghamshire—Sherwood Forest, Nottingham Castle, "The Outlaw's Trail," even a ride into the past called "The Tales of Robin Hood," which highlights the sights, sounds, and smells of medieval England.

The other "story hole" is the 8th, a very good 363-yarder through a chute of trees, with a forced carry from the tee first over a lagoon and then over a stream. After we had driven, Ian said, "I want to show you something." He detoured into a glade and down a few feet of rocky slope. I could hear water trickling over stone. He took a tin cup that was sitting on a little rock shelf there, filled it, and handed it to me, saying, "This is the holy well—Hollinwell, that's its derivation. This spring has been here for many hundreds of years, back to the Middle Ages at least, when it was the drinking water source for the monks in the abbey just over the hill about a mile from here. They would walk down and fill their jugs, then haul them all the way back to the abbey."

I tasted the water. It was wonderfully refreshing on this

warm summer day—clear, cold, free of any hint of chemicals, somehow delicious though there could not have been a flavor as such, nectar if not of the gods then surely of the monks. "Hollinwell," I said, "holy well." Then I drank the cup dry.

On the second nine, every hole merits praise, but a three-hole sequence beginning at 11 is especially fine. The 360-yard 11th, from a mildly elevated tee, plays along a gorse- and tree-framed valley in the early going. The second shot climbs up a draw, with rising rough ground on both sides corseting and narrowing the fairway, the shelf green at the top nestling in the defile of a high ridge. The playing value of this arresting hole is close to 400 yards.

The 430-yard 12th moves along the heights of the ridge. The drive, a lengthy forced carry over a no-man's-land valley, is blind. The full-blooded second shot to a hidden green must traverse a couple of dips, one of them quite hostile, and be kept much farther right than you could ever imagine on what is essentially a straight hole, because the ground we cannot see slopes away to the left—sand and trees down here—as we draw near the green. If ever a hole required local knowledge combined with scratch-level skill, this is that hole.

The complexity of the 12th is followed by the simplicity of the 13th: a 198-yarder from a towering tee, the view over the course breathtaking, our ball seeming to soar forever down to the green defended front, right, and left by six bunkers, not to mention mounding. It is all there below us—far below us—just waiting.

After the round, Ian and I had a sandwich in the deserted clubhouse. I said I was amazed at how quiet it was on this pretty Sunday afternoon.

"We do have days like this," Ian replied. "We're not overrun by visitors, though there are times when a golf society is here for an outing—then there's a lot of play. But even so, our members are rarely inconvenienced."

I asked if dinner were served regularly. British clubs can be counted on for cooked luncheon, but dinner is not often on the docket.

"Yes, whenever you want it."

I looked at him quizzically.

"We try to oblige our members. So dinner can be provided any evening, at the member's convenience. The stewardess lives here, and she is the cook. If for whatever reason you would like something to eat at ten-thirty in the evening—oh, I don't know, perhaps an omelet—she'll do it and be quite pleased to." Then he added, with a smile, "Understand, that sort of thing doesn't happen every day, nor even every month. But we wouldn't consider it an unacceptable request—unusual, yes, unacceptable, no."

About thirty minutes from Hollinwell is Langar Hall, circa 1837, an antiques-filled country house hotel with attractive gardens, a croquet lawn, sheep grazing in the surrounding park, a network of medieval fishponds stocked with carp, and an exquisite fifteenth-century church abutting the great house. Some rooms are cramped, an evening wedding reception can be noisy, and the excellent cooking inclines to be pricey. Nonetheless, we would go back.

Year in and year out, the Hotchkin Course at Woodhall Spa Golf Club is named one of England's top three inland courses, the other two spots usually accorded to Sunningdale Old or Wentworth West or Ganton or Walton Heath Old. For nearly a

James W. Finegan

hundred years, the great course at Woodhall Spa has sat there, a
diamond solitaire, polished and brilliant but utterly on its own
in the middle of nowhere, some twenty miles southeast of the
cathedral city of Lincoln. In 1995, having acquired the golf
club, the English Golf Union built here its administrative headquarters, plus a teaching and practice center, and a second
eighteen. As for getting to Woodhall Spa from Hollinwell, the
route is basically indescribable. You head in a northeasterly
direction to Newark-on-Trent and from there embark on an
exercise in map reading.

Golf has been played here since 1891, but today's celebrated
course is the result of a nine laid out by Harry Vardon over barren heathland in 1905, a second nine, in 1912, by Harry Colt,
and a sweeping redesign of this eighteen in the early 1920s by
Colonel S. V. Hotchkin, who owned the land. This is a heathland course: sand-based turf; heather, gorse, broom; mature
trees, chiefly pine and silver birch, framing most of the holes
individually. There are no hills and no water hazards; forced
carries over heather and thick rough are daunting enough. Still,
it is sand that is the villain in the piece, heaping doses of sand.
By actual count, there are 110 bunkers. They are the hallmark
of the course, and its glory. Few are small; the majority range
from moderate to large. All are deep, many are cavernous, some
require ladders. The deepest and most forbidding bunkers on
any inland course in Britain and Ireland are here on the
Hotchkin, eclipsing even the perilous pits of Ganton. And as at
Ganton, there is a decidedly links feeling to the game here.

From the regular tees, the course measures 6,501 yards. Par
is 71, with seven par fours ranging from 401 to 464 yards. This
is a severe examination. The first nine is merciless and, truth to

tell, a shade short of sparkling. This stems from a marked similarity among the 2nd (401 yards), 3rd (408 yards), 6th (464 yards), and 7th (409 yards), all of which head in the same direction and over level ground, and all of which are bunkered in much the same fashion. These are four strong and fine holes, but we could wish for some diversity. A chap from Johannesburg joined me on the 8th, an excellent 197-yarder, the green neatly sited on a low plateau, an unconscionably deep pit at the right front. He made no bones about his disappointment at being unable to keep the holes straight. I said I was optimistic that the second nine would be different.

And so it is. In fact, it is sublime, one of the very best nines in my experience, the holes of all lengths and strategies, heading toward every point of the compass, requiring an extraordinary variety of shotmaking, aesthetically beguiling, in short, full of Darwin's *sine qua non,* pleasurable excitement. And if every hole is superlative, three short par fours are especially lustrous. As you would expect here at Woodhall Spa, each features lethal greenside bunkering, and more. The 10th, in the space of a mere 328 yards, manages to jog both left and right through the trees. The 315-yard 15th presents a narrow, sand-corseted plateau green that puts unignorable pressure on the swing we are about to make with no more than a pitching wedge. And the 17th, 322 yards, adds gorse and mounds to the obligatory mix of big sand and little slopes to produce a very heady cocktail. By the time we had putted out on the magnificent 18th—a 442-yard par four with a huge gnarled oak tree edging into the right side of the fairway—and we had taken a seat in the bar of the intimate, old one-story clubhouse, my friend from Johannesburg was willing to agree that the Hotchkin had lived up to its reputation: it is a great course.

Next door lies the Bracken Course, designed by Donald Steel (the Jubilee Course at St. Andrews; the Carnegie Club links at Skibo Castle, Dornoch; Red Tail, near Toronto) and routed over level woodland and former farmland. It opened in 1998. The look and feel suggest American parkland layouts. The bunkers—there are only forty-nine here—are more sculpted, less natural, than those on the Hotchkin eighteen. Water, notably absent next door, endangers the shot on ten holes here. The new Bracken contrasts sharply with the old Hotchkin.

Probably the most enjoyable place to stay in Woodhall Spa is half-timbered Petwood Hotel, bordering the Bracken Course, a country house where royalty (King George V and King George VI) were once entertained. It served as the officers' mess for the RAF's 617th Squadron, the courageous *dambusters,* celebrated for flying their Lancaster bombers in World War II dangerously deep into Germany. By and large, guest rooms are spacious. You may want to specify the Oak Room, with its walnut four-poster bed, its Victorian sofa upholstered in raspberry velvet, and its broad bay window giving on the formal gardens. Have drinks in the paneled lounge (fireplace at each end) and dinner in the cozy dining room with its black-painted paneling, good cooking, and superior service.

If you can, set aside time to visit Lincoln Cathedral. John Ruskin called it ". . . out and out the most precious piece of architecture in the British Islands." Perched atop the small city's highest hill, the great church has dominated the landscape for 700 years. Take the "roof tour" for a complete view of the interior from a balcony high inside the west wall, where you can appreciate close-up the extraordinary Gothic vaulting of this masterpiece.

CHAPTER FOUR

Links, Clifftop, Heathland, Parkland: An East Anglian Smorgasbord

 IT IS TIME to return to the sea.

Leaving Woodhall Spa, we travel east very briefly to pick up the A16, then drive south to the A17, proceeding on it to King's Lyn. We now head north on the A149 to Hunstanton, the first of our four courses at the top of a terrestrial bulge in Norfolk thrusting at Holland, some 140 miles away across the North Sea. Two of them, Hunstanton and Royal West Norfolk, are classic links, seaside and sea level. The other two, Sheringham and Royal Cromer, are laid out on cliffs high above the sea.

The links at Hunstanton, which dates to 1891, is largely the work of James Braid, who in 1907 extensively revised the original nine, laid out by George Fernie, and added the second nine. Through the years the club has hosted numerous important competitions, including the British Ladies, English Ladies, English Amateur, and PGA Close.

The holes are routed over a strip of duneland between the river Hun, an easily overlooked stream, and the Wash, a vast indentation of the North Sea. The course meanders out to the 8th green over often level and featureless ground on the inland side of the property, then turns about to wend its way home nearer the shore and over linksland of character and interest. The four par fives, it must be admitted, lack spine.

Among the very good holes on the first nine are the tough 5th (430 yards, elevated tee, pair of "cartgate" bunkers 50 yards short of the green) and the dune-framed 7th (150 yards, platform tee, wall of sand across the front of the green). The early holes coming home include the excellent 11th, where, from the high tee, we enjoy a view of the sea and, in the far distance, Hunstanton town. Then we must tackle this exacting 402-yarder, which works its way along a shallow rolling valley, the hummocky ground on either side clad in the long bent grasses.

The finish at Hunstanton—16, 17, 18—is altogether wonderful. On the par-three 16th, from atop a dune ridge we play a falling shot of 188 yards across a rough-covered slope to a narrow and slightly built-up green ringed by bunkers. With the sea on our left and the shot paralleling the strand, we are generally called upon to bank the ball into a crosswind, starting it out over the left-hand bunkers and letting it drift back to the putting surface. The hole is regularly named in polls as one of England's best par threes. In 1974 it was the scene of what many feel to be the single unlikeliest occurrence in the annals of the game.

An amateur by the name of Robert Taylor came out to Hunstanton in 1974 to compete in the Eastern Counties Foursomes. On May 31, in a practice round, he aced the 188-yarder with a 1-iron. The next day, in the tournament proper and with the wind now at his back, he hit the ball into the cup with a 6-iron. That evening there was considerable talk in the club-house about the odds—how incalculable they must be—on a third consecutive ace. Taylor was actually offered a bet, at staggering odds—which, of course, he sensibly declined. Then, the following day, in the competition and once more with a 6-iron, he did it again!

No such improbable goings-on attach themselves to the superb par-four 17th, a 442-yarder which tends gently uphill all the way. Carrying a shallow dip of hummocky ground from the tee is not our principal problem. It is the second shot, uncomfortably more than 200 yards long to a narrow shelf of green carved out of a left-hand ridge, which disheartens us. There is strangling rough on the left, a ruinously steep and slick falloff into a deep hollow on the right.

Is the last hole easier? Well, it is eighty yards shorter. But the beach is on our right, there is broken ground on our left, and the second shot must clear a wide, sandy swale that functions as a bunker and a service road and a menace to our composure, particularly if the match is on the line and there are observers on the terrace immediately above the green.

Some seven or eight miles due east along the coast road, A149, brings us to the village of Brancaster, home of the Royal West Norfolk Golf Club, founded in 1891. A remote and tranquil place smack beside the sea, the club, familiarly known as Brancaster, is rich in atmosphere and tradition. Named "Royal" at its formation by the then Prince of Wales, later King Edward VII, it is the only golf club to have had four captains who were members of the royal family (a Duke of Gloucester, the Duke of Windsor, and two Dukes of Kent).

James W. Finegan

Interestingly, this most royal of golf clubs is, in a very real sense, one of the most democratic. When we first visited it, in the early 1980s, Squadron Commander H. E. Morrison, RAF (retired) was the secretary. Articulate, assured, and very proud of the club he ran, Commander Morrison took Harriet and me downstairs to the Smoke Room, a generous, high-ceilinged space on the ground floor. A fireplace and a number of round tables with captain's chairs gave the room a feeling of camaraderie.

"Everyone is welcome here," the secretary said, "men, women, children, visitors, even dogs. Notice there at the hearth, that metal bowl is filled with drinking water for dogs. And I should point out that our links is also home to the Brancaster Village Golf Club. The village club is made up of 120 townies who pay not a penny to play the course. Why? Because it is laid out on common ground."

As our chat in the Smoke Room was drawing to a close, the secretary gestured toward a heavily bound volume on a nearby table. We walked over to it and he casually riffled its pages, the great majority of them blank. "This is the Complaints and Suggestions Book," he said. "It has sat here on this table for nearly a hundred years. Only some twenty pages have anything written on them."

"Clearly," I said, "the members are satisfied with the way the club is run."

"It would seem so," he replied with a twinkle, and promptly made his exit.

The Brancaster links was laid out by Holcombe Ingleby and Horace Hutchinson, but the golf holes today owe more to the revisionary skills of C. K. Hutchison, Sir Guy Campbell (Killarney Golf & Fishing Club, both eighteens; remodeling of Prince's, Royal Cinque Ports, Rye, and Machrihanish), and S. V. Hotchkin. Nonetheless, it was Hutchinson—British Amateur champion in 1886 and 1887, and the first truly accomplished golf writer—who put Brancaster on the map.

Here we find ourselves playing a course that measures about 6,300 yards. Par is 71. On our most recent visit I ran into a problem: Arriving at the golf shop a few minutes before eight, I learned that the secretary's secretary had taken sick shortly after speaking with me on the phone several weeks earlier and had neglected to put my tee time in the book. But the woman who was in charge when I got there was determined to be helpful. Said she, "Go right out to the first tee. When you see a gap, whack your drive and run!"

I did as I was told, somehow even managing to carry the large sand pit that confronts us here on the first swing of the day. On this 402-yarder, we want to head right. This opens up the green and, equally important, keeps us clear of the remains of the pillbox for a six-inch gun battery that was built in 1940 to stave off a German landing. Yes, here on this marvelous links beside the North Sea we stand in the very front lines designed to repel the invasion that never came and to defend England against the Luftwaffe's bombers that did indeed come, in pitiless waves, night after night.

If the 1st hole is difficult, the 2nd is a killer. The forced carry from the tee over another deep pit shored up with railroad ties on this 447-yard par four is long, and though a solid drive gets us safely to the fairway, mere solidity is scarcely enough now that we are faced with an equally long second shot in order to get home.

The 405-yard 3rd is more of the same, this time with a two-tier green on a plateau beyond another powerfully intimidating boarded bunker. Fail to surmount this dreaded hazard on your long second into the prevailing wind and you are, in literal truth, in over your head, at the base of a wall of railroad ties. A thinned recovery attempt from the sand here can be life-threatening as the ball rockets back off the wood to skull you!

Brancaster is the last redoubt of bunkers faced with railroad ties. The intent was to keep the hazard intact despite high winds and strong rains. Once, such bunkers were commonplace on the seaside courses of Britain. Today they are rare, except at Brancaster.

Beyond the 3rd hole, brawn becomes less of a requirement, though the holes continue to challenge, particularly the famous 8th and the great 9th. The 8th is island golf at its most intriguing. This 480-yard par five is laid out through a saltwater marsh, with tee, fairway, and green all islands when the tide is in. It can be an unnerving odyssey. The 9th, at 400 yards, doglegs right as we again carry the salt marsh from the tee, biting off as much as we can chew. Looming ahead at the green are the railroad ties lining the face of another broad sandpit, and short of it a creek, so that once more it is a case of win or woe.

Brancaster has a number of elevated tees, particularly on the second nine, which is routed closer to the sea. Here we begin most holes from a little clearing high in the dunes and thus enjoy enthralling views over the links and the tidal marsh, over the beach and the sea. Among the outstanding holes here are 14, 15, and 16. On the 423-yard 14th, following a downhill drive to a landing area hidden in the dunes, we face the quintessential Brancaster second shot, a long carry over yet another deep and terrorizing boarded bunker sealing off the green. The 15th measures 186 yards to a narrow green with a cambered entrance where only a high, softly falling shot has any chance. At 16, just 334 yards, the drive from a lofty tee is inviting, but the hole now doglegs strongly right in the dunes and the pitch must be played to a high plateau green tucked around the corner.

Often marvelously testing and presenting many opportunities to negotiate shots along the firm turf, Brancaster is supremely natural, old-fashioned, full of spunk and, in its own way, of beauty and serenity—the seabirds swooping and crying over the dunes, the sea lavender and sea holly studding the marsh, and the sea itself murmuring beyond the range of sandhills.

Commander Morrison gave me a little booklet called "Hull Tide Tables," which, he emphasized, golfers at Brancaster find indispensable. The tidal flooding that can make playing the 8th hole a dodgy exercise in island-hopping also sweeps up to the clubhouse, cutting off access to it for up to three hours. As if anything more were needed to make this secluded jewel one of golf's special places.

Back on the A149 now, we head east along the coast for nearly twenty miles, to Sheringham and its grand eighteen high above the sea, between the railway line and the cliffs backdropping the beach. As at Hunstanton and Brancaster, the club here was founded in 1891. That September, Tom Dunn laid out the original nine, which was extended to eighteen in 1898.

Spotted with patches of gorse and an occasional tree, the land ranges from rolling to hilly. It is replete with natural sites for greens and tees, it is home to bedeviling breezes, and it is blessed, at 200 feet above the sea, with heartstopping 360-

degree panoramas of yellow sandstone cliffs, tawny beaches, the town of Sheringham, the farms, and the wooded hills.

Early on comes an exhilarating four-hole sequence. The 401-yard 3rd, which plays a good 430, climbs steeply as it brings the cliffs, on our right, into play for the first time. On the sporty 309-yard 4th—elevated tee, fairway sloping sharply right to left, elevated green—we may make a birdie or, rather more easily, a bogey. The 5th, 452 yards long, is one of England's great two-shotters. From its noble tee at the cliff edge, our drive lifts off, white against blue, seeming to defy gravity before finally touching down in the broad fairway dizzyingly far below. Now the long second shot, traversing restless terrain, must find a sand-free green with a steep falloff on the left and large mounds on the right. Against this thrillingly theatrical hole the 201-yard 6th manages to hold its own, thanks to another spectacular drop, this one of perhaps 100 feet.

The last stop on our coastal itinerary is four or five miles farther along the A149, at Cromer, the most attractive of the Norfolk seaside resorts. It became fashionable roughly a century ago and continues to be well-regarded for its tasty crabs, fine beach, pier and promenade, its fifteenth-century church with a tower 159 feet high, and more to the point in this book, its golf course. Royal Cromer is indebted to Old Tom Morris for the original design of the course, in 1888, and to James Braid and his partner John Stutt for the golf holes today.

This hilly clifftop eighteen, 6,280 yards long, plays to a par of 72. The fairways are generous, a necessity in view of the winds that rake this course, but the greens, fast and true, are stingy. Bunkering is moderate. Gorse, bracken, boundaries, and occasional blind shots all give pause.

All Courses Great and Small

The last six holes are attractively varied, beginning with the iron shot on the splendid 13th, 165 yards over a deep and inimical ravine. On the next hole, a 391-yarder, the drive should be sighted on the 150-year-old lighthouse; it's over the cliff and gone to sea for a slice. The hole doglegs left to a neatly bunkered green that lists to port and shunts away many a good-looking shot. Not too many years ago, Tony Jacklin chose this as one of his "eighteen holes on eighteen different courses, via helicopter." The 385-yard 15th is at least as testing. We drive over a road and some wild country into a gathering valley far below; the second shot bends right as it climbs steeply to a green bunkered right and left. Sixteen, 306 yards, and 17, 115 yards, are birdie opportunities. The home hole, 369 yards, is a memorable finisher: From another high tee, the drive is launched down into a billowing fairway, where a large concealed bunker lurks to trap the ball that lands even slightly left of center. The second shot, perhaps 140 yards, falls to a dramatic double-terrace green lined along the left with three sandpits.

There is plenty to engage us as we make our way around Royal Cromer. And who knows?—if the North Sea breeze is not too brisk, we may even pull off that rarest of feats, playing to our handicap on a course we've never seen before.

Now for two suggestions on lodgings out here on the East Anglian coast. First, the seventeenth-century Hoste Arms Hotel, on The Green in the village of Burnham Market. This twenty-one-room inn is an endearing hodgepodge of various-size public and guest rooms, creaky stairways, slanting floors, open fireplaces, old paneling, and up-to-snuff bathrooms. (Ask for Room #1.) The bar, highly popular with locals, is one of the legendary English pubs. And the restaurant, featuring fresh fish dishes, is equally admired. Less than fifty paces away is Fishes' Restaurant—first-rate seafood again, this time in a dining room that is simple to the point of being spartan.

The other hotel, Le Strange Arms, is all of a 5-iron from Hunstanton Golf Club. Less atmospheric than Hoste Arms, it is cheerful and comfortable, with lawns that sweep down to the dunes and to a beautiful sandy beach. Adjacent is the Ancient Mariner, a traditional fisherman's pub.

Simply wandering in this part of Norfolk is a treat: ancient and picturesque villages like Burnham Deepdale (carvings on the baptismal font in the parish church are eleventh century) and Blakeney (sailboat regatta in August); nature preserves such as Tichwell and Snettisham; stately homes like Houghton Hall and Holkham Hall (both huge, eighteenth century, Palladian style); and above all, Sandringham, where the royal family spends Christmas. Taken as a whole—the great house itself, the gardens, the perfect little church—Sandringham is the stuff of dreams.

With three additional East Anglian courses on our agenda, we're heading inland now, in a southwesterly direction, toward Cambridge. Thetford Golf Club's course (6,499 yards, par 71) was designed by little-known Charles H. Mayo in 1912. Here, ringed by woods, is classical heathland golf, where American airmen stationed nearby happily logged hundreds of hours during World War II.

The start is uncommon, a par three, in this case an excellent hole, the falling 194-yard shot crossing a valley to a bi-level green. The 365-yard 2nd doglegs left (gorse for the hook, heather for the slice). And then, surprisingly, we face another par three, this one of 147 yards. The 4th and 5th are serious two-shotters, with the drive on the latter having to be slotted between a bunker on the left and a chalk pit on the right. Then, after a 495-yard par five, where we might gain a stroke, and another par four where precision off the tee is critical, we meet the scary 210-yard 8th. From an elevated tee, the shot—often windblown—falls to a crowned green guarded at the left front by water, at the right front by trees. No drama on the 9th; what's needed in this backbreaking par four—452 yards, the ground rising in front of the green—are two stronger hits than I can muster.

Coming home, we are lulled by the start—305 yards, 312 yards, 369 yards (sporty drive on the 12th over a chalk pit, this one in the elbow of the dogleg)—into believing brawn will be unnecessary, but the 522-yard 13th promises sterner stuff. Making good on that promise are the 14th (429 yards), 16th (only 167 yards long, but sand every step of the way), 17th (521 yards, bending right, with a long forced carry over heather and gorse from the tee), and 18th, an endless par four of 467 yards, also curving right, and with a bunker guarding the right side of the tee-shot landing area to make the long hitter think twice.

There is a naturalness to this layout and a pleasing diversity of shots. And when the round is over we will find ourselves concluding that this lovely wooded course is, on the whole, quite testing.

Eight or nine miles south of Thetford lies the only nine-hole royal course in the world, Royal Worlington and New Market. The club was founded in 1893 and the course was laid out by Tom Dunn soon thereafter. Harry Colt revised the nine in 1906.

Among the game's many important figures who have hymned

James W. Finegan

the praises of Worlington are Herbert Warren Wind (". . . far and away the best nine-hole course in the world"), Pat Ward-Thomas, Frank Pennink, Peter Ryde, Donald Steel, and Bernard Darwin (". . . the sacred nine"). I could scarcely wait to get to the 1st tee. Alas, I walked off the 9th green profoundly disappointed.

Four holes are prosaic: the 1st (a level, straightaway, lightly bunkered, featureless, 486-yard par five) and 4th (another equally uninspired short par five); the 7th (165 yards, flat and forgettable); and the 9th (300 yards, with a large landing area for the drive and a large green). At the 2nd, a husky 224-yarder, the green is an inverted saucer, so chipping requires deftness. The 6th and 8th are two very long and excellent par fours—458 and 460 yards. The green is ever so slightly elevated at the left front of the 6th, and on the 8th it is heavy crossbunkering ninety yards from the green that can make us uneasy in a head-wind. The charming 3rd, 361 yards, has a ravine at the left of the tee-shot landing area that must be sedulously avoided. And then there is the unique 5th, which is very possibly great and which is undeniably outrageous. It is 157 yards long and offers no hazards of any kind—no bunkers, water, boundaries, ditches, ravines. The green is long and narrow. As we stand on the tee, sheltered in a glade, the hole, very gently rising, looks all innocence. In truth, it is satanic. Anything less than a perfect swing will not do. You see, the landing area for the shot is effec-tively no wider than five paces, fifteen feet. Touch down on either side of this mini-target and your ball scoots off, right or left, down a shaved embankment. You are now faced with a lit-tle pitch—or a scuffle—almost as demanding as the stroke from the tee, with the very real possibility now of skimming back and forth from side to side. You might well take 6 on this par three without making a poor stroke. It is a hole like no other. As to its basic fairness, that's not a question I would care to debate.

Let it be said at once that the greens at Worlington are superb—quick, true, undulating, very seaside in quality and challenge. But they cannot confer greatness on a course where the overall terrain—a pleasant meadow—is of no distinction and where too many holes are ordinary.

Now if my assessment of the nine is fair, why is the course renowned, admired, esteemed, in truth, beloved? Perhaps the key lies in that final adjective, *beloved*. Worlington is the home of the Cambridge University golf team, and it always has been. It is the graduates of Cambridge and of Oxford who have over the years emerged as the outstanding commentators on the game and its playing fields, in Britain. And Cambridge has produced more than its share of tastemakers—Darwin, Wind, Steel, Harry Colt, Henry Longhurst, and Leonard Crowley (golf correspondent of the London *Daily Telegraph* for twenty-five years and a Walker Cupper), to name the most prominent.

For generations, Cambridge undergraduates have seized every chance to slip away from lectures and tutorials in order to get in a game at Worlington. The club is not just around the corner from the university—it is twenty miles away. I suspect that the sense of escape—from books, from authority—led to the heavily nostalgic affection with which these otherwise clear-eyed men viewed this plangent nine. Those of us who do not share these old school ties should go to Royal Worlington with modest expectations; then we may enjoy the game, perhaps even more so the second time around.

On the outskirts of Cambridge lies the Gog Magog Golf

James W. Finegan

Club, which has twenty-seven holes, the original eighteen laid out in 1901 by Willie Park, Jr., plus a nine designed by Fred W. Hawtree in the late 1970s. Meadowland golf on rolling and at times even hilly terrain, the Park course is not especially testing—the tee-shot landing areas struck me as too generous and the rough as too light—but the bunkering is stringent and the holes are nicely varied.

On my visit to Gog Magog, very like twenty years ago, I was fortunate to play with the then captain, Gerald A. B. Turner, a man in his early sixties who must have been a 5 or 6 in his prime. He was helpful on distances, informative about the club and the course, and solicitous for Harriet's welfare. ("On the next hole we'll be coming right back to the green over there, just beyond that spinney, where you'll find a bench to make yourself comfortable while you wait.")

There were two moments in the round that I particularly recall, thanks in no small measure to Gerald Turner. Next to the 13th hole on my scorecard is just one word: "Terrific!" Two hundred and five yards long, with the tee on much the same level as the green and a gentle dip between the two, the hole at first glance is not impressive. But the green is perched on a modest rise, there is a steep falloff at the left front, a shallow falloff at the right, and a small clump of trees just left of the direct line. In the prevailing breeze, left to right, there is no way to gain the green except by hitting this long shot over the trees: hitting it over and hitting it up.

I commented on the excellence of the hole. Gerald nodded, hesitated for just a moment, and then, having made up his mind to set modesty aside, said, "I aced it once, with a 3-wood. On New Year's Day. It was a mild day, a beautiful day."

Then he added with a smile, "Cost me a pretty penny, that shot did."

On the par-four 5th the tee is high, the fairway slopes sharply left to right, and the vistas are glorious. "There are Gog and Magog," said my companion, pointing to two hills well beyond the boundaries of the course. "Gog and Magog, if you recall your Old Testament, represented the forces under Satan's leadership that were to war against the kingdom of God. Now I'll tell you why it's always so breezy on this course. Because those are the first hills between here and the Ural Mountains of Russia, the first hills west of the Urals, so there's nothing between here and Russia to block the wind that comes blowing across the plains of the Continent. Gog and Magog."

I was flabbergasted. While he was teeing up, I stared at those two hills. That is all they are, a couple of hills. I didn't know what to say, so I said nothing. It all sounded preposterous to me, but I loved the preposterous sound of it.

We played down the 18th in the last vestiges of twilight. While the three of us were enjoying a drink in the contemporary brick and red-tile clubhouse, Gerald said, "Perhaps I failed to mention it. Gog Magog's ground does not belong to the club. It's owned by one of the Cambridge colleges, Gonville and Caius. We have a ninety-nine-year lease, which is about to expire. But I'm confident it will be renewed."

CHAPTER FIVE

Old and New— North and West of London

 TURNING OUR BACK on East Anglia, we're now heading down to Greater London, where we are going to stay put for three chapters, playing more than twenty courses. The outskirts of the capital, like those of New York, Philadelphia, and Chicago, are extravagantly endowed with good golf.

North and west of the city, in Hertfordshire, Buckinghamshire, and Oxfordshire, are five notable courses. One of them is great, and it was laid out by an American ten years ago. Let's save it for last and start with the eldest of this quintet.

Huntercombe Golf Club is in Nuffield, Oxfordshire, five or six miles up the road from Henley-on-Thames, home of the famous annual rowing regatta. Willie Park, Jr., laid out the course here in 1901, and it is little changed to this day, which makes it beguilingly old-fashioned: crossbunkers, low mounding framing some of the greens, and far more grass bunkers than those containing sand. There is some gorse and less heather and, very occasionally, a tree to contend with. But the fairways are wide, the rough is not high, there is no water and only rarely a boundary. The greens constitute the course's chief defense: They are swift and they are sometimes dramatically contoured. The 13th, with its two tiers, is often pointed to as the first known double-level green. Park, who also designed or revised more than sixty courses in the United States, was an innovator.

Huntercombe measures 6,301 yards against a par of 70. It opens with a bland 150-yarder, but the 2nd (elevated tee with panoramic views of the Chiltern Hills) and 3rd (the green on this pretty dogleg left is in a natural dell) are testing two-shotters played over rolling terrain. The rest of this easy-walking course is rather level.

A look at both the topography and the scorecard suggests that we ought to have little difficulty playing to our handicap. But somehow, on this pleasant and secluded eighteen that puts little pressure on the swing, it doesn't necessarily work out that way. There are half a dozen strong par fours and a 214-yard par three, not to mention those perplexing Park greens.

On a visit to Huntercombe some years ago, I chatted briefly with the secretary, a retired lieutenant colonel who had been secretary at Royal Lytham & St. Annes (Chapter 15) for four years, during which the club hosted the Open Championship ("One is quite enough!"). He said, "Huntercombe is a golf club, nothing else. That's what we want, that's all we want. We serve lunch, no dinners. I'm told there was a dinner-dance about seven years ago. I rarely meet with the Board—they expect me to handle everything. Currently our roster shows ten MPs [Members of Parliament], ten justices of the High Court, and

James W. Finegan

several air marshals. Our members are wonderful. They never complain. If a door falls on one of them and I run into him ten days later he may mutter, 'You might want to look into that door in the changing room—doesn't strike me as quite sound.'"

Ian Fleming, a member of the club from 1932 until his untimely death in 1964, played here regularly. The guest register discloses that General Omar Bradley played the course in May of 1943. Perhaps "Ike," who would have been sympathetic, gave him the day off.

There can be little question but that the two most opulent clubhouses in England are those at Stoke Poges (Buckinghamshire) and Moor Park (Hertfordshire). Both clubs boast golf courses by Colt. Harry Shapland Colt studied Law at Cambridge, then practiced as a solicitor for a time, but golf was his first love. He served from 1901 to 1913 as secretary of newly founded Sunningdale, during which time he also managed to lay out some twenty courses, most of them in England, and to advise George Crump on the design of Pine Valley. (The terrifying 5th, 232 yards, and the electrifying 10th, 146 yards, can fairly be attributed to Colt.) He was the first course architect not to have been a professional golfer. In a career that saw him designing and revising courses for more than forty years, he created, often in partnership with C. H. "Hugh" Alison, such masterpieces as Wentworth's West Course, St. George's Hill, the New Course at Sunningdale (all to be discussed in succeeding chapters) and the championship eighteen at Royal Portrush. In his later years—he died in 1950 at eighty-two—gardening was his hobby, and he once won the gold medal for sweet peas at the Bath Flower Show. He considered this to be a more difficult achievement than planning any eighteen-hole golf course.

All Courses Great and Small

In 1908 Colt laid out twenty-seven holes for the newly minted Stoke Park Club, at Stoke Poges. The golf just may be put in the shade by the clubhouse *cum* hotel, an eighteenth-century Palladian-style mansion by James Wyatt, architect to King George III. This terraced and balustraded and pedimented and be-columned pale cream mansion is more magnificent today than at any time in its history, thanks principally to the full-scale restoration of the interior during the late 1990s. At every turn we encounter a veritable symphony of the decorative arts employed in traditional style: marble columns and parquet floors, crystal chandeliers and priceless antiques, fine tapestries and old oil paintings, handsome paneling and magnificent carved fireplaces, luxurious fabrics and equally luxurious carpets, and, lest it all sound rather overpowering, plenty of comfortable leather-upholstered club chairs for simply relaxing.

Colt's gently rolling layout here at Stoke Park is an ideal companion to the manor house in that it, too, is stylish and elegant. But Colt did not have a first-rate parcel of land (very little feature) and the result is good parkland golf but no better. There are some pedestrian holes—the par-five 1st and 13th, the par-four 6th and 16th, and the par-three 15th—and it seems to me that there are no inarguably great holes, though a number are very good.

The club points with pride to the one-shot 7th as the inspiration for the 12th at Augusta National. (Alister Mackenzie, for several years a partner of Colt's, would probably have been familiar with this hole at Stoke Poges.) Generally played at about 150 yards from a slightly elevated tee, the tree-framed 7th presents a very modestly falling shot to a generous green angled to the line of flight, a lot of sand along the left rear of the putting surface and, at the right front, a steep falloff to a narrow stream. There is no bail-out area. The shot must be well aimed and well struck. It is an altogether excellent hole and, I insist, altogether superior to Augusta's grossly unfair 12th, where the green is too shallow a target (about five paces too shallow), given the gusting breezes which bedevil the shot.

Distinguishing the course are the complex and silken-swift greens and, even more so, the bunkers, which are variously shaped and exquisitely sited, the sand often flashed up the face, the lip sometimes a swooping thin line. What we see here is a brilliant exhibition of the art—for surely it is an art—of classical bunkering. And it is strikingly on display in the tee-shot landing areas, at every green, and sometimes in between (crossbunkers on the par-four 4th and the par-five 5th).

In 1923, fifteen years after his work at Stoke Poges, Colt was hired to lay out two eighteens at Moor Park, in Rickmansworth, Hertfordshire, some twenty miles from Stoke Poges. Once again the master's work was overshadowed by the clubhouse, a massive pile built by the Duke of Monmouth, Captain of the King's Forces, in 1670. Expatriate Venetian artists were commissioned to paint murals and decorate the rooms in marble and gilt. It is overwhelming. The great hall, for instance, is a perfect cube, forty feet by forty feet by forty feet. Seated in it on an old leather chesterfield sofa, Harriet and I ate ham-and-cheese-on-rye sandwiches for lunch. Pheasant under glass would not have done the setting justice.

The High Course at Moor Park measures 6,370 yards from the regular markers. Par is 72. Stately pine and beech trees help to shut out suburban sprawl. The opening hole is quite good, a 360-yarder that finds us driving from a slightly elevated

tee into the opposite hillside, then climbing to the green. The 2nd is one of the best holes on the course, a dogleg-right 403-yarder calling for a goodly forced carry over a dip and then over sand, followed by a long second to a tightly bunkered green. The green on the knob-to-knob 3rd, 153 yards, is an island in sand, and the following two holes, a long two-shotter (420 yards, downhill) and a short two-shotter (315 yards, uphill) are first-rate. But three of the last four holes on this side are routine, with only the mighty 8th—440 yards, downhill off the tee, dogleg right, then uphill to a green defended by a pond short and left, trees short and right, and bunkers left and right—saving the day.

The second nine echoes the first, generous fairways and greens, plenty of bold ups and downs and distant views, most of the holes worthy but again three that are humdrum (13, 16, 17). Memorable are the two-shotter 11th, which plunges blindly from the tee and climbs near vertically to the green, and the 200-yard 12th, played over a deep, partly wooded valley to an immense two-tier green flanked by more sand than we might have expected on such a tester. The round ends unusually, with a pretty 134-yarder, a falling shot to a well-bunkered plateau green set on the diagonal.

We enjoy the round on the High Course, its periphery dotted with lovely houses and gardens, but, as at Stoke Poges, we had hoped for a bit more spark, a bit more originality. The West Course is almost a thousand yards shorter. Par is 69. The rolling land provides a number of attractive green sites, but with the eleven par fours averaging about 325 yards, this eighteen, no matter how agreeable, cannot be taken seriously.

Back to Buckinghamshire now, to a course that is eleven years old as this book goes to press. John Jacobs—noted teacher, two-time captain of the European Ryder Cup team, and occasional winner on the Senior Tour here in the United States—laid it out for the Buckinghamshire Golf Club, in Denham. It measures 6,401 yards from the regular markers against a par of 72.

John Jacobs is a big man (six feet three inches, 225 pounds, broad shouldered and muscular), and his Buckinghamshire is big golf—big fairways, big greens, big bunkers, seven water holes—that roams over 225 acres. There is little in the way of elevation change. Mature trees beautify parts of the layout, but this perfectly conditioned course is generally open in aspect, encouraging aggressive driving. The setting is serenely pastoral.

Good holes are plentiful. Some holes surprise us, like the 501-yard 18th, where a grand old beech tree stands defiantly dead on line a hundred yards short of the green. Some holes are rigorous, like the wonderful 413-yard 10th, doglegging right around a clump of trees, bunkers at the left in the tee-shot landing area, sand corseting the narrow green, water immediately right of the right-hand bunker. Other holes are a pure delight. In that category is the 332-yard 8th, which bends boldly left around a large pond stretching almost to the front edge of the heavily bunkered green. This hole is so short that we ought to be able to handle it, but it is mildly unnerving, which may be all that's required to trigger a chunked 9-iron or pitching wedge into the water.

The beautiful and substantial red-brick clubhouse is a Grade II-listed eighteenth-century structure. I chatted there with the professional, fifty-year-old Irish-born John O'Leary, four-time winner on the European Tour and a 1975 Ryder Cupper, and managing director Takao Miura, an employee of the Japanese company that owns the club. Cordial but somewhat guarded, Mr. Miura characterized the Buckinghamshire as an international club, with members from all over the world. He said that roughly half of the members are Japanese who live and work in Greater London. Visitors unaccompanied by members are welcome, but this type of play is not solicited. The clubhouse is quiet—indeed, the atmosphere is almost hushed. The gardens are impeccably maintained, and through them flows the river Colne, a gentle stream.

The Oxfordshire Golf Club, six or seven miles outside the university city, is also Japanese-owned. The course opened in 1993. Its architect is Rees Jones, who first came to prominence for his updating of a number of U.S. Open courses, including The Country Club and Bethpage Black, and who has further solidified his reputation with many outstanding original designs

James W. Finegan

(the Atlantic, the Green Course at Williamsburg Inn, Dacotah Ridge, Nantucket, Ocean Forest, et al.).

Routed over 260 acres of open and gently rolling countryside, dotted with countless mounds suggesting low dunes, marked only very occasionally by trees, and with the rough's long golden fescues whipping and shimmering in the wind, this course is even bigger—and far more adversarial—than the Buckinghamshire. Played at 6,307 yards, it offers quite enough golf unless your handicap is 5 or lower. Par is 72. On eight holes, ponds or lakes constitute a clear danger. There are 140 sand bunkers, some of them vast and fanciful, others tiny, shallow, circular pans (witness the cluster of nine just short of the 5th green).

My companion on a round here a couple of summers ago was Richard Moan, the club's forty-year-old manager of operations and an accomplished player. The wind blew at twenty-five to thirty-five miles per hour. I struggled just to make contact and was not disappointed with an 86. Richard, no taller than five feet eight inches but weighing at least 180 pounds, shot 76, consistently exhibiting the same smooth takeaway and full turn, never letting the wind prompt a short-circuited backswing or a rushed attack on the ball.

On a course with many superlative holes, three ought above all to be described. A longtime Pine Valley member, Jones has taken the great par-five 7th there as a direct inspiration for his 540-yard 4th here. As on the original, the drive calls for a forced carry over rough ground to reach the generous landing area. The second shot, again as at Pine Valley, must now traverse a vast irregular bunker well over 100 yards long to reach the safe harbor of a second landing area and get into position for the short third shot. Imperiling this pitch to a slightly elevated green—and here there is no borrowing from the New Jersey course—is a small natural pond just short and right of the putting surface. Jones's hole here is called "Hell's Half Acre," the same name given to the immense crossbunker at the heart of Pine Valley's 7th.

Two holes, 8 and 17, have been selected for *The 500 World's Greatest Golf Holes*. A lake skirts the right side of the 347-yard 8th from tee to green. The fairway grows progressively narrower as it buttonhooks so emphatically right around the water that both it and the green jut into the lake. Sand along the left side of the hole precludes any possibility of bailing out there. Into the teeth of what was at least a three-club wind, Richard struck two perfect 3-irons, the second one over the corner of the lake to the heart of the green.

The 17th astonishes. Squarely in the middle of the real estate devoted to this par five, which measures 495 yards from the regular markers, is a lake, an elongated oval. The high tee is some 200 yards short of the water. The green is at the far end of this 275-yard-long hazard. There are three routes to the hole: the long way round, to the right; the shorter way round, to the left; and as the crow flies. The right-hand route—the so-called safe way—still calls for a third shot of 115–150 yards, most of it over water. The left-hand route involves a forced carry on the second shot of at least 180 yards to reach dry land and then a 100-yard shot to the green. The ultimate risk/reward play— going for the green in two—demands two powerful and perfect swings, the second one to carry no less than 225 yards over the Lake. Rees Jones said to me, "When the Benson & Hedges International was played here in 1996—now remember, there were cold winds that sometimes blew at fifty miles an hour—

every score from 3 to 13 was recorded on this hole over the four days. That was a record for a European Tour Tournament."

The clubhouse at The Oxfordshire, where a high percentage of members are Japanese, is no centuries-old manor house but a blocky 40,000 square foot structure that, as the British say, was "purpose built." It is comfortable and welcoming, with lots of glass to provide good views over the great course. Richard and I had lunch in the spike bar and were later joined by Masahiro Obata, the general manager, a short forty-year-old wearing a shiny silver-gray double-breasted suit. They were at pains to convey the private nature of the club, which they view as comparable to Swinley Forest and Rye in that respect. The Oxfordshire, however, does host corporate golf outings with frequency. As for the individual visitor, club policy requires that he or she be accompanied by a member. But someone belonging to a recognized American club who telephones to express a sincere interest in playing the course has a good chance of being accommodated.

You could choose to stay at a London hotel and drive out daily to any of these courses. But there are also excellent lodgings rather more convenient. Less than thirty minutes from Moor Park and surrounded by forty acres of gardens is Grim's Dyke Hotel, which was the home of the great librettist/lyricist Sir William Gilbert for the last twenty-one years of his life. Bedrooms in the main house are more attractive than those in the lodge. Dinner in the Music Room—minstrel gallery and fireplace—is quite enjoyable.

Perhaps forty-five minutes from the Buckinghamshire Golf Club, thirty minutes from Heathrow, and just outside the picturesque town of Marlow-on-Thames stands nineteenth-century

All Courses Great and Small

Danesfield House, a chalky white crenellated castle perhaps 150 feet above the river. This is a great country house hotel in every sense: setting, appointments, accommodations (the Hurley Room has a ballustraded terrace looking down on the Thames), food, service.

In Woodstock, about thirty minutes from The Oxfordshire, is the seventeenth-century Feathers Hotel, which manages to be both chic and cozy (some rooms are small), with the added plus of wonderful cooking. Woodstock is a fetching village with small shops, small hotels, small cottages, and one very, very big house, Blenheim Palace, Sir John Vanbrugh's masterpiece. Winston Churchill was born there in 1874, and he is buried in the churchyard of nearby Bladon. Then, just eight miles down the A34 lies Oxford, town and gown, on the lovely Cherwell and Isis Rivers. With a population of 120,000, the city may be bigger and more bustling than many would prefer, but the university, architecturally and academically, is still one of the glories of Western civilization.

One final accommodation, the sumptuous clubhouse/hotel at Stoke Park, is only fifteen minutes from Heathrow. There are twenty-one luxurious guest rooms (most with a fireplace) and stylish dining in Stoke's Brasserie. And just beyond the Colt golf holes and the adjacent fields, its tower perhaps in view from your room, lies St. Giles Church, which dates mainly from the fourteenth century. Today it is revered by thousands of pilgrims annually as the place where in 1750 Thomas Gray composed "Elegy Written in a Country Churchyard," and where the poet himself is buried. Still to be seen there is the ancient yew tree under which, tradition says, Gray sat to write the imperishable verses. The opening quatrains call up a world that somehow seems little changed, lo these 250 years later, as we are reminded when the bells of St. Giles ring out over this idyllic scene again and again:

> *The curfew tolls the knell of parting day,*
> *The lowing herd wind slowly o'er the lea,*
> *The plowman homeward plods his weary way*
> *And leaves the world to darkness and to me.*

> *Now fades the glimmering landscape on the sight,*
> *And all the air a solemn stillness holds,*
> *Save where the beetle wheels his droning flight,*
> *And drowsy tinklings lull the distant folds.*

CHAPTER SIX

Harry Colt in
Berkshire and Surrey

DRIVE DUE WEST of London and you promptly find yourself in Berkshire. Head south and you immediately enter Surrey. In these two counties can be found the sandbelt shrines of Sunningdale, Wentworth, the Berkshire, and Swinley Forest, four clubs with a total of eight eighteen-hole courses, among them some of the most fabled heathland layouts.

We've already played three great heathland courses—Alwoodley, Notts (Hollinwell), Woodhall Spa—with their sand-based turf, heather, and variety of scrubby vegetation, perhaps including gorse. In season these courses are firm and fast, fairways as well as greens, with the play along the ground every bit as critical to the game—and our success at it—as the play through the air. True heathland golf, which emulates links golf, is found only in the British Isles and, to go a step farther, rarely outside England.

Sunningdale, twenty-two miles from Piccadilly Circus, is often pointed to as the surpassing venue for heathland golf. When I first visited the club, more than thirty years ago, I was able to appreciate only half of what awaits us here. Harriet and I and two of our three children, John and Megwin, had taken the transatlantic night flight from Philadelphia to Heathrow, where I picked up a rental car and headed dutifully into the city so that the ladies could check into the hotel and fall into bed. My sixteen-year-old son and I now turned around and drove straight back out, to Sunningdale. The secretary suggested that we play the Old Course first, have lunch, then play the New. It was at this point that my vaunted research collapsed: *I was unaware of the existence of a New.* Striving to conceal my ignorance, I said that this was just what we had in mind, and off we went to the 1st tee of the Old Course. We played it. Then, after a sandwich, we headed for the 1st tee of the New Course. By now, sleepless for thirty hours, we were zombies, semi-comatose, our swings lifeless, our games a travesty of what this marvelous course requires. More than once we found ourselves nodding off, our eyes briefly closing as we dozed momentarily while bending down to tee the ball up. I could not remember a hole—the course was just a vast blur of rolling terrain. When we got back into London, at nearly seven o'clock, Harriet and Meg were waiting impatiently at the hotel, four theater tickets in hand. On the first day of our trip to Britain in 1973, John and I managed to sleep through both the New Course at Sunningdale and Angela Lansbury's all-stops-out performance in *Gypsy.*

Sunningdale's Old Course, which opened in 1901, was laid out by Willie Park, Jr. It was Harry Colt, secretary during the club's first dozen years, who planted thousands of pine trees to create the enclosed look so characteristic of the individual holes today. He also extensively revised many holes. The Old has long been the scene of important competitions, including the Walker

All Courses Great and Small

Cup, the PGA Matchplay, the Dunlop Masters, the European Open, and the Women's British Open. Among the professionals who have won here are Gary Player, Greg Norman, Bernhard Langer, Ian Woosnam, and Nick Faldo. But it was the 66 here by an amateur, Bob Jones, in qualifying for the 1926 Open Championship, that is perhaps most memorable. A 66 was uncommon in those days, and this particular 66, made up entirely of 3s and 4s, was close to perfection: 33 going out, 33 coming in, 33 putts, 33 other shots. The golfing world was awestruck, and Sunningdale became famous almost overnight.

You will probably play the course at 6,308 yards, par 70. The 1st, an old-fashioned par five of 492 yards, and the 3rd, an old-fashioned par four of 292 yards, are birdie holes. The 2nd, a 454-yard two-shotter, is a bogey hole: a long forced carry over heather from the tee and a long, exacting second shot to a sloping green guarded by a bunker at the left and heather at the right.

The next five holes are fine and testing, beginning with a 157-yarder uphill to a well-bunkered semiplateau green. Following it come three superlative par fours, with the noble and heathery 5th, 400 yards, played from an exhilaratingly high tee, a pond shining well short of the green. The entire hole, together with the 386-yard 6th stretching clearly away into the distance beyond it, is spread out invitingly below us, framed by the dense dark-green pine woods.

The final two-shotter in this cluster has about as much up and down and up again packed into 383 yards as I've ever seen. Our blind drive must climb abruptly in order to clear the sharp ridge immediately in front of the tee. But if this shot should turn out to be a shade short, we may now be going for the green from a downhill lie, across a little valley. The lovely 168-yard 8th, over a heathery waste to a shelf green, is followed by a 267-yard par four that surely has been driven hundreds of times.

The second nine, almost 300 yards longer yet also with a par of 35, is crammed with difficult holes, including the 222-yard 15th and five rigorous two-shotters (459 yards, 416, 423, 417, and 411). At 459 yards, for instance, the great 10th calls for a powerful drive from a point so high above the fairway that we wonder if our ball will ever touch the valley floor. The second shot requires a cannon uphill to a green sand-menaced right and left. Twelve, 416 yards, is also inarguably great. Following a solid drive, we must carry a line of five bunkers running across the fairway on an acute left-to-right diagonal—Colt's version of a crossbunker—if we are to reach the green, a bold plateau tucked into a ridge, with sand at the left corner and a falloff at the right.

The home hole, 411 yards long, features another string of bunkers on a left-to-right diagonal to threaten the underhit second shot as we move uphill toward a sand-guarded green, the club's famous old spreading oak tree backdropping the putting surface and shading the red-roofed Edwardian clubhouse with its white-faced clock proclaiming whether we have dawdled.

It is pure enchantment that characterizes Sunningdale Old. Virtually every hole is played in splendid—and beautiful—isolation, and in harmony with nature. The overall elevation change must be about seventy-five feet, which is close to ideal. Power is valuable on half a dozen holes, but it is finesse that is essential. There is subtlety here, a measure of drama, and a wealth of that one indispensable ingredient, pleasurable excitement. This eighteen, where no two holes are alike but all are of a piece, has a greatness of its own. No wonder it may be the single most beloved inland course in the British Isles.

All that being said, there are those who like the New Course, which opened in 1922, at least as well. And let me assure you that the second time I played it I was wide awake.

The New is perhaps a bit more rugged than the Old, a bit more masculine, if you will. Following the higher ground, with the downs rolling away in the distance, it commands a number of striking vistas. It is also more exposed to the breezes and it is, on occasion, somewhat bleaker in prospect. But make no mistake about it: This is rich and handsome and challenging golf, Harry Colt in top form.

You will probably want to play the New also from the white markers, which add up to 6,443 yards. Par is 71. This is a superb driving course, the result of a potent combination of elements: elevated tees, long forced carries over the vegetation, sometimes to angled fairways, and the penalty of choking heather for the off-line tee shot. And even when we have managed to produce a strong, safe drive, we face a demanding second shot. Colt's green complexes, which may well include taste of heather "eyebrows" festooning bunkers, give us plenty to ponder as we stand in the fairway. The greens themselves are a bit smaller than those on the Old, and the penalty for missing them is stiffer. Even the very short uphill pitch on the 485-yard par-five 6th is unsettling: sand tight at the right of the green, sand plus a grassy hollow a shade less importunate at the left, and a green so violently sloped that the back edge must be at least seven feet higher than the front edge!

Though the Old may have the most acclaimed holes on the property (its 5th and 15th were chosen for *The 500 World's*

James W. Finegan

Greatest Golf Holes book), there is an especially worthy trio of holes on the New at the turn, beginning with the roller-coaster 9th, 424 yards. The blind tee shot must carry a dip, then sail over a ridge and reach the bottom of the hill so that we are in position to fire an uphill 190-yard shot from level ground The green is defended by rising ground at the left and a falloff feeding into a lone bunker at the right. The great 10th, also through a corridor of pine and silver birch, is a very gently falling 206-yarder. Here the green appears to be all but islanded by sand, but the bunker out front, dead on the line we must follow, is deceptively short of the putting surface. The patch of turf between this bunker and the green plays fast and inclines to draw to the left, where sand under that side of the green lurks to trap a shot that comes up short. The 11th may not have the dash of 9 or 10, but it is excellent in its own right. Persistently curving left, this 436-yarder begins with a blind drive that, if we play safely out to the right, away from the thick rough and the trees, makes the hole too long for most of us. It also sets up an uncontrollable second shot through a stretch of hummocky fairway short of the green. For any chance of reaching the green in regulation, the drive and the long second must be kept left of center.

Sunningdale has a number of well-to-do members, but many of relatively modest means as well. The club is made up of a quite eclectic bunch: investment bankers, insurance salesmen, lawyers, sports figures (for instance, Jackie Stewart, the legendary Formula One racing champion), actors (Sean Connery), academicians, broadcasters, in short, a breadth of people who have earned their success. Among them are those with a penchant for gambling, though there are a lot more low-handicap golfers than high-stakes gamblers.

All Courses Great and Small

Not ten minutes from Sunningdale, on Swinley Road, in Ascot, which is better known in certain benighted circles for thoroughbred racing than for golf, lies the Berkshire Golf Club. Until World War I, the acreage here was part of a vast forest. When many of the trees were felled for lumber to help the war effort, some people realized what had not been obvious: this rolling heathland could be the setting for golf. Happily, the Crown Commissioners—for this is Crown land—agreed, even to the extent of paying for the construction of the clubhouse as well as the golf holes, and then, not content with the prospect of a mere eighteen, insisted on thirty-six. Where are such men of vision in government today?

W. Herbert Fowler, who had established his reputation at Walton Heath (next chapter) in 1904, was commissioned to lay out the two courses, which opened in 1928.

The individual holes on both eighteens have an almost cloistered feeling—they are isolated from their neighbors by the pretty woods of chestnut, pine, silver birch, and sycamore. The fairways ripple in linkslike fashion. The Blue Course measures 6,260 yards against a par of 71. It opens with a stern one-shotter—217 yards, a forced carry over a heather-covered swale, which falls away steeply right to a belt of trees. Sand left and right at the green further complicates matters. This hole is a bear.

The 2nd, 344 yards, plays from a high tee, and once down we stay down, for the first nine tends to be flat. And despite the occasional dogleg and an even rarer creek, it is not sufficiently challenging.

The second nine starts as did the first, with a strong par three, this one of 200 yards, and other than the easy par-five 11th (478 yards), there is consistently testing golf here. I was playing this eighteen some years ago with a past captain of the club who had with him three small dogs, spaniels of some sort. Models of deportment, they sat together on the tee while we drove, then padded lightly down the fairway at their master's heels, never interfering with the play and, in their own way, adding a homey and easy flavor to the proceedings. I would not say that their obedience was dearly bought, but their owner did have a pocketful of chocolate cookies, which he doled out to the dogs at careful intervals. They got their last—and his last— as we trooped up the 18th fairway.

My notes show the following adjectives beside the last four holes: *fine, heroic, good, very good.* The 15th, 406 yards long and beginning on an elevated tee, bends left and then moves gently uphill to a small green bunkered at the front corners. The landing area for the tee shot on the 452-yard 16th has a bunker at the left and heather at the right. The punishingly long second shot on this par four takes us on a left tack to an elevated green defended by a creek. Mighty stuff.

I've long felt that uphill holes measuring 375 yards generally play more than 410 yards. The 17th is a case in point. It is an extremely pretty par four, and the only danger here is that of adding another 5 to your card. For me, the home hole is a dandy, but it is not everyone's cup of tea. The drive on this 402-yarder is launched from very high ground. The second shot, now that we are down, is blind, up and over a hill. We hit and, holding our breath as the ball sails over the crest, we hope.

Though the club insists that the two eighteens are of equal caliber, I prefer the Red Course, 6,379 yards, par 72. Maybe I'm unduly taken with its makeup: six par threes, six par fours, six par fives. As I write, the only other layout that comes easily to mind with this same combination is the Old Course at the Homestead.

Almost predictably, Fowler's par fives do not hold up for the contemporary golfer. At least four of the six are birdie holes. This is not true of the par threes and fours.

Several of the two-shotters are especially memorable. The 360-yard 6th, for instance, has earned a place in *The 500 World's Greatest Golf Holes* book. Doglegging sharply through the woods, it demands a drive that is long enough and straight enough to finish clear of the right-side tree line. The shortish second shot is played to a modestly raised green defended by sand right and left. Interestingly, the key shot is the drive.

The 428-yard 8th is beautiful and hard. A long tee shot—ideally a power fade around the tall pines on this gentle dogleg right—is required to set up a long second shot across a valley to a narrow, sand-squeezed green beckoning from well up the far hillside.

The 350-yard 11th is also a gem—a falling drive from a very high tee, then a short pitch up to a sturdily bunkered plateau green. One of the assistant professionals told me that the hole is exactly the length of the QE2 and that both Tom Watson and Greg Norman have driven it.

Appealing as the par fours are here on the Red, it is the one-shotters that are the hallmark of the course. Collectively, the six of them are wonderful, and three of them are great. We play the 7th, 195 yards, over a deep, heather-covered swale to a gorgeously contoured green with a large bunker at the left front and a steep falloff at the right. That's the easy one. The 188-yard 10th is harder—and thrilling. The magnificently sited green, reminiscent of the celebrated 14th at Royal Portrush, perches at the edge of a precipice that plunges to the right, some twenty-five feet below the level of the putting surface, into heather and tall rough. And the 16th is hardest of all. A 221-yarder, it is played into the prevailing wind from a low knob up to a plateau green. A deep pit well short of the green and on the direct line to it lurks hungrily. A smaller and shallower bunker awaits at the left front. Rarely are we called on, anywhere, to make a swing this pure.

Just how enjoyable is the game on the Red Course? So enjoyable that I would relish the prospect of playing it every day of the week.

Scarcely fifteen minutes away and this time back on the other side of the county line, at Virginia Water, in Surrey, lies the incomparable—as far as England is concerned—Wentworth Club, founded in 1923. The long rhododendron-lined drive, with splendid private houses at a discreet remove peeping through the foliage, leads to the extraordinary castellated clubhouse, once the home of Spain's Countess Morella. I suspect that even she would be bowled over today by the vast pleasure dome Wentworth has become: three outstanding eighteen-hole courses and a sprightly little nine-holer; thirteen tennis courts, among which are four different playing surfaces; a seventy-eight-foot-long indoor swimming pool and a ninety-five-foot-long outdoor one; gymnasium, aerobics studio, and spa; a ballroom; overnight accommodations for more than forty; lounges and bars and restaurants and shops; and parking lots so vast and various that they have names lest we misplace our car! Wentworth may strike you as more a resort than a club.

The World Match Play Championship, which has been played annually over Wentworth's West Course since its inaugural in

All Courses Great and Small

1964, numbers among its winners Gary Player and Seve Balles-teros, both five-time champions; four-time winner Ernie Els; three-time champions Greg Norman and Ian Woosnam; Arnold Palmer, Hale Irwin, and Nick Faldo—each victorious twice; and Jack Nicklaus, Tom Weiskopf, Colin Montgomerie, and Mark O'Meara, conqueror of Tiger Woods in the 1998 final.

Still, among the more than 100 important competitions that have been staged at Wentworth, it is the 1953 Ryder Cup and the 1956 Canada Cup that the club's more senior members are inclined to mention. The visiting Ryder Cup team, led by Sam Snead, Lloyd Mangrum, and Cary Middlecoff, was on top, 3–1, at the end of Day One (36-hole foursomes matches). But the British and Irish rallied furiously in the singles and seemed poised to regain the Cup until its two rookies, Peter Alliss and Bernard Hunt, managed to fumble away their matches. Alliss bogeyed 16, 17, and 18 to hand Jim Turnesa the win. Hunt then missed a three-and-a-half-footer on the home green to let Dave Douglas off the hook. The U.S. prevailed, 6½–5½.

In June of 1956 Wentworth hosted the Canada Cup (now the World Cup). Professional pairs from twenty-eight countries competed. Sam Snead and Ben Hogan were heavily favored to win. On the flight to London, Hogan, who had never played in England and whose painstaking preparation for important competitions is legendary, took advantage of the long hours aloft to ask his partner to brief him on Wentworth's West Course. For a considerable time Snead silently weighed Hogan's request, giving him the clear impression that he was about to present a thorough analysis of the course. Finally he turned to Ben and said, "It's a sonofabitch." Thus enlightened, Hogan returned cards of 68, 69, 72, and 68 to lead the American pair to victory, 14 strokes ahead of runner-up South Africa (Bobby Locke and Gary Player).

Wentworth's West Course, which opened in 1927, is one of the top fifteen to twenty courses in Britain and Ireland. Once again, as at Sunningdale, we find Harry Colt weaving his magic in a rolling expanse of heather, fir, and silver birch. Played at 6,739 yards, this layout is actually less arduous than it sounds. Par is 73; there are five par fives, four of them—465, 485, 475, and 496 yards—rather short. Nor are the four par threes hefty: 135 yards, 169, 174, 179. And of the remaining holes, nine par fours, only four of them—442 yards, 437, 425, and 458—are so long as to be often out of reach. Oh, there is plenty of golf here, all of it beautiful and much of it quite testing, but it is not overwhelming. The forced carries are not excessive, the bunkering is moderate, and water threatens only on occasion. Predictably, heather and bracken await the off-line shot. And there are opportunities for tree limbs to bat the ball about.

What Colt created here some seventy-five years ago are eighteen completely individual holes that combine to achieve an attractive unity. For example, the 7th, 380 yards, doglegs right, and from a tee tucked away in a little wooded corner we drive downhill over a choppy and heathery badlands, taking care to avoid a bunker on the right and a stream crossing the fairway where a 260-yard swat would finish. With the ground now rising, we fire our second over a broad belt of rough to a plateau green angled to the line of flight and featuring a very businesslike pit at the right front that is ready to trap the thinly hit shot trying to sneak home on the ground.

At 437 yards, the 9th is long, and with an opening to the green pinched right and left by sand, it is tough. A railway line runs down the left side of the hole. Our drive from a lonely tee in the brush must carry a forbidding wasteland of bracken and scrub to reach a shelf of fairway. The hole, played into the prevailing breeze, then seems to roll along beside the railroad at least as far as the next station.

Speaking of rolling along, the same phrase might be applied to the 17th hole, the one par five here that, at 549 yards (it's played at nearly 600 yards in the World Match Play Championship), calls for good hitting, good thinking, and good control. A strong dogleg left, with a boundary running the entire length of the hole, tall trees bordering both sides of the route, and a fairway canted from left to right all help to account for the selection of the 17th as one of the top 100 in *The 500 World's Greatest* compendium.

A good twenty-five years ago, when I first played the West Course, a man introduced himself as a member of the club and insisted on buying me a drink. Then, turning to several friends, he said, "This is the chap who's playing all the courses in England and writing a book about them."

"Well, no," I demurred. "I'm just playing six courses here in the London area and writing a magazine piece about them."

"Oh, no matter," he said with a laugh. "What did you think of our West Course?"

"Oh, I thought it was—"

"You played the West Course, did you?" another in the group interjected. I later found out that he was slated to be the club's next captain. "Don't you agree," he continued, "that it is the best course you have ever seen, the best course you have played anywhere in the world? Say it is. You must believe it is." He laughed, but if he was kidding, it was kidding on the square.

James W. Finegan

The East Course, which opened in 1924 and hosted the inaugural Curtis Cup Match in 1932, was Colt's first eighteen at Wentworth, and it is little changed over the years. Could it, like the West, also be labeled great? I believe so. Is it, as some observers seem to think, considerably easier than the West? I believe not. Admittedly, there is more room to swing away on the East, the woods do not press in on its fairways, and it does not punish so harshly the shot that is *almost* good enough. Also, there is the disparity in length—or is there? We play the East at 6,201 yards, the West at 6,739. Ah, but it is precisely this that brings us to the heart of the matter. Par on the West is 73; on the East, a mere 68. What is the average value of each of those five strokes in yards? Surely not less than 150 yards, or 750 yards overall. Add that 750 to 6,201 and you have, if the East were also a par 73, a course that would measure more than 6,950 yards. The net of all this heavy arithmetic is that the East is actually a long course, very long indeed for day-in, day-out sociable club golf.

There is only one par five here, a 526-yarder played by and large over level ground. The one-shotters make up a glittering quintet. The shortest of them, the 159-yard 12th, is a dropping shot to a narrow and vigorously contoured green defended by six sandpits. The other four—195 yards, 226, 191, and 215—include two truly great holes, the 195-yard 4th (mildly rising, extravagantly bunkered, the tee tucked maddeningly left of what you dearly wish were the line of flight) and the 226-yard 7th, an old-fashioned brute whose governing feature is a very low, heather-topped turf bank that runs diagonally across the fairway and past the right side of the green. Classic in its simplicity, unique in my experience.

All Courses Great and Small

Which brings us to the dozen par fours, with their wrinkled, linkslike fairways and their frames of pine, silver birch, and on occasion, holly and rhododendron. Five of them are short, but only one, the dramatically downhill 14th, 323 yards, is easy. So much for this course's lone birdie hole. The other two-shotters include the opener, a smoothly rising 384-yarder that we ought to make a 4 on (and sometimes we even do), plus half a dozen truly superlative holes, ranging in length from the 403-yard 13th (uphill, bending right, a playing value of 450 yards, sand endangering both shots, a two-tier green) to the 459-yard 16th (spectacular downhill drive over heather, long second shot to clear a bunker in the center of the fairway and forty yards short of the sand-flanked green).

What do you care whether par is only 68? This is great golf.

It was in 1990 that the Edinburgh Course, designed by John Jacobs in collaboration with Bernard Gallacher and Gary Player, opened. Winding through virgin woodlands, it measures 6,585 yards from the regular markers (par 72). It is contemporary in look and feel, particularly in the bunkering and in the use of water, which comes into play on nine holes.

A number of strong doglegs lend character to the course. The 385-yard 4th, for instance, a marvelous hole, swings right in the tee-shot landing area and then plunges to a green where a hidden bunker lurks at the right side and steep falloffs await at the left and rear. If the Edinburgh is not quite in a class with Colt's eighteens here, it is nevertheless well worth playing.

A final word about golf at Wentworth: A lot of people who are not members tackle these courses every day, whether as guests or on their own or in outings. You have to expect a crowded scene. Please don't let this dissuade you from playing here, where two of the three courses are great and the third is no less than very good.

Head down the road four or five miles, back to Ascot, and with a little bit of luck you will find Swinley Forest Golf Club, off heavily wooded Coronation Road. Its tiny sign, perhaps the size of a #10 envelope, is all but indiscernible down in the grass. A large black wrought-iron gate automatically creeps open as your car approaches. Nor is there a guard on duty to check your credentials. You are more welcome than you may have thought. Over the years, Swinley Forest, with its superlative course by Harry Colt, has had a well-deserved reputation for privacy, for exclusivity, for elitism. Outsiders, unless in the company of members, were *verboten*. But if it is still scarcely a neighborhood muni, it is also no longer the unassailable bastion of the privileged that it once was.

I've played there only once, on a Friday in the late summer of 2001 with the club secretary, Lieutenant Colonel Ian Pearce (retired), who had taken this post after twenty-eight years in Her Majesty's Army. A cultivated and urbane man of about sixty, he seemed eager to have the club known for what it is today. The *new* Swinley Forest, if we may call it that, has been taking shape since Lieutenant Colonel Pearce arrived in 1988.

Much of the course is laid out on Crown land. In 1988 the Crown Commissioners were charging the club £4,000 annually for the lease. When I visited, that fee had climbed to £45,000, and, the secretary confided, it was entirely possible that when the next five-year contract is signed, it might well be for £90,000 annually. Add in the substantially rising cost of supplies and employee wages and benefits, and it is obvious that dues would have to be boosted or the membership would have to be enlarged or the revenue from visitors would have to be significantly increased.

In fact, all three steps have been taken. Nevertheless, only on rare days will there be as many as fifty players all told on the course, which will sometimes be deserted, literally empty, on a Saturday or Sunday afternoon in high season.

As for the individual seeking to play Swinley Forest—say, an American who doesn't know a member—if he were to contact Lieutenant Colonel Pearce, either in writing or by phone, and be a member of a recognized club, the secretary may be able to accommodate him.

Swinley Forest was founded in 1909. A look at the membership list, which hangs on a wall in the changing room for all to see, emphasizes the patrician nature of the organization. The Duke of Edinburgh is a member, as is his son the Duke of York, a keen golfer who will be captain of the R&A not too long after this book is published. Also easily spotted are the Duke of Beaufort, the Marquis of Linlithgow, and numerous viscounts, earls, knights, and honourables. Swinley members mostly share the same background: Eton or Harrow, Oxford or Cambridge, and such prestigious London clubs as Brooks and White's. One story courtesy of John de St. Jorre, in his *Legendary Golf Clubs of Scotland, England, Wales, and Ireland,* can be said to sum up the membership: A visiting golfer is talking with a Swinley member in the changing room. "Yes," says the guest, "we have a nice cross section of people in my club." "Oh, do you?" replies the Swinley member. "We haven't got that problem here."

Swinley Forest is distinguished as much by what you will not find there as by what you will. The club has no captain, no club tie, no crest, no club silver, no club history, no suggestion book.

And it wasn't till Lieutenant Colonel Pearce took the secretary's job that par figures were established and a scorecard printed. For a good eighty years, there were no competitions. Now there are two, both played off scratch for the good reason that there are no handicaps. In his *Legendary Golf Clubs* book, de St. Jorre writes: "As a member at both Sunningdale and Swinley puts it, all the Berkshire members are gentlemen and love to play golf; all the Sunningdale members love to play golf but not all are gentlemen; and all the Swinley members are most certainly gentlemen but they don't give a fig whether they play golf or not."

Lieutenant Colonel Pearce could never be slotted in the "don't give a fig" category. He loves the game; he plays it well, very well, indeed, off 2; and his affection for the Swinley course is boundless. Introduced to golf when he was seven or eight, he has often been scratch. He won the Army Championship twice. I was not aware of this when we teed off, but after seeing him launch a smoothly drawing 255-yard drive from the high tee into the center of the fairway on the opening hole without taking so much as a single practice swing, I was not surprised to learn later of his achievements. And the golf holes here provide an ideal testing ground for shotmaking. Even its architect, the wry and serious-minded Harry Colt, had a soft spot for Swinley, referring to it as "the least bad course" he had ever built.

Swinley is very short—6,062 yards. Par is 69 in this interesting mix of eleven two-shotters, five par threes, and two par fives. Fairways are broad, forced carries are not cruel, and bunkering inclines to be light. Heather, however, seems to be everywhere that grass is not. And even to the keenest eye, the borrows on these superb greens are often unfathomable. To play along these beautiful corridors framed by pine and birch and heather (and occasionally by massive banks of rhododendron and azalea), indeed, simply to be abroad in this serene and silent world, so completely in harmony with nature, is to be inordinately blessed.

The five short holes that Colt has fashioned here may well equal his triumphant quintet on Wentworth's East Course. For instance, the 184-yard 4th, nicely uphill and playing at least 200 yards, presents a green with rising rough ground on the right, steeply falling rough ground and a deep bunker on the left, and two pits out front and deceptively short. On the knob-to-knob 170-yard 17th, the smallish plateau green perches a bit above us, defying us to hit and hold it. There is a sharp upslope in front, a modest falloff and sand at the right, and four pits, a rough-cloaked mound, and a steep falloff all on the left.

During his tenure, Ian Pearce, acting in the tradition of Harry Colt when he was secretary at Sunningdale, has felt the need to make improvements to the course, and he has not hesitated to do so, adding bunkers, tightening a landing area, putting in a new back tee or two. He even took advantage of the presence of a stream on the par-five 5th to fashion a little pond which, he assured me, the well-struck second shot will easily clear. I promptly struck my second shot well and it splashed ingloriously into his pond.

The incoming nine boasts a couple of especially fine par fours, with the double dogleg 12th probably the best hole on the course and, as it happens, the number one stroke hole. (Now that the club has a scorecard, there's no stopping it!) A hidden bunker just over the crest of a rise eats into the right side of the fairway on this 455-yarder to snare the powerful

drive that is only marginally off the hole's center line. A safer—
read *weaker*—tee shot leaves too much to do on our second.
The green relies solely on the uneven ground around it for
defense. The level and straightaway 16th, 415 yards, also has
some length going for it, but what gives it character is the bi-
level green, which, at forty-one yards, is the deepest on the
course.

The last hole, 368 yards, plays down from a high tee, then up
to a high green just below the clubhouse. The drive must carry a
stream, and into a breeze this can be taxing. Nonetheless, the
landing area is spacious. Too spacious, as it turns out, to suit Ian
Pearce. "I think some sand is called for on the left side," he
said, "probably three bunkers to put some teeth into the hole.
It's a trifle bland. I don't want people swinging away with
impunity from the tee."

One other course I'll mention, in passing, is Queenwood,
which opened in 2001, no more than fifteen minutes from
Swinley Forest, in Ottershaw, Surrey. The architect is David
McLay Kidd, designer of highly praised Bandon Dunes, on the
Oregon coast. Queenwood is quite open, though there are
trees, and water is used in the American fashion, which is to say
boldly. But it is heather on bunkers that is the player's primary
woe here. Kidd has taken the heather "eyebrows" so common
at the outstanding heathland courses and given them a whole
new dimension—on the lip, of course, but very broadly there,
and then on the fingers of turf invading the sand as well. Many
approach shots see us facing the terrible danger of missing the
green, itself usually vast and complex, by a foot and then,
assuming we find the ball, attempting to hack it, uncontrollably,
out of the heather to some point—*any* point—on the green. If

All Courses Great and Small

this is your idea of fun, and you have a friend or a friend of a friend who is a member of this club—Queenwood Golf Club is strictly private, with no green-fee paying visitors and no outings—by all means check it out.

For accommodations in this area, you're likely to be comfortable at the Berystede Hotel, set on nine acres in Ascot, twenty-five minutes from Heathrow and no more than fifteen minutes from any of the clubs in this chapter. This is an appealing old country house—red brick, some half-timbering, a couple of turrets, plenty of handsome mahogany woodwork in the public spaces, and if our experience in 2001 holds, good cooking. The majority of the guest rooms in this ninety-room establishment, while nicely appointed, are somewhat institutional in feeling. You may want to reserve a room with a four-poster bed.

Only eight miles from Ascot lie Windsor Castle, Windsor Great Park, and Eton. The castle, built on a cliff above the river, does not disappoint. Among its features are the State Apartments, St. George's Chapel, Queen Mary's Dolls House, and the Round Tower (stiff climb), with its magnificent view. A striking feature of Windsor Great Park (nearly 2,000 acres) is the Long Walk, planted with horse chestnut and plane trees and stretching away for almost three miles to Snow Hill and the huge statue of George III there. As for Eton College, it is probably the best-known of all English public (i.e., private) schools. The chapel and dining hall are both fifteenth century; the gatehouse, leading to the cloister, early sixteenth century. On a more commercial note, the town of Eton has several good antiques shops.

CHAPTER SEVEN

Ten More
London Courses—
Three of Them Great

 TWENTY MILES DUE SOUTH of Piccadilly Circus, near the village of Tadworth, in Surrey, lies Walton Heath Golf Club, with its two eighteens. When the Old Course opened in 1904, the club's head professional was none other than James Braid, who had won the first of his Open Championship crowns in 1901 and would win again in 1905, 1906, 1908, and 1910. The Scot, who hit the ball with what Horace Hutchinson called a "divine fury," would hold sway at Walton Heath until his death in 1950 at the age of eighty. Braid became a prolific golf course architect, designing or revising some 180 courses.

Walton Heath has hosted more than sixty important amateur and professional competitions, including five European Opens, twenty-three Match Play Championships, and the 1981 Ryder Cup. The 1981 U.S. team, captained by Dave Marr, is widely viewed as the strongest ever fielded by either side: Jack Nicklaus, Lee Trevino, Tom Watson, Raymond Floyd, Hale Irwin,

94

All Courses Great and Small

Johnny Miller, Larry Nelson, Ben Crenshaw, Tom Kite, Jerry Pate, Bill Rogers, and Bruce Lietzke. The European team included Nick Faldo, Sandy Lyle, Bernhard Langer, Mark James, and Sam Torrance. The U.S. won, 18½–9½.

Both eighteens at Walton Heath were laid out by Herbert Fowler, the Old Course marking his first venture into golf architecture, at the age of forty-five. In the world of outstanding heathland golf, the Walton Heath courses enjoy a distinction that should be made clear. They adhere far more closely to the classic concept of heathland, which the dictionary defines as a "large, open area, usually with sandy soil and scrubby vegetation, especially heather." Walton Heath's holes are indeed open, routed over high ground 650 feet above sea level and fully exposed to the wind. What trees there are here do not block the breezes.

Walton Heath has about it a sternness, at times even a bleakness. There is minimal elevation change, the course plays fast, and wind is a key consideration in our shotmaking. No wonder we are reminded of links golf. Darwin wrote: "Walton Heath has something of the fierceness and defiance which belongs to the sea and is apt to overwhelm us a little when we encounter it after being pampered by windless golf in a park."

There is an admirable naturalness to the holes. Putting is uncomplicated, and the framing of the greens offers almost none of the cunning little buildups that can fray the nerves of even a deft chipper. On occasion—one thinks especially of the 14th and 16th—sand and heather restrict the drive, but usually there is enough room. Bunkering is light to moderate, although the sixty-two pits, deep and steep-faced, are penal. Water and white stakes are nowhere to be seen. By and large, the double bogey is not a threat. But bogeys can be an all too abundant harvest, beginning with the opening hole, a 195-yarder (you may recall that Fowler's 1st on the Blue Course at the Berkshire is also a long one-shotter), the entrance to the green pinched by sand and rough mounds.

So we take our disappointing 4 and cross the Dorking/Sutton Road to the other seventeen holes—in fact, the other thirty-five holes—out on the expansive heath where for years, with nothing man-made to distract his eye at any point in the two rounds, a player could be alone with his golf. Today, while the view is unchanged, the tranquillity is marred just a wee bit by the ceaseless drone of traffic on the M25, which at least is mercifully out of sight.

The first nine on the Old Course has several very strong and fine par fours, none of them stronger or finer than the 2nd, 442 yards and doglegging easily right, where our good drive leaves us inevitably with a downhill lie and from it a long uphill second to a green at the top of a rise. The 4th, 430 yards, and the 6th, 390 yards, are also testers, in both cases with sand to be avoided on the tee shot as well as the approach. And the 381-yard 5th, a beauty chosen for *The 500 World's Greatest Golf Holes* volume, plays level off the tee, then curves left on the downhill second shot to a green tightly bunkered on both sides.

The last three holes are a stiff challenge. The 510-yard 16th begins with a forced carry of about 150 yards over a heather-infested hollow to a narrow landing area corseted by more heather. The bunker up ahead on the right that squeezes the fairway almost to extinction should cause little concern on our second shot unless we are contending with a headwind, but a huge, deep, and gathering pit awaits at the right front of the mildly elevated green. The gambling second shot with even a scintilla of cut inexorably finds its way into this monster's maw. Talk about risk/reward/ruin!

The 17th hole, 181 yards, with the putting surface at eye level as we stand on the tee, is straightforward: A solid semicircle of sand must be surmounted to gain the green. The only way on is up and on.

Nor is the finishing hole for the faint of heart. At 397 yards, it demands two sound strokes, the second one to clear a big crossbunker perhaps fifty yards short of the green. There is a bunker left and a bunker right at this generous putting surface, but since neither is truly vengeful we may swing with a certain abandon and—who knows?—maybe finish the round on this great course in style.

The New Course (1913), also par 72, is ninety yards shorter than the Old from the regular tees, 6,271 yards versus 6,361, though both can be stretched to about 7,000. Here there are several short par fours, not to mention shallow bunkers. Here also is more variety—no straight run out and back, as on the Old, but holes heading in all directions and some greens sited in hollows, others on plateaus. Among this eighteen's most memorable tests are the 422-yard 5th, which calls for a faded drive to a fairway encased by heather followed by a drawn second to a stringently bunkered green, and the characterful 14th, 400 yards, sweeping downhill on the drive while bending gently left and then turning a shade to the right as it rises to a plateau green.

In its early years, Walton Heath attracted to its membership media and political figures. Winston Churchill played here, as did Mrs. Churchill. David Lloyd George, Prime Minister during the latter part of World War I as well as for a couple of years after the horrific conflict, had a house near the club and played whenever he had a spare hour. On several occasions, cabinet meetings were actually held in the club's card room. It is also said that suffragettes, seeking the vote for women, once caught up with Lloyd George on the golf course and tried to remove his trousers.

If political figures were prominent at Walton Heath, it was a band of London barristers from the Inns of Court who founded Woking Golf Club, in 1893. This Surrey course was the first of the heathland layouts, predating Sunningdale by seven years and Walton Heath by eleven. The ubiquitous Tom Dunn laid out a workmanlike if unimaginative eighteen (square, flat greens, large crossbunkers scarring virtually every hole). Fortunately, two of Woking's most influential members, Scotsmen Stuart Paton and John Low, both excellent golfers, decisively revised Dunn's work, fashioning a course where strategic design replaced his harshly penal approach. The Old Course at St. Andrews was their inspiration. They completely rebunkered the layout and aggressively contoured the greens.

I played at Woking in the summer of 2001 with two members, Colin Howard and David Harrison. Colin, about fifty, is a computer wizard who runs his own small company. David, maybe a dozen years older, is a retired advertising executive who had spent a number of years heading a major agency in Japan. Colin's handicap was 14, David's 15. Both could hit the ball a long way, but neither was consistently on target. They joshed each other lightly from time to time, unpredictably conceding or not conceding a putt in question. Both were very knowledgeable about the course and, in an understated way, eager to have me appreciate it.

All Courses Great and Small

The sand-based fairways amidst dense stands of trees are generous, but to wander from them is to court serious difficulty in heather or gorse. The white markers add up to 6,340 yards against a par of 70. The beautifully rolling first nine is the stronger and more adventurous of the two halves. The second nine has rather too much flattish play, but, by way of compensation, it does have three water holes.

The round starts with a bona fide birdie hole, a two-shotter of only 278 yards. Play begins in earnest on the splendid 2nd, a knob-to-knob 201-yarder over a deep valley, which is followed by the even more splendid 3rd, 413 yards, a high tee encouraging an all-out drive, the fairway far below inclining to shunt the ball off to the left into gorse, while the hole, contrarily, is curving to the right. The green—protected by a large and defiant bunker squarely in front of and maybe a dozen yards short of the putting surface—is by no means gathering.

All of which brings us to the historic 4th, 336 yards long, commencing on a minimally elevated tee back in the trees. The pair of bunkers solidly in the fairway about 200 yards from the tee are riveting. They were put there by Stuart Paton, who had decided to simulate the celebrated feature of the 16th at St. Andrews, the Principal's Nose bunkers.

"I'm sure the choice—you may prefer to call it the dilemma—is obvious," said Colin with a smile as we stood on the tee. "Left of the sand is safe, but then your second shot must necessarily flirt with the bunker at the left of the green."

I nodded.

"On the other hand," David chimed in as though on cue, "take the line to the right—the railway is just beyond the white stakes—and assuming a good drive, you are left with a simple shot of 115 yards or so to a green that is wide open across the front. The brave line off the tee is rewarded with the easy approach. A very good hole, I hope you agree."

I agreed. Then, unhesitatingly selecting the coward's route, I aimed left and struck the ball squarely. What remained was a 125 yarder, which I had no difficulty popping into the left-hand greenside bunker, just as Stuart Paton, more than ninety years ago, devoutly hoped I would, fit punishment for having demonstrated such a shameful want of courage on what is generally viewed as the first deliberately strategic hole in English golf.

David Harrison had to get back to the clubhouse when we finished the 11th because he was being counted on to play in a match against a visiting club that afternoon. Colin and I bade him a reluctant goodbye, then drove on the excellent 12th, 409 yards, curving pleasantly right, the second shot over a gentle dip to a green protected by crossbunkers some thirty-five yards short of it and by more sand at the right front. There is plenty of golf in the dogleg left 13th, 426 yards, a bunker at the right front of a vigorously undulating green. Then come a couple of breathers, back-to-back par fives of 510 yards, level and straightaway.

It was on the 15th, as we were about to play our long second shots, that we paused for some local traffic near the green. A very elderly woman who wished to follow her dog across the fairway took a couple of tentative steps, then stopped, apparently fearful that we were about to hit. Colin waved her across, saying to me, "It's Mrs. Preston. I'm not absolutely sure I recognize her, but I do recognize her dog. She lives nearby and is obviously out for a walk. I have two Labs and I often come over in the evening with them from our house, just beyond the 17th

All Courses Great and Small

tee. I'll play four holes—17, 18, 15, and 16, which brings me back home. Sometimes we run into Mrs. Preston and her dog."

Our shot on the 156-yard 16th must carry a lagoon, which really ought to be lengthened in order to come closer to the green, but the bunkering and a two-tier putting surface do give the hole spice. The level 421-yard 17th calls for a couple of good hits, and now we head down the home hole. Only 338 yards long, it is every bit as welcoming as the graceful and unpretentious clubhouse just left of the green, itself menaced by a pond at the right.

It was at the 18th hole, in 1904, that Hugh Alison executed the most extraordinary shot in Woking's history. For the first and only time, the annual match between Cambridge and Oxford was being played here. When Oxford's Alison pulled his second shot sharply, the ball wound up on the roof of the clubhouse veranda. Calling for a ladder, he gained the roof and played his next shot over a gable and onto the green, halving the hole in 5. Alison went on to serve for a time as secretary at Stoke Poges, where he met Harry Colt, who was laying out the course there. After World War I, he became Colt's partner, designing courses mostly in North America (two of his best are Milwaukee Country Club and North Shore Country Club, outside Chicago) and the Far East.

Woking is special. The golf course itself, however attractive and testing, may not be truly great, but the club and the course put together do add up to a great golf place.

Some seven or eight minutes from Woking, and just off the A322 (the Guildford/Bagshot Road), lies West Hill Golf Club, outside the Surrey village of Brookwood. Willie Park, Jr., and Jack White, 1904 Open champion and Sunningdale's longtime professional, are credited with the routing. Carnoustie-born-and-bred Cuthbert Butchart, West Hill's first professional, provided the architectural details.

West Hill is a typically pretty and rolling heathland course studded with gorse, the holes less densely tree-lined than at Woking. It measures 6,325 yards from the white tees against a par of 69—five par threes, only two par fives. Sand and water (a stream must be avoided on five holes) give the course bite. Among the many solid holes are the 454-yard 3rd, a two-shotter where the stream runs diagonally across the fairway and then turns toward the green to endanger the long second shot that is hooked; the 392-yard 11th, uphill, the second shot blind over an expanse of heather; the par-three 15th, which amply demonstrates the difficulty of hitting a 212-yard shot onto a green defended left and right by sand; and the very strong finishing hole, a 440-yard uphill two-shotter where the putting surface cannot be seen but the flagstick can. Squarely behind the green stands the black-and-white clubhouse with its telltale clock.

Worplesdon Golf Club, the last of the three "Ws" in this wooded corner of Surrey, is located on Heath House Road, in Woking, five minutes from West Hill. This course is altogether delightful and, in the bargain, challenging. The club gained considerable fame from the mixed foursomes scratch competition that has been held there each October beginning in 1921. The great Joyce Wethered shared the cup a total of eight times, with six different men. On one of the winning occasions, Bernard Darwin was her partner. There is a famous photograph of Darwin, his back turned apprehensively to Miss Wethered, unable to force himself to look as she attempts a particularly delicate little pitch—that he has left her with—over a deep bunker.

All Courses Great and Small

I recall with particular pleasure my first visit to Worplesdon, in June of 1991. Harriet accompanied me. Because I arrived wearing neither jacket nor tie, both of which were de rigueur in the dining room and the mixed lounge, the assistant secretary, a young woman, was kind enough to procure for me a navy double-breasted blazer and a striped tie. Her source? The bartender, who kept three jackets and three ties on hand for just such emergencies. The blazer was ludicrously large on me, but we wasted no time finding seats in the lounge, so perhaps no one noticed.

John F. Abercromby took up golf as a boy and became a scratch player. At about the age of forty he was hired as a private secretary to a man who owned a large estate in Surrey. When in 1908 his employer said he would like to have a golf course, Abercromby obliged by laying one out for him. That eighteen is Worplesdon, and though Harry Colt would make some changes twenty-four years later, the holes we play today can, by and large, be attributed to Abercromby.

From the white tees, the course measures 6,440 yards against a par of 71. Once we reach the 5th, each hole is isolated in its own broad *allée* of pine and chestnut trees. The first nine is quite rolling, the second nine flattish. Fairways are roomy, but heather, gorse, and thick rough await the wayward stroke. The adroit bunkering—some pits are framed with heather—may owe much to the elegant hand of Colt. Sophisticated strategic demands are set up from time to time by the greenside bunkering (e.g., at the 3rd, 4th, and 18th), which calls for precise placement of the drive if we are to have a reasonable chance of hitting the green. The putting surfaces, swift and true, are spacious, sometimes concealing quite subtle borrows, at other times presenting bold undulations or slopes.

James W. Finegan

Following an inviting 365-yard opener—down, then up—we are confronted with one of Worplesdon's toughest par fours, a 414-yarder where a blind drive is followed by an uphill second, generally from a downhill lie, to a green with diabolical contours. Does a 4 *ever* lose this hole? The 3rd is a solid two-shotter, downhill and doglegging gently right. And now we return to the clubhouse, on the great 4th, 168 yards steeply uphill to a beautifully bunkered plateau green. The 412-yard 5th is also a honey, a fine driving hole that encourages us to bite off a chunk of the heathery rough as the hole bends smoothly right.

On the inbound nine is that attractive circumstance we encountered on both nines at the Berkshire's Red Course—three par threes, fours, and fives. The first of the par fives, the 520-yard 11th, moves downhill to a deftly bunkered green tucked teasingly left. It was chosen as one of *The 500 World's Greatest*. The one-shotters, including the 193-yard 16th, are also especially good. The round concludes with a very strong par four of 451 yards, its slightly elevated green bunkered at the right front.

With its spirited and lovely course and its hospitable clubhouse ambience, Worplesdon is, like Woking, one of the special places in the game.

In 1911, three years after he laid out Worplesdon, the now fifty-year-old tyro J. F. Abercromby got a chance to design a second course, Coombe Hill, in Kingston, only nine miles from Hyde Park Corner. It is shut off from the world by its thickly planted firs, oaks, and silver birches, to say nothing of its 2,000 rhododendron bushes.

The Duke of Windsor, then Prince of Wales, notched his first win in a formal competition here. When in London, Bing

Crosby and Bob Hope played the course from time to time. Bob Jones also admired it, citing the 341-yard 14th, where the second shot falls to a closely bunkered green that is actually larger than it looks, as one of the finest of its length he had ever played.

Nonetheless, Coombe Hill—6,293 yards, par 71—may strike us at times as too well mannered. A stream meanders through the course but is never really in play. Heather is on hand but not in profusion. A shot that is hit weakly or off line will produce a bogey but no worse. There is not quite enough pressure on the swing. And surely the 1st and 2nd holes, two very short downhill par fours, provide the easiest start imaginable.

Counterbalancing the obvious birdie opportunities is a clutch of punishingly long, uphill two-shotters—the 5th, 8th, 11th, 16th, and 18th—all of which measure more than 420 yards and play no less than 450 yards. Add to this occasional need for brawn two or three blind shots, plus the subtleties of the large and beautifully contoured greens, and you have an eighteen that, despite the paucity of originality and tension, will provide pleasure, if not powerful memories.

Down in a corner of southwest Surrey, forty-three miles from central London, is an unusual heathland course. Its name is Hindhead. The club was formed in 1904 and golf holes were laid out then by five founder members. The course can fairly be said to have a schizophrenic personality, or at the very least, a split between "top" and "bottom." The 1st hole and the entire second nine are routed over the high ground, a gently rolling plateau some 800 feet above sea level. Conversely, holes 2–9 are played down in a valley, through a couple of long gullies and over ground with abrupt ups and downs.

Hindhead measures 6,365 yards, which, against a par of 70, puts it on the long side. However, in season the ball bounces briskly along, and some holes on the first nine, with their sloping sides, become funnels that throw errant balls back into the narrow bottoms. The heather, bracken, and long bent grasses are penal. Greens, of medium size, incline to be flat. There are no water hazards, and bunkering is rather light.

Still, Hindhead is not easy. Half a dozen of the par fours range from 410 to 442 yards. Two of the one-shotters, the superb 3rd (198 yards, steep falloff left of the green, sand right) and the 238-yard 8th are also man-sized. And the short par-five 2nd, 478 yards, is unforgettable: Standing toward the back of the high tee here, it is all you can do to convince yourself as you drive off into space that there really is a golf hole way down below in that gully.

All Courses Great and Small

By now you may be wondering whether there is any justification for devoting a day to Hindhead. Well, how about the club history? With any luck, you will be able to acquire a copy. It is called *Hindhead's Turn Will Come—The Unauthorized History of a Golf Club*. The author is one Ralph Irwin-Brown, and the use of "Unauthorized" is just one of Mr. Irwin-Brown's many little jokes. The title itself is borrowed from George Bernard Shaw's *The Misalliance* (Shaw lived in this neighborhood for a while): "The writing is on the wall; Babylon fell, Rome fell, Hindhead's turn will come."

Irwin-Brown is an urbane and stylish writer, a painstaking researcher, and one of the three or four ablest chroniclers of a golf club's doings in the history of that inconsequential literary category. You have to love a man who opens his book with this quotation from T. S. Eliot:

> *And the wind shall say, "Here were decent, godless people,*
> *Their only monument the asphalt road*
> *And a thousand lost golf balls."*

Within the next two pages we learn that the Hindhead countryside was derided on a number of occasions long before there was golf here. Tennyson wrote of ". . . those gloomy gladed slopes." And Defoe pulled no punches whatsoever: "Quite sterile, given up to barrenness, horrid and frightful to look on, not only good for little but good for nothing."

So the book is off to a rousing start—I should mention that Arthur Conan Doyle was the club's first president—and it never falters as the author escorts us engagingly through every facet of the club's existence, from its founding in 1904 down to 1991. And how saddened we are to see him finish.

Now we retreat to the capital, to the borough of Eltham, where awaits Royal Blackheath Golf Club, which proudly claims to be the oldest golf club in the world. Is it? Hmmm. In any event, the club does manage to trace its lineage all the way back to 1608, when James I gave his approval to the Society of Blackheath Golfers. But next to nothing comes down to us from the next 168 years, and it is not till 1776 that we can truly say Royal Blackheath was up and running. Certainly it is the oldest club in England.

Blackheath was redesigned by James Braid in 1926. The course measures 6,209 yards against a par of 69. Most holes are laid out on level ground, some move up or down the gentle hill crowned by the clubhouse. There is neither heather nor gorse, bracken nor broom. Bunkering is light. The greens, though generally flat, are the one reason why the course might test us, for they make poor targets, simply sitting there, a small, closely cropped extension of the fairway.

Three holes linger in memory. At 400 yards and playing uphill all the way, the 17th is long. It can also be hazardous: fifteen yards short of the green is a vast and deep crossbunker. The 1st and 18th are also unforgettable. The 1st is a shocker, a downhill par four played to a tiny green 452 yards in the distance. What we remember, however, is not the extreme difficulty of the hole but, squarely in front of the tee, the charming little beech hedge we must drive over. Which brings us to the home hole, only 290 yards long and working its humble way gently uphill to a green that sits not merely in front of the clubhouse but almost flush against its foundation. Defending the putting surface are bunkers, a ditch, a boundary, and, right back where we started, that beech hedge again.

Royal Blackheath's clubhouse, a perfectly symmetrical red-brick structure with a hip roof and eight chimneys, is so superlative an example of late Renaissance architecture that it is maintained by the Ministry of Public Works. It was built in 1664 for a merchant banker who had assisted Charles II during his exile on the continent. With its noble rooms, its handsome fireplaces, its old paintings, trophies, and medals, this great house is surely fit for a king, or for a king's banker, or at the very least, for England's oldest golf club.

Not thirty minutes southwest of Blackheath, in Croydon, lies The Addington, one of my all-time favorites. J. F. Abercromby designed only a dozen courses; The Addington is his masterpiece. He laid out the holes in 1914 and ran the club in autocratic fashion until his death in 1935.

When I arrived at The Addington on a pretty June morning in 1998, I spoke first with the bartender, who said, "This club is in a time warp. It's still the 1930s here—no photocopier, no fax, no computer, not even a TV. There is a typewriter, I think."

The club's owner and chairman, Mrs. Moira Fabes, a small, dark-haired woman in her early seventies, now materialized at my elbow, cutting short my exchange with the bartender. She led me to her office, making clear with every step and every word that she was functioning with the same absolute authority that had characterized Abercromby's reign. She spoke at once of the bartender: "He isn't a full-time employee; he knows nothing about the club and even less about golf. Pay him no mind."

She told me that in 1963 she had inherited the club from her father, a solicitor. Her husband, she added, was an accountant.

James W. Finegan

On the heels of these two vocational revelations came a short, sharp, knowing laugh suggesting that the two key men in her life had had the two most important bases—the law and money—neatly covered and that she had learned a thing or two from both of them.

In her office Mrs. Fabes reviewed a large map of the course for my benefit, pointing out the several bridges over ravines and warning me to be careful of the wooden planks, which local children sometimes loosened out of devilment. She traced Abercromby's career from when he got into golf course architecture till he got out. The chairman who preceded her in office was, she believed, misguided. "He thought he knew more about golf course architecture than Aber," she said disdainfully, "and as a result undertook many revisions. I undid his changes, and the course today is just as Aber made it."

I had noticed a sign on the clubhouse when I parked my car: "Professional Shop and First Tee," with an arrow pointing the way. The sign was only half right. Said Mrs. Fabes, "We have no golf professional, nor do we have need of one. The bartender collects green fees and sells golf balls."

I did not see her after the round, nor in fact, ever again. About two years later, I read that this diligent keeper of the flame had died.

The site which Abercromby chose for The Addington is ideal— high and rolling sand-based ground where the holes are carved out of a forest of oak and beech, silver birch and cedar, mountain ash and chestnut. The course measures 6,242 yards against par of just 68. The result is a number of long holes. So if you cannot belt the ball, be prepared to save strokes around and on the greens, which are generally not tough to putt, even for a stranger.

110

All Courses Great and Small

But length is only one consideration. This is one of the very greatest of the English courses. It has everything: superlative shot values from start (a sharply uphill 166-yarder that plays 185 yards) to finish (a gently uphill 430-yarder, adroitly bunkered); the occasional death-or-glory shot; a remarkably diverse assortment of holes, including six par threes ranging from 134 to 225 yards; a brilliant and unpredictable routing plan that takes full advantage of the rolling terrain; heather, bracken, ravines, and trees to menace the weak or off-line shot; the proper amount of pressure on the swing (quite a bit, indeed, but nothing like what one faces at, for instance, Carnoustie or Doonbeg); more than its share of the essential Darwinian ingredient, pleasurable excitement; and implicit in all the foregoing, a number of genuinely great holes, perhaps as many as ten (2, 3, 5, 7, 9, 10, 12, 13, 15, 16), certainly no less than seven.

Only two of this dazzling collection will be described here. The par-four 12th, 472 yards, doglegs smoothly left (the only smooth aspect of this rugged, pulse-quickening hole). We drive blindly over bracken, necessarily taking the aggressive line left in an effort to find one of the fairway shelves at the corner of the dogleg. If successful, we are now in position to swing out of our shoes on a 3-wood shot that must traverse a stunningly deep valley and reach a pinnacle plateau green that is mercifully free of sand. Make no mistake about it: This is one of the most heroic two-shotters in the world, worthy to be spoken of in the same breath with the 14th at Dornoch, "Foxy," also without artificial hazards.

And immediately following comes the equally great par-three 13th, a 225-yarder that plays from a knob down over a rough-clad swale to a somewhat lower knob that hosts the green as well as bunkers left and right. Henry Longhurst, who believed The Addington to be the finest inland course in Britain, wrote evocatively of this majestic hole: ". . . with the exception of the fifth at Pine Valley, near Philadelphia, [this is] the greatest one-shot hole in inland golf. To see a full shot with a brassie, perfectly hit and preferably with a new ball, sail white against the blue sky, pitch on the green and roll up towards the flag, is to know the sweetest satisfaction that golf has to offer."

You will want to move heaven and earth for a game at The Addington.

Less than twenty miles southwest of Trafalgar Square lies Britain's first housing community *cum* golf course, St. George's Hill, in Weybridge, Surrey. Carving the holes through a dense forest of deciduous and evergreen trees, Harry Colt laid out the course in 1911 and 1912, some eighteen months before he briefly assisted George Crump at Pine Valley. The kinship with the peerless New Jersey course is readily apparent: the vigorously rolling terrain, the isolation of most holes in tree-framed *allées,* the sweep and spaciousness of the fairways, the imaginative contouring of the vast greens, the boldness of the bunkering, the appealing naturalness of it all, even the occasional glimpses of handsome houses on the periphery.

But one overriding difference is also apparent: at St. George's Hill there is not the intense pressure on the swing that sometimes brings us to grief at Pine Valley (and, it must be admitted, helps to account for the greatness there of hole after hole). A mistake at St. George's Hill is not calamitous; it costs a stroke, no more, with the result that the round is an unalloyed pleasure.

From the regular tees, the course measures 6,322 yards

against a par of 70. There are half a dozen two-shotters over the 400-yard mark. The start is grand, a majestically beautiful 384-yarder from a lofty tee, with the second shot played steeply uphill from the opposite slope of the valley. The par-four 2nd hole, 452 yards, is one of the glories of St. George's Hill. A blind drive over the crest of a hill sets up a strenuously long second shot. This must be fired from a downhill lie, over a stream, then uphill to a plateau green with a deep pit at the left front. And thus it continues: a pulpit tee down to a Redan green on the 180-yard 3rd; a ferociously bunkered but driveable par four (that is, if you drive the ball 270 yards), followed by a steadily uphill 383-yarder that plays 410 and presents a crossbunker to be hurdled on the second shot; and a monster two-shotter, this one of 464 yards with, fortunately, a high launching pad for our tee shot and, unfortunately, in a bow to St. Andrews, a "Valley of Sin" at the front of the green.

The two par fives—one only 455 yards long but uphill and into the prevailing breeze, the other 525 yards and rolling gently along on low ground from tee to green—are both sorely needed birdie opportunities. As for the one-shotters, they are alike in one respect: All make the blood race, with the 175-yard 8th perhaps the most thrilling of the quartet. The tee is on a ridge and the green is on a somewhat lower ridge. In between is a deep dip. The green is fronted by four sandpits scooped out of the hillside. Two of them are large and cruelly deep, but since they are not actually greenside, the carry over them is no more than 150 yards. A tribute to Colt's skill—did he fashion more terrific par threes than anyone else?—the hole looks considerably more frightening than it actually is.

The entire course is studded with great holes and grand vistas. Add to the golf the charms of the imposing yet graceful, many-chimneyed, red-brick clubhouse. There can be few views more captivating than the long and wooded one from the terrace, where we incline to linger over a postround libation when, in fact, we ought to be getting on over to the 1st tee of Harry Colt's altogether excellent *third* nine.

After hither-and-yonning around the suburbs and exurbs of London for three chapters, it is high time to come to the heart of the capital. A recommendation—just one—about where to stay: the London Outpost of the Carnegie Club, itself headquartered at Skibo Castle, in Dornoch. No need to be a Carnegie Club member in order to avail yourself of its London Outpost, a surpassingly elegant small hotel in Cadogan Gardens, Knightsbridge. Eleven spacious and charming bedrooms, many with fireplaces, are furnished largely with antiques. The collection of paintings and prints by eighteenth- and nineteenth-century English masters is a good one. There is no restaurant, but breakfast, light lunch, afternoon tea, and supper can be provided, either in your accommodation (you may want to request the Turner Room) or in the glass-roofed conservatory. And if you are wondering just where Cadogan Gardens is, the answer is simple: within a very few minutes walk of Prada, Gucci, Armani, Versace, Dior, Georg Jensen, Van Cleef & Arpels, Bulgari, Harrod's, and the Victoria and Albert Museum.

We had dinner one evening at Floriana's, in lively Beauchamp Place. The decor is smartly current, all of it creams and beiges (an Armani palette). The cuisine is Northern Italian (tomato sauce reared its head just once on the entire menu). Among the excellent dishes was a seafood ravioli with a shellfish ragout.

All Courses Great and Small

Herewith, half a dozen of our favorite London "moments" that may tickle your fancy: (1) the Inns of Court, or legal London, an intriguing maze of courtyards, cloisters, passageways, and gardens, plus occasional glimpses of wigged and robed barristers (Rumpole at the Old Bailey?); (2) Hay's Galleria, an architectural stunner on the South Bank of the Thames, with stalls that sell everything from lingerie to toys; (3) the London Eye Ferris Wheel, a spectacular thirty-minute ride that giddily commands the vast cityscape; (4) the Banqueting House, in Whitehall, a 1622 design by Inigo Jones with a sumptuous ceiling by Rubens; (5) the Burlington Arcade, built in 1818, a block-long covered passage lined with smart mahogany-fronted shops; and (6) the central courtyard of the British Museum—redesigned by Sir Norman Foster under a faceted glass-and-steel roof, it is one of the city's three or four most brilliant contemporary architectural achievements.

A final London note: If you wish to splurge on a dinner, and do so in a hopelessly romantic way, try the Ritz Hotel, which may well have the most beautiful dining room in Europe and which purveys very good food. A small orchestra plays for dancing. Before the evening is over, the vocalist may offer a song for you (and the others on hand), with an indelible moment in the lyric: "I may be right, I may be wrong / But I'm perfectly willing to swear / There were angels dining at the Ritz / And a nightingale sang in Berkeley Square." This dinner could be one of the high points of your London golfing trip.

CHAPTER EIGHT

Kent and England's Greatest Course

 TIME NOW TO HEAD DOWN into Kent, which is contiguous to London and extends on a south-westerly thrust to the English Channel. This chapter will take a look at five Kentish courses—one inland, four seaside.

A little more than an hour south of London, in rural Bidden, is Chart Hills Golf Club, where Nick Faldo has laid out a course on the grand scale. This 1993 design, his first in Europe, clearly reflects Faldo's worldwide experience, particularly his extensive play in the United States. A big, good-looking course dotted by ancient oaks, it boasts dramatically undulating greens, water on fourteen holes, and massive doses of sand. For example, the 210-yard-long snakelike Anaconda Bunker on the par-five 5th, skirts the right side of the hole for a time (a long time), then bisects the fairway to complete its journey on the left side.

I played at Chart Hills with three members, all in their late forties to early fifties, handicaps ranging from 8 to 14. I expected that we would play a better-ball-of-partners match.

All Courses Great and Small

Not a bit of it. Each of us played the other three an individual one-pound nassau, but not at match play; Stableford was the scoring method. Using your handicap, you got one Stableford point for a net bogey, two points for a net par, three for a net birdie, and four for a net eagle. At the end of nine holes, if you had accumulated, say, 19 Stableford points and one of your three opponents had come up with only 18, you had won the first leg of that nassau. If you tallied 18 points on the second nine, but he had come up with 20, you had now lost the second nine and, by a total of 38 to 37, the third leg of the nassau as well. Imagine playing three such matches simultaneously and, in the bargain, paying a pound to a player making a natural birdie and a pound to the player closest to the hole on each par three, unless that chap should happen to three-putt, in which case he earned nothing for his good tee shot.

Since my sole interest in this round was getting a handle on the golf course, I agreed to participate fully and then privately decided to ignore all these goings-on, to make notes on my scorecard as usual, and to trust that when the final accounting was rendered I would not go straight to debtors' prison. Against a worst-case scenario of losing £15, I actually won £2, which came in handy to help buy a round of drinks.

We played a course that measures 6,449 yards. Par is 72. What with all the sand and all the water, not to mention the doglegs and the angled greens, good thinking is almost as essential here as good hitting. There is a trio of excellent holes in the middle of the round that embodies this course at its best. The 399-yard 8th, essentially level, is one of two holes without sand. Flanking the fairway are artificial mounds that look fairly natural. There is a pond in the trees on the left, but it should

James W. Finegan

not prompt any uneasiness. No, it is the sinuous stream that the second shot must carry, some twenty-five yards short of the green, and the shallow swale immediately at the front of the green, that combine to demand a solid swing. A par here is well earned.

As it is on the 327-yard 9th. The hole is steeply uphill and backdropped by the clubhouse at the top of the rise. The forced carry from the tee, into the prevailing breeze, must clear a cluster of five sandpits and some very nasty vegetation. The second shot, albeit much shorter, is much steeper. And the green slopes dangerously downhill from back to front. We *must* keep our approach short of the hole, an injunction that somehow gets lost in our determination to put the ball somewhere—anywhere—on the heavily bunkered green.

The 10th, 405 yards, is classic and beautiful, at first rolling along without any real elevation change, sand left and mounds right, then turning left and drifting downhill. The green, modeled loosely on the Road Hole green at St. Andrews, has steep little falloffs left and right and not enough depth to hold a shot that comes in even tepid. A teasing business.

After the round, the view from the clubhouse prompted me to say that Faldo's use of sand was extravagant.

One of my three playing companions, a landscape architect, responded, "A hundred and thirty-seven bunkers."

"But," I said, "I thought it was a hundred and thirty-eight."

"It was," he said, laughing, "but Faldo took one out."

In the historic town of Tenterden (a number of Tudor structures here), ten minutes from Chart Hills, is the White Lion, a fifteenth-century coaching inn. Creaking and atmospheric, its pub crowded with locals, it offers good food and sometimes cramped accommodations at reasonable rates. For contemporary comfort, consider the Hilton, in Maidstone, with its 146 guest rooms, health club, and swimming pool.

I should mention the London Golf Club, in Ash, which also opened in 1993. Jack Nicklaus provided two eighteens, personally laying out one, called the Heritage. Both courses, which take full advantage of the pretty and pleasantly rolling countryside, are strong, but, unfortunately, visitors may play here only if they are guests of members or if they are prospective members invited by the club.

A forty-five-minute drive southwest of Tenterden brings us to the English Channel and the Littlestone Golf Club. What we find here is authentic links golf with more character than a cursory look at the terrain might suggest. The course architect was Dr. W. Laidlaw Purves, whom we'll encounter in a rather more important endeavor before this chapter is finished. He laid out the holes in 1888. Subsequently, revisions were carried out by F. W. Maude, James Braid, Tom Dunn, and then, in 1921–22, Alister Mackenzie.

The course measures 6,460 yards against a par of 71. The early holes are routed over ground that is for the most part flat and featureless. The ten holes from the 8th through the 17th offer variety, challenge, and even an occasional moment that lingers in memory, like the site of the green on the 413-yard 10th, in the lee of a dune.

Still, the two best holes come almost at the end. The 468-yard 16th, a big par four even by today's standards, curves left around a bunker on the drive. The fairway for the second shot rises smoothly as it reveals folds and slopes and hummocks that have been denied us through much of the round. This agitated ground frequently diverts our long shot from the straight and narrow path to which it must hew if we are to have any chance of reaching the green in regulation.

The 17th, at 180 yards, plays from a mildly elevated tee—when the day is crystalline, the coast of France may hover on the horizon—to a green at about eye level and set in the shadow of a low hill on the left. The ground slopes severely to punish the shot that slips even a wee bit right. This hole calls up Donald Ross's outstanding 17th at Seminole.

Now we follow the coast road (first A259, then A20, finally A258) on a northeasterly heading, through Hythe and Folkestone and Dover to Deal, a picturesque old seafaring town and the home of Royal Cinque Ports Golf Club. The drive should take just under an hour.

Founded in 1892 and commonly known as Deal, Royal Cinque Ports has hosted two Open Championships—1909, when J. H. Taylor easily won the fourth of his five crowns, and 1920, when George Duncan, 13 strokes behind Abe Mitchell at the start of the final day's thirty-six holes, got them all back in the morning round (his 71 against Mitchell's 84) and wound up winning by four strokes.

Tom Dunn laid out the original nine, a second nine was soon added, and over the next forty years the links felt the ministrations of J. S. F. Morrison (longtime partner of Harry Colt), Harry Vardon, Guy Campbell, and Henry Cotton. Still, the routing is little changed from the club's earliest days—we play out along the sea, then come home just inside. The holes on what is one of the great natural links of England, treeless and stark, often take their shape from a ridge of grass-covered dunes that starts near the 1st green and extends the entire length of the property. Lies are tight, bunkers are deep, greens are fast and full of unreadable little curls. Stances incline to be awkward—sidehill, uphill, downhill, every imaginable cant and angle. This land is, of course, nature's grand deposit, very little altered by the hand of man or the iron of his machines.

The course measures 6,467 yards against a par of 71. It's been a long time—in truth, twenty-five years—since I've played here. On that cold, windy March day—gusts up to thirty miles per hour—my companion was a fellow in his late thirties by the name of Tony Smith, a dentist in Deal and one of the club's top players. Undiscouraged by the conditions, tucking his chin down against his chest and striding determinedly on, he calmly went about the business of shooting an altogether wonderful 76.

I could do no better than 84. Following a three-bogey start (a stream in front of the green on the 346-yard 1st was just unsettling enough to induce a pulled short-iron; the 453-yard par four 3rd is blind to the punchbowl green, with wildly tumbling terrain more than half of this hole's considerable length), I managed to make a clutch of pars and finish the nine with 40. Par is 35. We must get our figures on this nine.

The 10th, a 359-yarder that plays out to sea, bends gently left. The drive moves freely on the crumpled ground, and we are left with a 7- or 8-iron to a slightly elevated green set at an angle to the fairway. There seems to be nothing original or pulse-quickening about this hole—yet, inexplicably, it is superb. Sir Guy Campbell once wrote: ". . . surely one of the great holes of golf. What in particular puts it in this class I have never been able to define, but the first time I played it its quality hit me like 'the blow of an angel's wing,' and each time I have played it or seen it since, the blow has been just as keen and refreshing."

James W. Finegan

It is on the 12th that the long and inexorable trek home, paralleling the coastline, commences. If we hook our second shot on this rigorous 432-yarder, it may come to rest on a rutted and sandy road. We have turned the clock back 2,000 years, for it was Julius Caesar's legions that built this road in their conquest of Britain. We get a free drop from what the scorecard calls "the Ancient Highway." It is doubtful that Caesar would have been so generous.

In any event, we are now heading right into the prevailing wind, with velocities of ten to twenty miles per hour on an ordinary day. There is no letup on this murderous "beat back": 432 yards, 406, 214, 416, 465, 359 (the breather, which, after all, plays no more than 410), and 397.

Length, of course, is only part of the examination. On the 14th, for instance, at 214 yards, anything less than string-straight slips off into sand on the right or a grassy hollow on the left. At 465 yards, the 16th ought surely to be a manageable par five, even into the teeth of the wind. But it calls for a tee shot, aimed at an old wartime gun turret, that must be slotted precisely into a gullylike patch of fairway, followed by a second and third climbing toward a green capriciously sited on a steep dune. And on the last hole, 397 yards, the underhit second shot, wind-pummeled, will not clear the stream in front of the green, while the shot that does get over may not hold the low plateau green. This classic and mighty links, with the wind blowing from its customary direction, the southwest, is a cruel taskmaster.

Harriet and our then thirteen-year-old daughter, Megwin, came out to the club to join the secretary, John Honnor, and me for lunch that day. When we told him we were driving into Canterbury, he said, "You'll be passing quite near a house I once occupied, in Barham. I mention it because it's rather well-known in these parts. It's very old, twelfth century. One of the four knights who slew Thomas à Becket is supposed to have owned it. But don't make too much of that. I'm not at all sure it could be authenticated. Still, it is interesting. We seem always to be surrounded by history here in England. This sort of thing occurs again and again, wherever you go. Probably because we're an old nation and a lot of things have happened, and there isn't all that much space—not like that vast country of yours—for these things all to have happened in. So you keep bumping into them."

Not fifteen minutes northeast of Deal on the coast road lies Sandwich, home of two more celebrated links courses; Prince's and Royal St. George's. Let's go first to Prince's, venue for the 1932 Open Championship and scene of one of the game's most poignant stories.

In 1928 Gene Sarazen finished two strokes behind Walter Hagen in the Open at Royal St. George's. He had been fortunate to have as his caddie Skip Daniels, then in his mid-sixties. When Sarazen arrived at Prince's four years later, Daniels was waiting for him—but he was almost seventy now and his eyesight had failed. Sarazen's friends urged him not to take Daniels: He would be a burden, not a blessing, and why throw away what might be your last good chance to win the British Open simply for the sake of sentiment? So Sarazen told the old man he would not be using him. However, the caddie he chose turned out to be a poor fit, as the practice rounds made clear. Sarazen was swinging poorly, his timing was off, he was blaming the caddie for suggesting the wrong club, and the caddie was equally insistent that Sarazen was not striking the ball squarely. The day before the championship was to begin, Sarazen fired the young man and handed his bag to Daniels, who had stood loyally by, day after day, convinced that only he could bring Sarazen home a winner.

With Skip Daniels at his side, Sarazen shot a 70 in the opening round—par was 74—for a one-stroke lead that he extended to three strokes with a 69 in the second round. Another 70 sent him off in the final eighteen with a four-stroke cushion, and he finished five ahead of perennial runner-up Macdonald Smith.

This was Skip Daniels's finest hour. After the presentation ceremony, the new champion gave Daniels his beautiful polo coat. Wrote Sarazen later: "I waved to him as he pedaled happily down the drive, the coat I had given him flapping in the breeze, and there was a good-sized lump in my throat as I thought how the old fellow had never flagged for a moment during the grind of the tournament and how he had made good his vow to win a championship for me before he dies."

Skip Daniels wore the coat proudly everywhere he went, retelling, shot for shot, "how Sarazen and I did it at Prince's." The next three months were wonderful for him, the culmination of a lifetime of caddieing, and then after a short illness, he passed away. Wrote Sarazen: "When old Dan died, the world was the poorer by one champion."

Prince's Golf Club was founded in 1905 by London businessman Harry Mallaby-Deeley, who, together with the club secretary, P. M. Lucas, laid out the golf holes. In World War II, slit trenches, concrete tank traps, machine-gun posts, and a battle-training area guarded by minefields all contrived to devastate the course. There was no choice but to build a new one.

All Courses Great and Small

Guy Campbell and J. S. F. Morrison were hired to lay out three nines. It is their holes, with minor revisions, that we enjoy today. And if you are able to play only 18 of the 27, it really doesn't matter which nines you choose.

Morrison was especially optimistic about the course he and Campbell were creating. In a letter to Harry Colt in July 1949, he wrote: "Prince's will be terribly good; in fact, I feel sure it will be the best course in the world and be adjusted to meet any change in the golf ball, whether it is allowed to go further or shorter." Morrison seems to have anticipated accommodating both the Pro V1 and the Cayman ball.

I last visited Prince's in mid-summer of 2001. My companion on the Shore nine—despite its name, it is not noticeably closer to the sea than the other two nines—was Bill Howie, the club's general manager, whose handicap was 12. Early on, he mentioned the frequently voiced criticism of Prince's: The holes are featureless. He did not agree with this sweeping assessment, but I do. The holes have teeth and test, but they have little in the way of distinguishing characteristics. Images of individual holes do not come unbidden. We have to summon them, generally with the aid of the scorecard and maybe some helpful notes as well.

The explanation for this lies principally in the minimal elevation changes, together with the obvious instinct of the architects to accept the land as they found it. Put another way, there are no hills, there are no water hazards, and there is no sign of a bulldozer's depredations. The naturalness is palpable. Long, wispy grasses cloak the low dunes that frame the hummocky, tumbling fairways, which tend to run parallel to the dunes, almost never clambering over them. These fairways are always

James W. Finegan

generous targets, which is necessary if we are to have an honest chance of hitting them in the winds off the Channel that regularly pound this wholly exposed links. Bunkering is light and strategic. The undulating terrain itself provides the course's first line of defense, and it is a stout one, particularly in summer, when, over fairways that have a wonderfully old-fashioned burnished sheen, the course plays fast.

The greens are often sited on very low plateaus; at other times they will be set snugly into a gentle elevation; and sometimes they are mere extensions of the fairway. In any case, they incline to shunt the ball away, frequently down into shaved surrounds that call for nerveless chipping or putting. And in the clear air off Pegwell Bay, these greens seem closer than they actually are.

Although the holes at Prince's never clamor to be noticed, a handful of them, when we stop to think for a moment, do stand out. Like the 6th on Shore, a 378-yarder where the green is neatly tucked left in the modest sandhills at the top of a little rise. Or the 385-yard 4th on Dunes, where a cluster of five bunkers must be carried to reach an elevated green with steep falloffs all around. Or, on the same nine, the 8th, a 192-yarder rendered quite difficult by the prevailing right-to-left wind off the water that invariably shoves our ball toward the sand at the left front of the green.

If, as I believe, Prince's has very few memorable holes, I believe with equal conviction that the golf here is very good. Yes, we miss variety and unpredictability and drama. But there is a purity, an integrity, and a challenge to this collection of links holes that I think you will find genuinely satisfying. The "pleasurable excitement" here is of a subtler, cumulative nature.

All Courses Great and Small

P. M. Lucas, Prince's first secretary and the codesigner of the original eighteen, had five children, among whom was P. B. (Laddie), one of the outstanding left-handed amateurs in the first half of the twentieth century and a Walker Cupper in 1936 and 1947. Laddie was born in the clubhouse at Prince's, and it was there—and on the links—that he was reared. In 1922 the British Open was played next door, at Royal St. George's. Over from America for the championship came "Long Jim" Barnes, Jock Hutchison, and Walter Hagen, who would win the claret jug. A couple of days before the Open began, the three decided to try Prince's. Laddie followed them for the full eighteen holes. When the round was over, Barnes asked the child whether he was a golfer. When Laddie said proudly that he was, Barnes instructed him to be on the 1st tee at five o'clock and to bring his clubs.

At the appointed hour, the little boy and the great professional met on the first tee at Prince's. Barnes had brought along two boxes of brand new golf balls imprinted with his name. "Tee them up," he told the boy, "and drive them off. Each one that finishes on the fairway you can keep."

The wind was blowing powerfully off Pegwell Bay as the six-year-old took his stance. Laddie remembered playing safe and letting each ball fall gently, with the wind, from right to left. All twenty-four balls came to rest nicely in the fairway. Barnes was astonished. The child raced out and gathered up the lot. They would last him for two years, until he went away to school.

Laddie's father died in 1927, and the family soon left Prince's. The son, however, was to come back—dramatically—during World War II. An RAF pilot, Laddie was returning from a mission over France when a shell from a pursuing Messerschmitt hit an ammunition drum in his Spitfire. With the right wing all but ripped off, Laddie somehow cleared the Channel and brought his crippled plane safely down on the first stretch of land in sight.

As Jack Whitaker told it in the telecast of the 1993 British Open, Laddie overshot the fifth fairway of his beloved Prince's by about half a mile. Clambering out of the cockpit, he said, "Never could hit that fairway with a driver, don't know why I thought I could hit it with an airplane."

Cheek by jowl with Prince's is the greatest course in Kent and, for me, the greatest course in England as well as one of the ten greatest courses in the world, Royal St. George's, or, as some still call it, Sandwich.

The Open Championship has been played here twelve times, with the thirteenth scheduled for mid-July of 2003. The Amateur Championship has been contested here twelve times. The roll call of those who have triumphed at Sandwich includes a number of the game's most celebrated champions: J. H. Taylor, Harry Vardon, Walter Travis, Walter Hagen, Henry Cotton, Bobby Locke. Then add to this the number of firsts that the club can lay claim to: the first in England to host the Open, the first in England to host the Walker Cup (Bob Jones captaining a victorious American team in 1930), the scene of the first American triumph in the British Amateur (Walter Travis, 1904), the scene of the first victory by a native-born American in the Open (Hagen, 1922). Small wonder that we approach this extraordinary links with something akin to reverence.

It was in 1885 that Scottish-born scratch golfer Dr. William Laidlaw Purves, the same man who would lay out Littlestone, looked down from the 900-year-old Norman steeple of St.

Clement's upon the most tumultuous linksland a golfer could ever have spied, and promptly determined to lay out holes on it. Substantive revisions to the Purves design were made by Harry Colt and Hugh Alison, by Alister Mackenzie, and in the 1970s by Frank Pennink.

From the white tees, the course measures 6,607 yards against a par of 70 (6,947 yards from the championship markers). The round begins with two very good par fours. On the 1st hole, 413 yards, a necklace of three deep revetted bunkers is draped carefully in front of the green. On the 2nd, 339 yards, two crossbunkers threaten the drive, the approach is blind over a ridge, and the green undulates conspicuously.

The 3rd is the first of the great holes—198 yards from a slightly elevated tee over a no-man's land of broken ground to a plateau green nestled in the dunes, fronted by a swale and with sand at the left. This hole is now rather easier than when I first played it, in 1973. Then it was 228 yards and *blind*.

By the 4th hole we have reached the country of the giant sandhills that give Sandwich its renown. On this 417-yarder, the drive, launched from an elevated tee, must be kept left of a veritable tower of dune into which have been clawed two ferocious bunkers, one of them almost certainly the single most horrific pit ever to confront players in a major national championship. The face of the shallower one is twelve to fourteen feet high; the real shocker, beside it, is nearly thirty feet. But the solid tee shot sails serenely by these diversions to disappear into the fairway beyond, which doglegs left. The green is clearly in view for our second shot and a compelling target it is: a two-tiered plateau with an out-of-bounds fence right behind it. The shot must be kept well left, for both the green and the surrounding

129

ground tend to kick the ball smartly right. A splendid hole every foot of the way, and chosen as one of the top 100 in *The 500 World's Greatest Golf Holes.* It is also the root of a wonderful story. In the 1979 English Amateur, Reg Glading, then fifty-four and the oldest scratch golfer in the country, finished all square with his quarter finals opponent after eighteen holes. They halved the first three extra holes. Then, alas, Glading drove high into the face of *the* pit. He could not come at his ball from above for fear of causing a sandslide that would dislodge it. So he slowly inched his way up from below, club in hand. Now he gingerly took his stance, then set his grip. He swung. At the top of his backswing the sand suddenly shifted under him and, in a grotesque reverse cartwheel, he and the club and the ball collapsed down the slope to finish in a heap at the bottom of the pit. As to how many penalty strokes he may have incurred—testing the sand, grounding his club, moving the ball—neither he nor his opponent would venture a guess. What we do know is that, in one inglorious moment, Reg Glading gave new meaning to the term "sudden death."

The 5th, 421 yards, also doglegs left. The sandhills now begin to draw in upon us, and our drive—we are playing out to sea from a high tee, enjoying for the first time a view of the waters of Pegwell Bay—carries down into a narrow, dune-framed valley made to seem even narrower by a cluster of hidden bunkers at the left side of the landing area. A perfectly placed drive opens up a glimpse of the green through a little gap in the sandhills. Any tee shot less than optimum leaves a blind second shot over huge dunes. The remaining four holes on the nine are fine and memorable: the 156-yard 6th, the sea at our back this time, a long, tri-level green beckoning, ringed by deep bunkers and set with perfect naturalness in the dunes; the 487-yard 7th, a par five commencing from high ground that looks directly over a giant sandhill scarred with three terrifying pits; the 410-yard 8th, its tee just inland of the road along the beach to Prince's, its second shot an exacting downhill medium-iron to a well-bunkered green; and the 376-yard 9th, where a dangerous pit easing into the right side of the landing area for the drive forces us to shy away from the ideal spot for playing our second up to the narrow, elevated green, with its steep falloff on the right.

So much for what I have no reluctance to call my favorite first nine, a purely subjective judgment that doubtless is influenced by such inconsequential things as the tee benches themselves—old, weathered, formal, roomy, a barely readable plaque commemorating some individual or some golfing society. Oh, make no mistake about it, the holes are superb, quite superb, and sometimes, as in the case of the 3rd, 4th, and 5th, they can justly be termed great. Yet in the end it is the topography itself that so delights me, this landscape of mountainous sandhills, with the holes sometimes leaping off from atop the great grass-swaddled dunes, more often routed fascinatingly through them, and all of it so beautifully fitting, producing a combination of splendor and naturalness and solitude that is utterly beguiling. We often feel sheltered, better yet, secluded, more so than on any links I can think of. The holes wind among the sandhills, leading us through charming hollows and protected dells. We walk on and on without ever being aware that others may be on the course. Are there no distractions? Only the lilt of the lark or the enchanting seascape that awaits when we climb out of a dune valley to stand on a high tee and gaze across Pegwell Bay toward the cliffs at Ramsgate. It is all delicious stuff, and we drink it down in great draughts.

And what, you may wonder, about the second nine? Well, it provides another series of superlative holes, though it is played over much more level ground. There continues to be an admirable separateness about each hole—one can imagine a lifetime at Sandwich without once hearing the cry of "Fore!"— but it is generally the result of vast spaces between fairways rather than the walls of high dunes. This nine is not so private, nor so majestic. But it is still remarkable, it is immensely challenging, and it is more heavily bunkered. Against some forty pits on the outward half, the inward nine has almost seventy.

I note on a scorecard that beside the 13th hole I've written a single word: "Impossible!" It is 438 yards long, and when the prevailing breeze becomes the prevailing wind, this normally formidable hole becomes downright unplayable. Called for are two career woods (metals), both arrow-straight, the second one to a green with only a footpath cleaving two substantial bunkers.

The 14th is another Sandwich contribution to *The 500 World's Greatest Golf Holes.* A boundary fence close along the right separates this 539-yarder from Prince's. A ditch called the "Suez Canal" crosses the fairway some 300 yards out. On a pretty day, with the breeze at our back, this hole may be our best birdie chance. But a headwind, especially if it is violent, can transform this Jekyll into a Hyde, as was the case in the 1938 Open, amidst a gale so furious as to make a mockery of the players' most resolute efforts. Gusts exceeded sixty miles per hour. Four-putting was commonplace (in fact, there were instances of six-putting). Normally worthy par fours were driven—Alf Padgham, 1936 champion, reached the green on the 380-yard 11th with his tee shot and got the putt down for an eagle. On the other hand, par fives could not be reached in four shots. Into the teeth of the shrieking blasts on this, the Canal Hole, the same powerful Padgham swung four times with his driver and still failed to gain the putting surface!

It is just possible that the par-four 15th, generally played into a left-to-right crosswind, is even harder than the par-four 13th. The bunkering at both sides of the tee shot landing area is merciless, and the long second shot on this 442-yarder must carry a trio of pits blockading the front of the green. Like the 4th and 14th, it, too, was chosen one of *The 500 World's Greatest.*

At the 16th, 163 yards, the green is set charmingly in the dunes and surrounded by bunkers, eight of them. Seventeen and 18 are splendid closing holes. After a blind drive on the 413-yard 17th, we play along a beautiful curving valley; again there are eight bunkers to keep us honest. Incidentally, it was on the 17th at Royal St. George's, thinly disguised by Ian Fleming as "Royal St. Mark's," that the wicked Goldfinger, who had pushed his drive "far out to the right into deep rough," made a last desperate effort to cheat 007 of victory in their £10,000 grudge match in the famous James Bond novel. Fleming was captain-designate of the club when he died suddenly during a visit to Sandwich in 1964.

The home hole is a long two-shotter, 455 yards. It is also straight and hard. There is enough room for the well-struck second shot to chase onto the green if we can keep it on line. But the pit at the right front awaits greedily, the green falls away on both sides, and a boundary prowls behind.

The red-roofed Victorian clubhouse is rambling and comfortable, filled with overstuffed leather armchairs, dark paneling, old portraits, silver trophies, medals, antique golf clubs,

James W. Finegan

and memories of the club's rich history. Visitors, having made arrangements with the secretary in advance, are welcome on weekdays. Men must have a handicap no higher than 18 and women no higher than 15. There are no women members and no women's tees. The very presence of women, in fact, is so little acknowledged that they pay no green fee. And though they do not have the run of the clubhouse, they do have access to the dining room and the writing room.

Well-entrenched as some of the old ways still are at Royal St. George's, these considerations are not of much moment where visitors are concerned. The noble course is what counts. It is emblematic of seaside golf at its best: natural, demanding, surprising, often thrilling and beautiful, skillful short work along the ground immensely satisfying. It is not easy for me to place any links above it. I'm inclined to let Bernard Darwin have the last word: "This is perfect bliss . . . as nearly my idea of heaven as is to be attained on any earthly links."

All Courses Great and Small

In the very center of the town of Sandwich is the Bell Hotel. As long as there has been golf in this corner of Kent, the Bell has been taking good care of golfers. Though not luxurious, it is thoroughly comfortable and the cooking is good (delicious char-grilled sea bass).

Kent is a treasure trove for sightseers. Sandwich itself is a medieval jewel—narrow, cobbled lanes, half-timbered houses, the Guildhall, ancient churches, and the Stour River with its lovely quayside. Deal is also winning, with its fishing fleet, several streets lined with eighteenth-century houses, and its castle. But then, Kent is full of castles: Dover (overlooking the fabled white cliffs), Walmer, Hever (Anne Boleyn's birthplace), and perhaps above all, Leeds. Set in a small lake and surrounded by a picturesque nine-hole course, with the moat as a hazard, Leeds just may turn out to be the castle of your dreams. And for those with a green thumb, Kent is even more irresistible. There are 180 gardens open to visitors, including Chartwell, which Winston Churchill created for himself.

Not to be missed under any circumstance is Canterbury. The sublime cathedral, with its Great Cloister and extensive monastic buildings, may be the magnet, but there is much else about this ancient small city on the Stour that is appealing: a goodly stretch of medieval city wall, the Hospital of St. Thomas, the Buttery Market, and Christ Church Gate, to mention its most prominent attractions.

Add the well-nigh limitless charm of Kent to the excellence and historical importance of its most celebrated links and we find ourselves wondering what other county in the realm is more richly endowed.

CHAPTER NINE

The Channel Islands

THE VERY MENTION of the Channel Islands, some seventy-five miles off the southeastern coast of England and a mere fifteen miles from the Normandy and Brittany coasts of France, has always carried with it for us an ineffably romantic feeling, though what exactly is romantic about dairy cattle (Jersey, Guernsey) or a tax haven for the rich or an archipelago of nine islands occupied by the German Army from July 1, 1940, to May 9, 1945, I'm sure I cannot say. Still, the lure is there, perhaps in part because they are islands, graspable and knowable and beautiful; in part because they are convenient to London; in part because the immortal Harry Vardon came from Jersey (so a worthy course or two must be there); in part because of the influence of France (Jersey French, a blend of Norse and Norman French, is still spoken in the countryside); and in part because of their unique relation to Britain: They are "peculiars to the Crown," owing their allegiance to the Sovereign herself and not to the government.

We flew to Jersey from Gatwick. The airport on Jersey is not ten minutes from La Moye Golf Club, often a professional tournament venue over the last forty years. Among the winners of the Jersey Open here were Tony Jacklin, Sandy Lyle, Ian Woosnam, Christy O'Connor, Jr., and Sam Torrance.

The setting for the game is spectacular, on an exposed headland 250 feet above St. Ouen's Bay, its frothing combers a powerful attraction for the hundreds of thousands flocking to Jersey from the UK and from the Continent for their annual holiday at the sea. The first golf holes were laid out in 1902 by George Boomer, but the course we play took its overall shape and feel from James Braid in the early 1920s, with subsequent revisions by Henry Cotton and David Melville.

Despite its location high above the sea, La Moye can fairly be called a links—its quick-draining turf is sand-based and its natural features include dunes and hummocky stretches. Fairways are uncharacteristically narrow for a course so open to the wind, but the rough is generally light and there are only thirty-three bunkers.

I played La Moye with Nick Le Couteur, on a breezy June day in 2001. A member of the club's Committee (the governing body), Nick is also the owner/operator of a golf course (nine-hole par-three parkland layout) and a small hotel, two miles from La Moye. Dark-haired, fit looking, of average height, he appeared to be in his late forties. He is quick to smile and a ready conversationalist.

I was curious as to how he came to be in the golf resort business, even on such a modest scale.

"My mother and father had farmed their forty-acre plot for close to thirty years—in the fifties, sixties, and seventies," he said. "It was very hard work—the land is hilly—and it just didn't produce enough income. After my father died, it occurred to my mother—this was her idea—that with tourism so much a part of the economy here on Jersey—did I tell you that 50,000 rounds a year are played here at La Moye?—we might be able to build a decent little par-three course at Wheatlands and make it pay. We had to get planning permission to convert the farm into a golf course. This sort of thing has to come up before the island's parliament. I know that may sound strange to you—forty acres changing from crops into a par-three golf course requiring a vote of the legislature—but that is the law. The vote went against us. After a couple of years, we applied again. Again no luck. After another interval, we filled out the papers once more and once more our request was turned down. But we would not give up. Finally, in 1993, the parliament voted in our favor, twenty-three to nineteen, just a four-vote difference. We had our official opening in the summer of 1994, a grand opening, with Ian Woosnam—at that time he was a Jersey resident—doing the honors. This got us a lot of coverage in the newspapers here and even some mention in the UK golf magazines. And when you put the course together with the hotel, it's turned out to be all we could have hoped."

Nick and I played La Moye from the regular markers, 6,411 yards, par 72. The start here, on this island that is "peculiar to the Crown," is a bit peculiar itself: a par three, a par five, and a par three. Not till the 4th do we encounter a two-shotter, and what a strong hole it is, at 406 yards, bending left, out of bounds left and right, the level second shot heading straight out to sea and straight into the sea breeze. The 6th runs in the same direction, but this is a short par five, only 460 yards, and we can handle it if we don't allow the St. Ouen's Bay views to distract us. The delightful 368-yard 7th, commencing from a high tee beside a gorge plunging to the beach, has a hummocky landing area for the drive and a blind second shot over rough ground to a long, narrow plateau green with a steep falloff left. Eight and nine, each about 400 yards, are also demanding par fours.

The 353-yard 10th finds us driving between low dunes, then playing a shortish iron to a two-tier green defended by a couple of deep bunkers. A deceptively rigorous short par five (479 yards) follows, first curving elegantly right, then left, along a dune-framed valley to a pear-shaped and severely sloping green. Each of the three shots calls for careful placement. Two level and well-bunkered one-shotters bracket the 13th, 382 yards. Here, following a drive to an exposed fairway plateau, we turn left and play downhill to a sheltered green.

The final four holes hardly look intimidating on the card— 331 yards, 464 yards (yet another short par five), 390, and 390—but playing them is not easy, especially the short 15th, where the drive must carry a dangerous rough hollow in order to reach a shelf of fairway with a steep falloff to the right, and the 17th, which heads directly toward the sea from the shadow of the clubhouse and plays longer than 390 yards because of the wind and the big dip immediately in front of the green.

Offering a number of serious and satisfying holes in a beautiful setting, La Moye consistently provides the exhilaration of first-rate golf by the sea.

The drive to Royal Jersey Golf Club, along the south coast, past St. Aubin's Bay and through the vital capital, St. Helier, takes about half an hour in light traffic.

Only three British players have won both the U.S. and British Opens: Harry Vardon, Ted Ray, and Tony Jacklin. Astonishingly, two of them, Vardon and Ray, were born on Jersey, both in Grouville, the location of Royal Jersey Golf Club, and Jacklin actually made Jersey his home for five years.

Vardon, who learned the game as a caddie at Royal Jersey, was the greatest of the three. Not only is he the one man to have won the Open Championship six times, between 1896 and 1914, but his influence on how the game is played was profound. He stressed first of all the importance of the grip, preferring the little finger of the right hand to overlap the index finger of the left hand, thus encouraging each hand to do its proper work (the Vardon grip). Instead of the closed stance his contemporaries employed, he opened the toe of his right foot slightly and the toe of his left foot to nearly thirty degrees. He then took the club back in a much more upright arc than displayed by any golfer who preceded him, promoting a full shoulder turn and a more rhythmic release. No one—from grip through stance to swing—had gone at the ball the way Vardon did. It would be the template for virtually all of the finest players who followed.

Considering Vardon's extraordinary record of championships and his perhaps even more extraordinary impact on the technique of striking a golf ball, you will not be surprised to learn that a nearly nine-foot-high statue in bronze of the great man completing his graceful swing stands at the entrance to Royal Jersey Golf Club.

The club was founded in 1878 when a cadre of local golf enthusiasts mapped out eighteen holes on seventy acres of mostly sand-based land bordered on the east by the Royal Bay of Grouville. The links was little changed until World War II, which saw the Germans transform it into a minefield. When peace was restored, the scars soon healed and the game came back to life on this lovely spot.

I played there with three members of the club, Mike Tait, of the Jersey Tourist Bureau, Sue Dufty, owner of Longueville Manor Hotel, and Elaine Peoples, a travel agent. Mike's handicap was 11, Sue's 14, and Elaine's 8. Mike suggested a match pitting the men against the women, better ball of partners, no handicaps, the women to play from the forward markers (5,431 yards), the men from the back (just 6,100 yards). Par is 70. Then he announced the stakes: "We'll play for £20,000." Now he turned to me. "That's the grand prize in the Jersey Lottery. To have a chance of winning it, you've got to have a ticket, which costs £1. So whichever side wins our match here today, each of the two partners is given a £1 lottery ticket by the losing team. Then, when the weekly drawing takes place, perhaps one of the tickets will turn out to be worth £20,000. In which case, the 20,000 will be divided between the two partners."

"Yes," Elaine added, "we always play for 20,000. Wouldn't bother for anything less."

I dearly loved the course, which, despite its shortness, has a number of testing holes. And if the opening hole, a par five of 476 yards, is scarcely intimidating, it is nonetheless unforgettable. It rolls along beside the sea wall, about seven or eight feet above the beach. As I teed up my ball and stepped back to survey the requirements of the shot, Mike said to me, pointing down the fairway, "You will want to split the difference between the German gun emplacement on the right and the Napoleonic fortress on the left." And so, with two reminders of the island's colorful history framing the hole, we begin the game at Royal Jersey. The landing area for the drive is generous, our shot comes down comfortably in it, and we are away on an altogether delightful round. The 143-yard 2nd was a Vardon favorite: paralleling the strand, a carefully bunkered and rather narrow plateau green with a steep falloff at the left. The 3rd, at 554 yards much the longest hole on the course, is superb. A mildly downhill drive leads to a cloistered fairway framed by dunes and bending right over tumbling ground, finally to fetch up at a partly concealed green. The level and sand-free 4th, 180 yards, completes this run along the shore. From the tee there is a view of the sailboat-filled harbor just down the coast at Gorey, with the cottages on the hill and magnificent Mont Orgueil Castle serving as the backdrop. It is all what we envision when someone speaks of "holiday golf at the sea."

The best holes on the back nine are a couple of par fours, 12 and 17. The uphill 12th, 389 yards, has two memorable moments: the huge fairway-filling mound short of the green that makes the second shot blind and effectively turns away the short ball, and the low, gray granite Vardon memorial marker just right of the fairway, which spells out the years of his six British Opens and one U.S. Open and begins with a pointed "locator" statement: WITHIN PUTTING DISTANCE OF THIS STONE HARRY VARDON 1870–1937 THE GREAT GOLFER WAS BORN.

The 404-yard 17th is hard, the tee shot aimed at the gates of Fort Henry (Mike's "Napoleonic fortress"), the second shot rising to a large green with a steep falloff into sand at the right front. The last hole, only 321 yards, climbing while curving smoothly left, gives us a chance to improve our score. Most days it also gives us a clear view of the coast of France, fourteen miles away.

Ah, I've neglected to keep you posted on that dog-eat-dog match. As it happens, Mike and I simply proved too tough for the ladies, taking an early lead and closing them out on the 181-yard 16th, 3 and 2, when my partner bravely holed a two-footer for bogey. Our vanquished foes presented us each with the prescribed lottery ticket. I must assume that neither ticket turned out to be the winner, because the £20,000 was not forthcoming.

There is no shortage of good lodgings on Jersey. Beside the 2nd green at La Moye is the fifty-room Atlantic Hotel, on high ground looking out to St. Ouen's Bay. Public spaces, highlighted by antiques, are sparkling and stylish. Guest rooms are smartly appointed, and even the smaller ones do not feel cramped. The cooking is imaginative and excellent. The Atlantic is what a top-notch hotel by the sea ought to look like and feel like and be like.

At the opposite end of the island, a short run from Royal Jersey, is vine-covered Longueville Manor, dating to the fifteenth century and set on sixteen acres. In the exquisite gardens is a little lake graced by black swans. Public rooms are filled with tastefully chosen antiques. Guest accommodations, individually decorated, are spacious and very like sumptuous. Food and service were outstanding. By any measurement, a superlative small luxury hotel in the great country house tradition.

Sightseeing on Jersey (forty-four square miles) is immensely rewarding. We managed to take in the cliffs of the north coast and the sandy bays in the south and west, to get happily lost a couple of times on the twisting country lanes, to relish the picturesque little harbor of St. Aubin's, and to catch our breath at a sidewalk cafe in St. Helier's Royal Square.

The flight from Jersey to Guernsey takes twelve minutes. The taxi from the airport to Royal Guernsey Golf Club (1890), at L'Ancresse, takes twice that long. The German occupation of this twenty-five-square-mile island, from 1940 to 1945, inflicted damage not only on the links but on the clubhouse as well, where the first act of one of the soldiers was to throw the con-

James W. Finegan

tents of the secretary's office, including the historical records, out of the window.

The course today is largely attributable to Philip Mackenzie Ross, who was responsible for the resuscitation of Turnberry's Ailsa Course after World War II. Alterations were made to the Ross layout here some twenty years later by Fred W. Hawtree.

L'Ancresse, as the course is generally referred to by Channel Islanders, is bounded by the beautiful bays of Grand Havre and L'Ancresse. It doubles as a pasture—by law, the Guernsey cattle have grazing rights. This is authentic links golf: duneland that sometimes tumbles violently, sometimes scarcely undulates at all, and boasts tall golden-fescue rough, plus more than its share of gorse. The course at its longest measures 6,215 yards; par is 70. There is a sharp contrast between the two nines, to the clear detriment of the outbound half, which is too often level and uninspired. Oh, there are a couple of very stiff two-shelters, 438 and 461 yards, and a couple of first-rate par threes, 181 and 190 yards, each very good in its own right but similar in length and design. Still, the first nine is a disappointment.

All Courses Great and Small

Fortunately, the second nine comes to the rescue. Here the holes range from good to great, thanks to land full of feature and dramatic elevation changes (the dizzying drop on the short par-four 13th, the exhausting climb to the green on the 306-yard 17th, which, into a stout breeze, can play 425 yards!). The 407-yard 15th is a great par four, our drive from an elevated tee piercing the prevailing wind to pass a huge, old stone tower on the right and land amidst heaving terrain on the lower ground, the long second shot now scaling a steep embankment to gain the green.

As for the 18th, I don't know where we will ever play a hole quite like it. Talk about a top-of-the-world tee—well, walking onto it, the first thing we think of is not the shot but the panorama of this entire end of the island and, if the day is sunny, its surrounding cobalt seas. It is heart-stopping. Then comes this simple shot, just 156 yards but falling, falling, falling through a zephyr or a breeze or a wind or a gale to a green that would like to be hospitable, not too many paces from a spiffy new clubhouse where you can be assured of a warm welcome.

The cobbled streets and historic architecture of Guernsey's capital, St. Peter Port, cry out to be explored, but we barely scratched the surface. Maybe you'll agree that we had a good excuse. We stayed at La Fregate (The Frigate), an eighteenth-century manor house in St. Peter Port. The public spaces are not appealing. Our room, #10—large, comfortable, cheerful—was not attractively furnished. Still, we cannot imagine staying anywhere else on the island. Why? Because the setting and the view add up to enchantment. This thirteen-room hotel is tucked away on a garden hillside with surpassing views of the harbor (small pleasure craft, big ferry boats, a fishing fleet, and thirteenth-century Castle Cornet on guard at the seaward end). The sitting area of our room opened through full-length glass doors to a broad terrace commanding this scene. The hotel's principal patio, one floor below, with its stylish white sun umbrellas, is blessed with the identical view. So is the dining room, every table in the dining room, where, I hasten to add, the classic French cuisine is widely regarded as the finest on Guernsey. Only one other time in our wandering throughout Britain and Ireland have we come upon a location to equal La Fregate's, and to equal its cooking. That was in Cornwall (Chapter 12).

CHAPTER TEN

Is Rye the Toughest Course in England?

IT IS LIKELY that Royal Ashdown Forest, in East Sussex and thirty minutes from Gatwick, is the most truly natural of the world's outstanding courses. The reason is clear to see: no sand bunkers. The Conservators of the New Forest, which is common ground and thus belongs to the people of England, long ago decreed that the club must not alter the terrain. Mow the grass for fairways and tees and greens, if you insist, but dig no holes, please!

The club was founded in 1888 by a group of Tunbridge Wells golf enthusiasts led by an Anglican parson, Reverend A. T. Scott, who himself located the land, in Forest Row, laid out the course, and struck the first ball. This is heathland golf, on sand-based soil, the holes isolated in rolling corridors framed by pine and silver birch. From the back tees, it measures 6,500 yards against a par of 72. We are immediately taken with the course's beauty and tranquillity.

Twenty-five years have passed since I first played Ashdown. I have returned on several occasions, always with a sense of happy anticipation and never to be disappointed. The secretary in the late 1970s was R. L. Griffith, who gave me good counsel on my initial visit: "I think you'll want to play the long tees throughout. The great feature of Ashdown is the driving, the need to carry the ball over all that mess out there, the heather and the gorse and the bracken—it's much the same on most holes—in order to reach the fairway. Quite enough room out there, but you do have to get out there."

The drive on the 332-yard 1st, from a hillside tee, is wonderfully inviting. There is all that rough country below, with even a tiny stream, and then there is a vast and welcoming landing area on the opposite slope that, in fact, is shared with the 18th, for the two holes crisscross.

Without explicit directions from Mr. Griffith, I seriously doubt that we would ever have found the 2nd hole. But now we wound our way around the lovely Shalesbrook house and garden and down the lane past the barnyard to the clearing at the foot of the hill where the tee awaits. At 384 yards and playing over a steep ridge smack in front of the tee, the hole then rises almost imperceptibly to a green with a creek in front of it. This is one of the course's premier two-shotters.

The pretty 334-yard 3rd, doglegging left to a green in the corner of a wood, is followed by a boldly uphill 385-yarder, where the second shot is blind. On the downhill 5th, 512 yards, the powerful hitter will get up in two if he can carry the trouble-strewn swale, complete with stream, just short of the green. It is purest risk/reward.

Ashdown's shortest hole, the 126-yard 6th, is its most famous. Thanks to a meandering ditch, the extremely narrow "island green" has water on three sides. Mr. Griffith, his young black Labrador retriever tightly on a leash, had come out to walk with Harriet and me for several holes, and now told us that in 1897 a nonmember endowed the hole with the sum of £5. The interest was to be allowed to accumulate and this money was to be paid to a member making a hole-in-one here in a club competition. Not until 1947, fifty years later, did someone finally pocket the proceeds. And then, as luck would have it, just one month later a second ace was scored, but this time the cupboard was bare.

The second nine, like the first a par 36, is, however, 350 yards longer. The culprits are a hefty 568-yarder, steeply sloping from right to left much of the way, a 472-yard par four, and both one-shotters, the 249-yard 11th and the 200-yard 14th. When the three of us walked off the 10th green, Mr. Griffith suggested that Harriet also make the short walk up the slope to the 11th tee in order to enjoy the views.

In truth, from this vertiginously high platform, they take one's breath away, so glorious are they, stretching across peaceful wooded valleys toward East Grinstead and beyond, all the way—a good forty miles—to the North Downs. There is no moment at Royal Ashdown that is not appealing, but the vistas from the 11th tee are intoxicating: that wonderful wedding of beauty and serenity and grandeur.

Probably the finest hole at Ashdown is the 17th, which I particularly recall from a visit ten years later, in 1987. I found myself paired with a member of the club's artisan section, a strapping 200-pound nineteen-year-old who within the space of twelve months had reduced his handicap from 24 to 4. The blind tee shot on this 472-yard par four gets some benefit from a gentle downslope. The long second shot must steer clear of woods on the left and, ideally, drift from left to right on its path

James W. Finegan

to a green cut into a right-hand hillside. I hit an excellent drive followed by a lifetime 3-wood to reach the very front of the putting surface. My young friend—why does the image of L'il Abner pop up?—now went into the green with a 6-iron that sailed, on the fly, somewhere between 215 and 225 yards to finish twenty feet beyond the cup. That was more than fifteen years ago, pre-Daly and pre-Tiger, to say nothing of pre-titanium and pre-Pro V1.

I can almost guarantee that Royal Ashdown Forest will provide one of your warmest memories of golf in England. Not only will you be charmed and challenged by this highly regarded course, but you will be equally taken with the club as well—the small membership, the focus exclusively on the game, the homey Victorian clubhouse dating to 1893 (lunch is the only meal served), and the modesty of the overall operation. Said Mr. Griffith, "The course requires very little maintenance. No bunkers to consume a lot of man-hours. As for the rough, we never tend to any of that. The fairways are not the lush carpets you Americans are used to. They're mowed only a couple of times a month, I should think, even less when it's very dry, as it was last summer."

We're leaving East Sussex for the nonce and heading across the county line on a southwesterly tack and down to the West Sussex Golf Club, at Pulborough, the name by which the club itself is generally known. Founded in 1930, Pulborough boasts a very strong heathland course—and an exceptionally beautiful one—designed by Guy Campbell, Major C. K. Hutchison, and S. V. Hotchkin, partners in several important undertakings, most notably the remodeling of both Woodhall Spa and Royal West Norfolk (Brancaster).

Don't be misled by the overall length here, a mere 6,156

yards, for par is an equally meager 68. The lone par five is the opening hole, only 481 yards. There are also a couple of short-ish par threes. What this means is that half the holes here are strenuous. In fact, seven two-shotters range from 403 to 448 yards. Two of the par threes are 210 and 220 yards. Vigorous hitting is actually at a premium on this gently rolling eighteen, where the routing uses the terrain to excellent advantage and there is a very attractive diversity to the holes. There is little drama on the greens but plenty of danger in the bunkering, whether greenside or in the tee-shot landing area.

On a course that has many very good holes, three seem to me to be inarguably great. One of them, the 6th, can also be lethal. A 220-yarder that, depending on conditions, may call for anything from a 5-iron to a driver, it plays moderately downhill, first over an expanse of heather, then over marshy scrub that merges into a natural pond. Between the far side of the water hazard and the green, there is some landing room, but this is not generous and it is corseted by sand on the right and heather and gorse on the left. This hole is an authentic card-wrecker.

The 7th, a 442-yard two-shotter, is equally superlative. The tee shot is blind. But it is what we *can* see that is intimidating: roughly (not a casually chosen adverb) 180 yards of uphill heather and scrub capped by an enormous steep-faced bunker just short of the hidden fairway. Succeed with the drive and you will have earned the right to play a 4- or 5-wood to a sloping and adroitly bunkered green.

The star of the inbound nine is the 363-yard 13th, more often than not played into the wind. It rises gently and curves right. Menacing the drive is a bunker at the left and heather at the right. The second shot, much longer than the card suggests, must be fired across a massive expanse of sand to an elevated bowl-shaped green that, if it does not channel our shot toward the cup, will leave us with a dismaying putt or two.

Pulborough has cultivated a low profile over the years, but in no sense should it be viewed as snooty. Visitors are greeted graciously.

If West Sussex is a relatively young club, East Sussex National is young without the qualifier. Located in Uckfield—we're back over the county line now—maybe three quarters of an hour east of Pulborough, East Sussex opened in 1990 with two excellent eighteens designed by Bob Cupp. Nicklaus's senior designer from 1973 to 1985, Cupp has been on his own since, with his most admired courses the two at Pumpkin Ridge, in North Plains, Oregon.

At East Sussex National, Cupp was given a tract of beautiful, rolling countryside, some of it wooded, and he has made the most of it. Both East and West Courses can be played as long as 7,150 yards and as short as 5,200 yards. They are fashioned in contemporary American parkland style, where doglegs abound, fairways breathe in and out, water frequently threatens, trees come into play from time to time, a shot landing in a bunker does not automatically signal the loss of a stroke, the greens are swift, and the turf is close to perfect.

It is difficult to choose between the two eighteens. The East, which hosted the European Open in 1993 and 1994, is the more penal. Water is in play on ten holes and there are ninety bunkers (not an inordinate number), as contrasted with the West, where water imperils the shot on six holes and there are only sixty-seven bunkers.

With its spectator mounds, the East is a so-called "stadium

course." Its par fives are outstanding. The straightaway 507-yard 2nd gives us a roomy landing area for the drive, but the second shot is bedeviled by oak trees right and a rough-covered mound left, and the green, closely bunkered at the right, presents steep falloffs in the front and at the left. On the 7th we swing hard: Measuring 569 yards, the hole climbs all the way—its playing value is never less than 600 yards. There is a dip in front of the green, a green that is only eighteen paces deep and all but sealed off by sand. This is a legitimate three-shotter. The 10th, on the other hand, is short stuff, only 489 yards, the blind tee shot clearing a crest and coming to rest on one of several "decks" stepping down the hill toward the green. The second shot aimed at getting home here is death or glory: It must be lined between two oak trees (goal-post fashion) and carry water fronting the green. And the final par five, the 525-yard 14th, is yet another beauty, clusters of sand traps both left and right at the tee-shot landing area, a second shot that must avoid a pot bunker in the center of the fairway, and a neighboring pond, plus a deep swale in front of the green. What a grand quartet of long holes Bob Cupp has assembled for us on the East Course!

The West Course is less open in aspect and feel than its sister. The surrounding woods are denser and the elevation changes are sharper. There are genuine hills here, and the climbs result in entrancing views over the South Downs. Among this course's many top-notch holes is an especially appealing trio to start the second nine. The 403-yard 10th—played from an elevated tee, old oak trees right and left constricting the drive—curves right, around a lagoon that is entirely too close for comfort to the raised two-tier green. The 11th bends the opposite way and, at 422 yards, is demanding enough without the added problems of hillocky rough on both sides of the fairway and a vast, complex green full of double-breaking putts. Which brings us to my favorite hole at East Sussex National, and wouldn't you know it's a par five, the 519-yard 12th. The entire length of the hole is all but intertwined with Little Horsted Creek. We must clear it on the drive, a carry of some 175 yards, clear it on the second shot, another 175-yard carry, and steer clear of it on the third, with the green perched just above the water on a shelf, below which, for good measure, is also a six-foot-deep stacked-sod bunker. This is as much tension on one golf hole as the law allows.

I should mention that, in the best upscale American tradition, the sprawling brick clubhouse has paneled locker rooms and marble-clad showers; the huge pro shop is a veritable temple of merchandising; and the halfway house can take your order for hot snacks by intercom from the 9th tee.

Allied with the golf club and set on a rise behind the 9th green of the West Course is Horsted Place, built in 1850 and one of the finest examples of Gothic Revival architecture in Britain. While it was the home of Lord Rupert Nevil, from 1965 to 1984, the Royal Family spent long weekends here from time to time. It is now an idyllic country house hotel, elegant and luxurious, each of the spacious guest accommodations with a character and charm of its own. Service is faultless, and the food is of a very high standard.

East Sussex is full of interesting houses, gardens, and villages, including Kidbrooke Park, a sandstone house and stables built in the 1730s; Sheffield Park Garden, its series of five lakes linked by cascades; and the picturesque village of West Heathly, with its 13th-century church.

All Courses Great and Small

There is no mistaking our final golf club in this chapter for nouveau East Sussex National. It is Rye—old guard, old school, a throwback to the days of empire, and custodian of one of the greatest links courses. Frank Pennink's succinct characterization of the links is spot on: "True seaside golf of championship calibre."

Still, other than a couple of English Ladies' Amateurs (1970 and 1990), Rye has never hosted an important championship. Some claim it is too short in season. But it is the home each January—yes, January, possibly for the pure cantankerousness of it—of the President's Putter, a four-day match play knock-out competition among the members of the Oxford and Cambridge Golfing Society.

This gathering, which began in 1920, is marked by some very good play in frequently wretched weather. The gallery is sometimes smaller than the field, itself 150–160. In 1993 a couple of friends of mine flew from JFK to Gatwick, then drove down to Rye for the sole purpose of watching this event. The *Times* reporter was so struck by the presence of the two Americans that she wrote her opening piece mostly about them:

> Harrie Perkins, of Dallas, Texas, and Martha Reddington, of New York, will never play in the President's Putter, but they were the undoubted stars when the 66th edition . . . of the annual outing started at Rye yesterday. On a damp, mizzly day, with visibility at a premium, the two Americans, golfing traditionalists to their frozen fingertips, fetched up to watch shadowy, muffled figures do battle with their own rickety bones and the elements as well as

their opponents. Perkins and Reddington knew none of the competitors. If the participants are widely regarded as crazy to compete at such a place at such a time, where does that leave people who have crossed the Atlantic simply to watch?

Rye was founded in 1894, and it was Harry Colt who laid out the course, his first. Much altered over the decades since, Rye today reflects above all the fine hand of Guy Campbell. There is also an attractive relief nine here, which Frank Pennink designed in 1975.

I played Rye for the first time twenty-five years ago, on a mid-March morning. There were two other players on hand, a pair of women in their sixties who preceded me to the 1st tee by thirty seconds. They teed off as I stood there twiddling my thumbs or twirling my driver. They held me up on the 481-yard opener, which rumbles promisingly along; on the heavily bunkered 180-yard 2nd, which is both grand and supremely testing; and on the 437-yard 3rd, which is uphill, also grand, and also supremely testing.

As they approached the 3rd green, I impulsively decided to wait no longer but instead to dart directly to the 4th tee, cutting in ahead of them. Swiftly off, I did not hold them up for an instant. As it turned out, however, I had not made the clean getaway for which I was congratulating myself.

Two holes later, as I headed down the 6th fairway, the elder of the ladies veered sharply off the parallel 5th and struck out directly to intercept me, head on. Terrified now, I simply marched straight ahead. She fired a reprimand at me from a distance of perhaps ten paces. "You played a smart number on the fourth, sir," she barked, "cutting in ahead of us, didn't you?" Head held high but eyes averted, I strode past her in mortified silence, my pace quickening. She called after me, "How dare you? What you did is against the rules. And as a singleton you have no standing whatsoever on the links. You may be certain that I will bring your conduct to the attention of the secretary."

I never doubted it for a moment. My only thought now was to complete the round and get on the road. An appreciation of the unpretentious but comfortable clubhouse would have to wait for five years, till my next visit, by which time perhaps both my identity and my nefarious deed would be forgotten.

Rye measures 6,308 yards against a par of 68. It is, for me, the most difficult course in England and second only to Carnoustie in all of British golf. It is like Pulborough in that it has only one par five, the opener, and five par threes. These one-shotters, ranging from 159 to 222 yards, rank among the very best short holes in the world, their greens cocked up in the dunes so elusively that it is often said, only half in jest, that the toughest shots at Rye are the second shots on the par threes. What about the par fours? There are twelve of them. The 8th, 9th, and 11th measure 391, 300, and 324 yards, respectively. The other nine two-shotters, beginning with the 3rd, are 437 yards, 411 yards (chasms right and left to swallow the errant drive from a high tee), 468, 420, 420, 430 (spectacular blind second shot over sandhills), 458, 419, and 439. Even a forceful hitter grows weary fighting these battles, especially on this tumultuous terrain, where capricious bounces and awkward stances are endemic.

Two prominent dune ridges serve as the spines of the links. Holes are routed through the dune-framed valleys or from the top of one ridge to the top of another or along the flanks of the

James W. Finegan

sandhills. We are thus confronted by a cavalcade of hillocks and hummocks and hollows, natural duneland that ranges from wrinkled to hilly and includes billowing, rumpled, and broken. All of this on perhaps the fastest great course in the world, with the ball inclining to skim over the closely mown, sand-based turf, racing everywhere, persistently frustrating the player and requiring him to fashion short shots along the ground with imagination and consummate finesse.

Then stir into the mix the wind, which seems never to be with us. In fact, almost all the holes must be tackled in a crosswind, and nothing is more destructive of the golf swing than repeatedly having to allow for twenty to twenty-five miles per hour gusting from right to left or, even worse, from left to right. Our swing, fragile at the best of times, is in tatters before we have made the turn.

This triple harassment—length, topography, wind—produces a sternly exacting course, but what profound satisfaction is ours when we have somehow fought Rye to a standoff, all the while reveling in one of the most severely beautiful panoramas in the world of golf: the splendid bent-covered sandhills, the gray-green Channel seas, the lonely Romney Marsh with, here and there, clusters of grazing sheep, and the ancient town itself atop its hill, beaconlike and welcoming.

Speaking of welcoming, how accessible is Rye Golf Club to the player with no acquaintance among the membership? The candid answer is, "not very." The club's basic policy is that a visitor may play only in the company of a member. But is the door really barred otherwise? Or are there times when the secretary may make an exception to the rule? There are such times. Perhaps in the off-season or on a day in season—say, Monday—

when relatively light play is expected. Or maybe in mid- to late-afternoon on a weekday. Or if there are just two of you or four of you willing to split up and play in twosomes. Clearly, you will have to be flexible and fortunate. But with the planets properly aligned, you just may find yourself on the 1st tee, under the warning eye of the clubhouse clock, ready to embark on the splendid adventure. For this is the authentic stuff, the definitive duneland golf that, perhaps more than anything else, will color your memories of golf in England forever.

Believe it or not, of the hundreds of thousands who travel to this corner of East Sussex annually, only a handful are here for the golf. Tiny Rye Harbour, a haven for sailboats at the mouth of the river Rother, delights. Then there are those who come chiefly for the pleasure of overnighting at the legendary Mermaid Inn, which is so ancient that it was *rebuilt* in 1420. It is all here in this atmospheric hostelry: antique paneling, blackened oak beams, immense stone fireplaces, husky fourposter beds in some guest rooms (none of them more captivating than Dr. Sym's Bedchamber, which we once occupied), and good cooking.

But in the end it is the hilltop town itself that is the draw. Many visitors simply browse, for an hour, a day, or a weekend, and it will be obvious why. True, most of the medieval wall that once encircled Rye is gone, but the main entrance, the Land Gate, is still intact and still flanked by two tall stone towers. Nearby is beautiful St. Mary's Church, dating to the twelfth century. Rye is one of the best-preserved ancient towns in England. Many of the narrow streets are still cobbled, and the medieval street plan is unchanged. There are roughly a hundred timber-framed structures going back to the sixteenth century and even earlier. That avid Anglophile Henry James lived here in Lamb House, a handsome red-brick Georgian residence, from 1898 until his death in 1916. It was here that he wrote some of his most respected fiction, including *The Turn of the Screw* and *The Wings of the Dove.* Though not a golfer, James was elected a member of the club in 1898. He visited it often, but only for high tea.

CHAPTER ELEVEN

Hampshire: An Unknown Links and a Well-Known Hotel

WE ARE NOT LEAVING the English Channel quite yet. Instead, we head due west on the A27 past Brighton and into the county of Hampshire, to reach Hayling Island and the Hayling Golf Club. Founded in 1883, it nestles on the shores of the Solent, the narrow body of water separating Hampshire from the Isle of Wight.

The course we play today began to take shape in 1905, when five-time Open champion J. H. Taylor made substantive revisions to a very rudimentary layout devised by a couple of members. An intensive remodeling under the direction of Tom Simpson took place in 1933.

Elevation changes are minimal at Hayling, and there are few blind shots, though a number of shots are semiblind or ill-defined, making club selection difficult. The wind is often powerful. We tackle an all but unbroken succession of holes routed through duneland of folds and humps and hollows, of ridges and shallow valleys, all of it studded with gorse and heather and the long bent grasses. Now mind you, this wonderfully natural links is no monument to meticulous greenkeeping. In truth, it is somewhat scruffy. Golfers of all description come here. The day I played, in late summer of 2000, there were rank beginners (a couple of ten- or eleven-year-old boys with their fathers as instructors), a mixed foursome of the elderly towing trolleys, and scratch collegians cracking 270-yard drives and then landing little knockdown 9-irons short of the green to commence the necessarily long skip and run over the thin turf toward the flagstick.

The course measures 6,300 yards; par is 71. The opening hole is indicative of the test. It is 173 yards long. A lone bunker—and not at all a large one—awaits at the left front of the green. Beside it is a rough-covered mound. Because the prevailing wind sweeps off the Solent and across the hole from left to right, both the mound and the sand lie precisely where we must aim our shot, banking it up into the crosswind, if we are to have any chance of hitting and holding the flat, unreceptive green. This is a highly exacting play.

That solitary bunker is a forerunner of many such to come. For here at Hayling is the most brilliant—and beleaguering— collection of single bunkers I've ever seen. On eleven holes we encounter one of these "orphans," cunningly sited just where we do not want to go but are in grave danger of going because of the wind or the topography or our swing. Again and again these solitary pits give pause, introducing an element of doubt when what we dearly need is certainty.

On a course with a number of forceful holes, there is a par-

All Courses Great and Small

ticularly memorable trio early on the second nine. The 11th, 144 yards, plays straight out to sea from a slightly elevated tee, the Isle of Wight a pretty backcloth, the green a simple shelf ringed by sand, the wind into us. The 435-yard 12th is Hayling's longest par four, also its hardest and best, working its secluded way along the shore, with framing dunes, scrub, and gorse, the mildly raised green set against the sandhills and defended on the left by a single deep pit and a steep falloff. Then comes the 327-yard 13th, with an immense and ragged bunker to trap the cut drive, a sometimes blind (depending on the wind) second shot over the hill, and beguiling views of the sailboat-filled bay from the crest. The nautical flavor of this moment is reprised at the home hole, with its striking white clubhouse instantly calling to mind the luxury-liner clubhouse at Royal Birkdale (Chapter 15 and front cover). But the panoramic views here, across the water to Wight through the window-walls of the lounge, are more captivating than those at the great Lancashire club.

Nearly an hour's drive west of Hayling Island—first skirting Portsmouth and then Southampton on the M27—brings us to Barton-on-Sea Golf Club, with its twenty-seven holes of exposed clifftop golf some eighty to 100 feet above the English Channel. The club was founded in 1897.

Two nines, called Needles and Stroller and laid out by Scottish-born J. Hamilton Stutt (Ireland's Wexford course, Scotland's Murrayshall) have little in the way of elevation change and are quite similar in look and feel. But the third nine, Becton, which is largely the work of Harry Colt, has its full share of delightful ups and downs. So if you're playing only eighteen holes you will want to make sure that Becton accounts for half the round.

The opening hole on the Becton nine is a flat, dull, straight-away par four. The 2nd, however, is everything the starter is not. From a high tee on this 365-yarder, the drive is launched down into a narrow fairway corseted by a stream on the right and sloping rough ground on the left. The stream turns left to cross the fairway about eighty-five yards short of the green, then straightens out as it heads toward the putting surface to imperil the pulled approach shot. A very sporty business from start to finish and an honest indication of the exuberant nature of this nine, where water, sand, hills, and gorse (the par-three 8th lying in a sea of it) all take turns challenging us.

The other two nines provide the built-in variety that stems from three of each, par threes, fours, and fives. Needles is the tougher of the two. It offers a couple of stout, rippling par fours more than 400 yards long; a lovely 517-yarder with the green nestling in a dell of dunes; a pair of discouragingly long one-shotters, including the superb 225-yard 2nd, where a vast bunker seals off the green and water swallows the hooked shot; and, finally, a 130-yarder with an island green, water churning around it courtesy of a pump inside the glass-walled clubhouse.

Barton-on-Sea is pure holiday golf: the salty scent of the Channel, the muted roar of the waves pounding on the beach far below, the wind always to be wrestled with, a good score possible yet far from automatic. And, of course, there are those ravishing views: When the day is brightly clear, we actually feel that we might reach out across Christchurch Bay and touch the chalk cliffs of the Isle of Wight.

A twenty-minute drive north on the A337 brings us to Bro-kenhurst Manor Golf Club and another meeting with the redoubtable Harry Colt. Laid out in 1920, this is not one of his celebrated courses, but it is thoroughly satisfying. The holes are routed over rolling ground in the very heart of the New Forest. The world is at a far remove.

Even from the medal tees, the course measures only 6,200 yards; par is 70. On half a dozen holes, a stream endangers the loose shot, as is the case on the 2nd, crossing the fairway from the right about eighty-five yards short of the green and then sidling up along the left side of the putting surface, exactly as he designed it for the 2nd hole at Barton-on-Sea. It is all right to borrow from yourself.

There are eight potent holes here, six of them in a row beginning at the 8th. This series includes a pair of excellent par threes, the shorter one a knob-to-knob beauty of 171 yards, plus a quartet of rigorous two-shotters. The 8th, for instance, at 446 yards, moves gently downhill, so we have a chance of reaching it in regulation. The 9th, at 459 yards, moves steadily uphill, so we have no chance of reaching it in regulation.

One other par four should be singled out, the splendid 421-yard 17th. A stream must be carried from the modestly elevated tee. The hole doglegs right, through the trees, and the green, bunkered only at the right front, is smaller than is comfortable on this long second shot. John Jacobs names this hole on his best eighteen in England, but we cannot count on him to be objective in this instance: He is a member of the club.

I played the second nine with another member of the club, a robust chap in his early sixties who had worked as a manufacturing executive for Ford Motor Company. "After I retired," he said, "my wife and I bought the Roselyn Hotel in Bournemouth. We ran the place, the two of us, for seven years. It was a twenty-four-hours-a-day, seven-days-a-week job, and we grew to dislike it intensely. I can tell you that serving the public on an intimate basis is an awful way to make a living.

"Then we bought an older cottage that needed a lot of modernization, which I enjoyed doing. But when I'd finished it, I couldn't just sit there and stare at the telly, so about eighteen months ago I took a job at the Meyrick Park Municipal Course in Bournemouth. I'm supposed to be a ranger, but I do everything from keeping play moving to picking up trash to sometimes even working as a starter. I love it. I love the place, love the job. Meyrick's the oldest municipal course in England. And it's not even 6,000 yards from all the way back, but it's still tough. The first hole's a 243-yard par three. Some people consider it the toughest opening hole in the country."

When we parted in the car park after the round, he said to me, "I hope you'll come to Meyrick Park one of these days. I'll be there somewhere on the job."

I promised to seek him out if I should get there. Here was a man who had been an automobile maker and an innkeeper and a cottage remodeler, but none of these occupations—or so it seemed to me—had been quite so rewarding as his present post, all-purpose ranger at a municipal golf course.

Fifteen minutes south of Brokenhurst Manor, on the outskirts of nondescript New Milton and about a mile from the sea, is Chewton Glen, a five-star hotel that *Gourmet* magazine named "Best Country House Hotel in the World" for 2000. It is beautiful—the three-story, red-brick, vine-covered house dates from the early 1700s—and luxurious and expensive. In season, expect to pay at least $700 a day for two, dinner and breakfast included. Chewton Glen epitomizes the English Country look (chintzes, tassels, antiques, oriental rugs, and old oil paintings).

All Courses Great and Small

French doors lead to trellised terraces and an immaculately maintained croquet lawn. In our lovely accommodation, three old books sat atop a Chippendale-style chest. One contained Shakespeare's sonnets. A second offered four of the Bard's most famous comedies and an intriguing inscription penned on the flyleaf: "Grace Bromley Allan, Wellesley College, Tent mo. 15, 1906." The third book was pragmatic and to the point: *Teach Yourself Beekeeping.*

As for the kitchen at Chewton Glen, it has a Michelin star. We were quite bowled over by an Emmenthal cheese soufflé appetizer (kirsch-flavored fondue sauce), char-grilled fillet of duck, and a greengage plum tart topped with walnut ice cream and homemade honey. The wine cellar houses 400 labels ($2,100 for the Pomerol Chateau Le Pin 1986).

A few words about the amenities at this 130-acre, sixty-two-room demi-paradise: outdoor and indoor tennis courts, outdoor and indoor swimming pools, a sybaritic health club, and a charming little nine-hole par-three course with plenty of opportunity to sharpen your wedge play.

The southern part of Hampshire is full of places to see and things to do. To name just a handful: 17th-century Kingston Lacy, one of the National Trust's prized stately homes; Lymington, a picturesque old port that, be forewarned, the world flocks to on weekends; Jane Austen's home at Chawton; and above all, the New Forest, 93,000 acres between Southampton Water and the river Avon. In 1079 William the Conqueror set it apart as a royal hunting preserve. Spend an hour or two driving through its stretches of majestic oaks, beeches, and yews, and across its heaths and farmlands (this forest is not *all* trees). Chief among the grazing stock here are the fabled New Forest ponies, thousands of them, all sizes, colors, and ages. They sometimes disrupt automobile traffic, but only in the friendliest fashion. A widely read historical novel called *The Forest,* by Edward Rutherford, is a portrait of this special world from the Conqueror's time down to the present. Reading it will enrich your visit to southern Hampshire.

CHAPTER TWELVE

Cornwall, Starring the One and Only St. Enodoc Links

WE ARE BIDDING HARRY COLT goodbye in Hampshire and driving 200 miles southwest— A35 to A30, then A389 for the last leg—to Cornwall, where we will renew our acquaintance with the master at Trevose, just outside the old fishing village of Padstow.

The Royal Duchy of Cornwall: We have only to articulate the full name of this land to summon a flood of beguiling images: Tintagel Castle, Bodmin Moor, Land's End, Daphne du Maurier's *Rebecca* and Winston Graham's *Poldark,* wildly romantic cliff scenery, and the utter serenity of winding lanes that link ancient villages. We'll play four courses here, all of them seaside. One, St. Enodoc, is among my dozen favorites in the world.

Colt laid out the eighteen at Trevose Golf & Country Club in 1926, and Guy Campbell provided minor revisions a decade later. The regular markers add up to 6,435 yards; par is 71. On this tract of undulating linksland there is neither gorse nor heather. Bunkering is light, so is the rough, and the fairways are quite broad. Three of the four par threes play knob to knob (no surprise on a Colt layout). The 199-yard 11th, its two-tier shelf green bunkered left and right, is especially good. Of the three par fives, which are potential birdie holes because of their length, the shortest of them, the 450-yard 4th, is memorable. It bends steadily left, on rumpled ground and through low dunes, to a green overlooking the Atlantic combers that surge onto the tawny sand beach of Booby's Bay. Trevose Head, uncompromisingly bleak, rears out of the sea in the background.

The appeal of the short and long holes notwithstanding, it is the two-shotters that are the backbone of this links. Five of them call for our strongest, soundest swings. The opening hole, downhill but into the prevailing wind, measures 443 yards. The closing hole, 416 yards, is aggressively uphill. And in between are the 461-yard 5th (gently uphill to a sand-free green), the 467-yard 10th (from a high tee and into the prevailing wind, a monster with a playing value many days of 520 yards!), and the 448-yard 12th (mercifully, wind-aided on the smoothly uphill second shot). With its friendly, open aspect and its exhilarating sea views, Trevose may look like holiday golf, but it doesn't play that way. It should be noted that there is also a third nine here, designed by Peter Alliss, plus a par-three course, not to mention a variety of overnight accommodations, a swimming pool, two tennis courts, a boutique, and heaven knows what else.

In marked contrast is West Cornwall Golf Club, an hour and a half south on the coast, in Lelant. Here there is an eighteen-hole links, period. From the medal tees, it measures only 5,884 yards—par is 69—and it cannot possibly occupy as much as 100 acres. It is natural and unpampered, rugged and hilly.

All Courses Great and Small

The club was founded in 1889 by Reverend Richard Frederick Tyacke, Vicar of Lelant and pastor of the Church of St. Uny, which dates to the sixteenth century and is an unignorable presence during a round here on the southern shore of St. Ives Bay. It is not possible to attribute the course to any individual golf architect. The best thing to do is simply enjoy it, as it tumbles along, for the most part on the dizzying heights above the vast golden beach and the Hayle estuary, surprising us at every turn, thrilling us with the grandeur of its views, frustrating us with the more than occasional blind shot over a dune or ridge, and rewarding us handsomely whenever we make a truly good stroke.

West Cornwall is quirky. Four shots on four different holes (1, 3, 14, and 18), coming from four different directions, are aimed on the Church of St. Uny. Three holes—5, 6, 7—are shoehorned into a tilted scrap of land just beyond a single-track railway, with two of them, 5 and 7, crisscrossing, and the drive on the 6th having to be kept clear of the rusted skeleton of an old warehouse. The 1st hole is a par three—in truth, a *great* par three, 229 yards long, much of it a forced carry over humpy ground and tangled rough, an out-of-bounds road tight on the right every step of the way, the shot calling for a driver as often as a 3-iron. And since it is lined squarely on the church tower, a silent prayer for smooth tempo would not be amiss. To put the ball on the green here with this, our first swing of the day, is to make our best swing of the day.

The holes going out that follow the great opener have plenty of spine and sport, culminating with the grand 9th, at 406 yards the longest hole on the nine, where we drive over the 8th green (space is in short supply here beside the railroad track). The hole edges left as it climbs emphatically to a plateau green with, on the right, a very steep falloff and three menacing pits.

Coming home there are several outstanding holes, 12, 13, and 14 being particularly attractive. A lofty tee on the 494-yard 12th affords a distractingly beautiful view of sea and sand and of the elusive plateau fairway. The very short par-four 13th, a mere 264 yards and commencing atop a sandhill, is drivable by the big bashers, but the green is cunningly sited beyond a hollow, the rough is punishing, and a small greenside pit lurks at the right to snare the bold hit that *almost* gets home. Fourteen, the longest (446 yards) and best of the two-shotters, doglegs right among the dunes—the temptation is to cut the corner— and requires a very long and very precise second to a gently raised green defended by sand at the left.

The game ends as it began, with the drive reminding us of the reverend founder as we take aim once again at the old church. A downhill 394-yarder, with a boundary along the right the entire length of the hole and a well-bunkered, narrow opening to the pear-shaped green, the exacting 18th is not often lost with a par.

Lelant is the birthplace of "Long Jim" Barnes, who learned the game as a lad on the links. He emigrated to America in 1906 and went on to win the PGA Championship in 1916 and 1919, the U.S. Open in 1921, and the British Open in 1925. Barnes memorabilia is displayed in the clubhouse, where the welcome extended to visitors is a notably warm one.

A little less than an hour north of Padstow lies the pleasant seaside resort of Bude. The Bude and North Cornwall Golf Club course was laid out by Tom Dunn in 1891 and revised several times since. It is the town's centerpiece. The round actually begins and ends, as it does with the Old Course at St. Andrews, right in the heart of town.

Bude just may require more patience than some players are inclined to grant it. Though the 3rd, with its plateau green, is an attractive short par four, the game does not begin in earnest until we stand on the 6th tee. From that moment on, there is a whale of a lot of challenging golf to be savored here. Still, our patience continues to be tested, now by a veritable barrage of blind shots. They are the order of the day at Bude, the price that is paid for the naturalness of the links. The terrain is vigorously rolling, at times almost hilly. Bunkering is light and the fairways are generous. The sea is often in view, but at a considerable distance. Like West Cornwall, Bude is short—at full stretch only 6,057 yards against a par of 71. What gives this eighteen much of its character is the heaving and tumbling of the ground, with the attendant capricious bounces and stances. We are frequently called upon to fashion creative little pitch-and-run or bump-and-run shots, which are such an appealing feature of true links golf.

St. Enodoc Golf Club lies directly across the broad estuary of the Camel River from Padstow, perhaps a mile away, its astonishing sandhills in view from the harbor. Many golfers simply shoulder their bag, board the ferry for the five-minute crossing (the tiny craft does not carry cars), and walk 200 yards up the steep hill to the clubhouse.

In all the world of links courses there are perhaps a handful—Cruden Bay, Royal County Down, Ballybunion, The European Club, Doonbeg, Sandwich—that prepare us for St. Enodoc. The holes here are imaginatively routed through and over—and up and down—some of the most mountainous

James W. Finegan

sandhills known to the game. After his first visit, Bernard Darwin wrote: "The golf had been described to me as eminently natural . . . in a country of glorious and terrific sandhills . . . and yet I was not prepared for quite such mighty hills nor for quite so many of them." Not only are the elevation changes extreme, but the springy fairways themselves range from merely undulating to tempestuously heaving. And because no bulldozer ever shaped things here, there are blind shots to spare, a good dozen, with all the suspense inherent in them. For sheer exhilaration, for downright delight—the entrancing views to Daymer Bay and over the Camel estuary to the rooftops of Padstow are all part of it—very few courses are in St. Enodoc's class.

The club was founded in 1891, but the course we play today was laid out by James Braid in 1907 and substantively revised by him in 1936. Measuring 6,243 yards from the back (par 69), it is crammed with superb holes, including six that are great by any standard, and a couple that are unique.

There is no easing into the challenge of this sublime links. The 518-yard opener is a jewel—a modestly elevated tee, consecutive blind shots over one of the most outlandish humpty-dumpty fairways imaginable (or unimaginable), then an eighty to ninety yard pitch to an unbunkered but tiny plateau green with a steep falloff at the left. In the distance is the first of the many transfixing views for which St. Enodoc is justly celebrated, this one disclosing the widest part of the Camel estuary merging with the Atlantic Ocean. The next three holes are par fours. Picking a favorite is difficult. The 438-yard 2nd climbs into the wind to a plateau green just beyond a swale. The 3rd, 436 yards, bends left as it plunges, out of bounds tight on the right for the second shot. As for the 4th, at only 292 yards it must be a breather, but that turns out to be very heavy breathing, our own. Since a boundary threatens on the right, we incline to drive too far left, leaving a mean little pitch that has to be landed on a pie plate if it is to hold the shelf green. The 161-yard 5th is rather more straightforward: knob to knob over a deep valley to a large and hospitable putting surface.

Which brings us to one of the game's true curios, the 378-yard 6th. To my knowledge, there is nothing like it. The blind drive is followed by a blind second—nothing unusual about that at St. Enodoc. But this time the second shot—a 6- or 7-iron with soaring aspirations—has to clear the fearsome Himalaya bunker, which, seventy-five feet high, must be far and away the tallest sand hazard in the game. This naturally eroded sandhill—for no one would ever construct such a thing!—rears tauntingly above the fairway about a hundred yards short of the hidden plateau green, demanding, whichever club we choose, a thoroughly solid hit to clear it.

The 10th is also unique and, in the bargain, great. Then, too, it has a certain reflected glory. Unlike the 6th, sand is not a consideration on this dogleg left par four, but length is—at 457 yards and into the prevailing wind, the hole is pitilessly long—and so is water and so is topography. Launched from a nobly high tee, our drive seeks a safe harbor in a fairway abruptly grown narrow and now following its cloistered route between an overgrown marsh that runs all the way along the left side of the hole and a steep bank on the right smothered in heavy rough. The green is set on an angle to the line of flight and falls off to a hollow at the left. Accept your 5 and proceed directly to the 12th-century Church of St. Enodoc, just beyond the green, to which the body of John Betjeman, poet laureate of England

James W. Finegan

from 1972 until his death in 1984, was carried—there is no access by road—across his beloved links ("A glorious, sailing, bounding drive that made me glad I was alive."). He was the last to be buried in the graveyard here, which is now full.

The holes in this "parish" are among the least distinguished on the course, meadowy in feeling at times, so I'll pass them by and concentrate on the three that bring us back to the clubhouse—a great long hole, a great short hole, and a great par four.

The 16th, 495 yards, has no dominant feature. It simply rolls along naturally on the heights, virtually sand-free, pitching and tossing, full of wonderful golfing folds and wrinkles, the estuary and the red roofs of Padstow captivatingly in view. A teasing little hollow just short of the green lends flavor to our pitch, especially if the cup is cut well forward. This wonderfully engaging hole was cited as one of *The 500 World's Greatest* in *the* book.

The 17th, though not chosen for this compendium, is every bit as deserving. A 206-yarder, it requires a perfect stroke from an elevated tee across a valley to a shelf of green a bit higher than eye level. Low dunes edge in from the left to cut off that access route. A ball that comes up just short will retreat at least fifteen paces down the hill.

And so to home, via one of the surpassing finishing holes. The drive on this 446-yarder is blind, from a high tee, vanishing over a rise and down into a boldly undulating dune-framed valley. The long second shot, possibly a 5-metal from a downhill lie, climbs to a defiantly raised green squarely beneath the windows of the clubhouse. This is a hole for champions on a links to spellbind all of us, however well or ill we play the game. I suspect that if a genie were to appear before me at this moment with an offer to transport me magically to any course in the world, I just might—notice I say *might*—choose this nonpareil on the wild north coast of Cornwall.

In Padstow we have stayed at two places, rather next door to each other. The Metropole Hotel offers a pretty garden, good food in a dining room with harbor views, and comfortable guest rooms. Room 103, with its high ceiling and its bay window giving on the estuary, is particularly nice. The late Duke of Windsor, then Prince of Wales, stayed often at the Metropole in the 1920s and 1930s, occupying Room 26 when he came out to the royal duchy for golf at St. Enodoc, where he was president for many years.

The second place is the Seafood Restaurant, which falls into that category of "restaurant with rooms." In this instance, eleven rooms, most of them overlooking the harbor, all smartly done in ecru, putty, and soft gray. It is Rooms 5 and 6 that are the most sought after (we occupied 6), each of which has a spacious rooftop terrace that commands the Padstow harbor, the sailboat-dotted estuary beyond, and on the far side of the water, the majestic sandhills of St. Enodoc. It is for us the single best accommodation a traveling golfer could ever envision: the combination of comfortable indoors and expansive outdoors, the vibrant water scenes in the foreground and the middle ground, and the grandeur of the great links backdropping it all.

The Seafood Restaurant is widely recognized as one of the two or three best fish restaurants in Britain. It is situated directly across the quay from where the lobster boats and trawlers tie up; the fish comes straight off the boats and in through the kitchen door. The restaurant is bright, crisp, chic—

white walls, black wicker seating, contemporary watercolors. Roast monkfish wrapped in Parma ham and on a bed of sauerkraut is just one of the highlights of the innovative menu. At St. Peter's Bistro, owned by the Seafood Restaurant and just a block up the hill, the cooking is simpler, the atmosphere is homier, and the prices are lower.

As for sightseeing on the coast of Cornwall, no golf book could begin to tell the tale. Tiny Padstow itself, with its twisting cobbled lanes, is a charmer (the ideal after-dinner stroll is a circuit of the harbor). Golf takes us up and down the coast from St. Ives in the south (a good sandy beach, a gathering place of artists, and a numbingly commercial scene in high season) to Bude in the north, where the old canal, elevated above the broad beach and running parallel to it, is an intriguing anachronism. Between these two extremes are many places of interest, including Trerice, a small Elizabethan manor house near Newquay, with fine furniture and equally fine carved-plaster ceilings; Port Isaac, where the road corkscrews breathtakingly down to a postage-stamp beach; and, of course, Tintagel itself, with its evocative ruins of the castle believed to be King Arthur's birthplace set dramatically on the somber slate cliffs high above the sea.

CHAPTER THIRTEEN

Turning Back the Clock at Westward Ho!

 THE DRIVE NORTH from Padstow into Devon, where our goal is Saunton, takes about two hours, unless we are doing it in July or August, when England's West Country is thronged. But go in the spring or the fall and you will skim easily from point to point.

The Saunton Golf Club was founded in 1897, "with a membership of eighty comprising fifty-eight gentlemen and twenty-two ladies." Bravo, Saunton! The local post office doubled as clubhouse. First there were nine holes by Tom Dunn, then twelve, then eighteen. In 1919 Herbert Fowler completely redesigned what is now called the East Course, and in 1951 C. K. "Ken" Cotton effected further changes. It might be mentioned that American tank divisions arrived in 1943 to use the links as a training ground for the Normandy invasion. The West Course, which opened in 1975, is largely the work of Frank Pennink, who, as it happens, won the 1937 English Amateur here on the East Course.

The two eighteens, on Bideford Bay, are backdropped by a

long range of inordinately high sandhills, among the most majestic in all of Britain. However, the golf holes are not routed through these imposing dunes but over less rousing ground in what might be called the foothills. Measuring 6,373 yards from the regular markers, 6,729 from the tips, the East Course is the championship eighteen, having hosted the English Amateur, the English Stroke Play, the British Ladies, the British Boys, and the British PGA. Except for the 17th, there is little measurable elevation change. Bunkering is light.

From the outset, the seriousness of the test is made clear: The 1st hole is a 470-yard par four, bunkered right and left. If no other holes on the first nine are quite so rigorous, there are several where par is well earned, including the 428-yard 4th (because of low dunes, only drives held carefully down the left side set up a view of the flagstick on the long second shot) and the 402-yard 7th, with sand at both sides of the green.

The inbound nine is the finer of the two. Many holes are highly exacting, like the 345-yard 11th, a sharp dogleg right, with a stream and adjacent boundary (double jeopardy) along the right side of the green; the superb 14th, a 432-yarder where our long second shot must string its way between the dunes to an ever so slightly raised green; and the last three holes.

On a course that has only three blind shots, here on this 406-yard 16th, which doglegs determinedly left through the sandhills, are two of them, the second shot having to clear a giant hillock blockading the green. Seventeen is a falling 186-yarder from the only high tee on the course, sand right and left and very uneven ground across the front. The home hole is a worthy companion to these two, 387 yards, curving smoothly right around a low hill, our second shot aimed on the clubhouse clock. There is a lot more of that humpy ground, and a slightly raised green with just one bunker, short and right.

The possibility of Saunton's East Course as a venue for the Open Championship pops up from time to time. Admittedly, this is an excellent layout, but it is not a great one for that simplest of reasons: It lacks great holes. It cannot be discussed alongside Sandwich, Birkdale, Lytham & St. Annes, or Hoylake, the four English courses currently on the rota.

Also a par 71, the West Course is 240 yards shorter than its sister. We notice the difference especially on the par fours, with only two of them over 400 yards. Promisingly, the 1st hole leads straightaway from the clubhouse into the grand dune country, but the 2nd turns around and comes right back out. There is actually very little involvement with the bolder topographical features from that point on. Still, this is sprightly golf, with water, generally in the form of very narrow streams, in play on at least half a dozen holes. Several muscular doglegs call for careful placement of the drive, and the shots to the green are often endangered by steep falloffs. The second nine has that attractive combination of three par threes, fours, and fives. The round ends with a memorable 183-yarder played from an elevated tee through a narrow gap in the sandhills.

On the opposite side of the bay and in view on a clear day lies the links of Royal North Devon Golf Club, generally referred to as Westward Ho!, the village in which the club is located. It had been twenty-one years since I last played Westward Ho!, in 1977, when we had stayed at the fourteenth-century, thatched-roof Rising Sun Hotel, in Lynmouth, a secluded spot where the river Lyn trips musically over its rocky bed to enter the Atlantic Ocean. The hotel was then run by a diminutive man called Billy. Quick with a smile and a story, Billy was an engaging rough diamond whom we found ourselves remembering from time to time over the years, wondering whether he still managed the 600-year-old inn. So on this pretty day in May of 1998 we drove to Lynmouth for lunch to get the answer.

The assistant manager at the Rising Sun, a woman in her early fifties, told us that Billy had retired "when his ship came in." She said, "You would not have known it, but he was a compulsive gambler, oh yes, addicted, betting on the horses, on the football, on anything he could get a wager down on. And then, one day, didn't he hit the lottery! Three hundred thousand pounds the prize was, about ten years ago. He quit the hotel—no need to work anymore, he was a rich man, at least in these parts. The first thing he did was take his family—and not just his immediate family, because I think there must have been eleven or twelve in the party—to New York on the QE2. It was a very rough crossing and they all got seasick! Then they went to Disneyland, which they loved. When they got back home, to Lynton [Lynton, Lynmouth's sister town, is on the cliffs above the estuary, the two towns connected by a funicular], Billy decided to buy the council house [government-built-and-owned housing] he'd been living in for years. Said he loved the location. He spent a great deal of money enlarging it and remodeling it. He must be about seventy-three or seventy-four now. He doesn't come down here very often, and I can't say for sure how his health is. I do know the two towns were thrilled when he won the lottery."

The word *shrine* can properly be applied to the Royal North Devon Golf Club, one of the four or five most important golf clubs in England. It is the birthplace of links golf in England and it is the oldest golf club in the country still playing over its original ground. Golf got its start here on Northam Burrows in 1854. Six years later, Old Tom Morris laid out a proper course at the suggestion of Reverend I. Gosset, Vicar of Northam, who, in 1864, founded the club (holy shades of Notts and Royal Ashdown Forest and West Cornwall) and was named captain. In those times, the first players off the tee in the morning used their pocket knives to cut the holes for that day, which they then marked with seagull feathers.

The great Horace Hutchinson learned the game here. In 1875, at the tender age of sixteen, he won Westward Ho!'s most important annual event, a scratch competition. By a rule of the club, the lad thus became its captain, presiding over the meetings for twelve months. This rule was changed the following year.

In 1910 Herbert Fowler extensively remodeled the course. It is little changed since, although much restoration was necessary after World War II, when it was used for bombing practice. The British Amateur, the British Ladies, and the English Ladies Championships have all been played on this storied links more than once. And it has seen the top British professionals in important competitions on a couple of occasions.

However, not many of us are quite ready to be confronted by a course that is such a throwback to the distant past. No other outstanding layout in Britain and Ireland, with the exceptions of Prestwick and North Berwick, is such a monument to golf as it was played well over a century ago.

This supremely natural links is laid out on common land. Since the local farmers still cling to their ancient rights, sheep and horses graze here. We are indebted to the sheep for the neatly trimmed fairways; the horses seem to prefer to munch in the rough, rendering it rather easy for the wayward golfer to handle. The greens are ringed by a light tape strung on little iron poles to ward off the livestock. These relatively simple putting surfaces are swift and true.

The course measures almost 6,400 yards from the regular markers, 6,650 from the back tees. Par is 72. The look of this linksland is flat and barren, and the overall elevation change is no more than twenty feet. On the other hand, the average width of the fairways is scarcely less than a hundred yards. What other important course can be this wide open?

The first two holes—a short par five with a ditch to cross on the drive and a similar ditch in front of the green; the 2nd, a long slog of a par four—are relentlessly unattractive: a vast gray-green sweep of level ground, the marshy turf marked occasionally with hoofprints. Our instinct is to believe that on this primitive patch golf would simply never be played since there is no definition whatsoever to the land, no suggestion of the shaping or outline of a golf hole. The unwitting visitor must be tempted to return at once to the parking lot, climb into his car, and be gone.

The 3rd hole, 413 yards, is not much more reassuring, though it does have some character, thanks in part to an all but invisible bunker solidly in the left side of the fairway just where a good drive might come to rest.

But with the 344-yard 4th, the game is on. And it never lets up, challenging and puzzling and charming us every foot of the way. The 4th presents one of the legendary moments in golf as we stand on the tee, staring at the infamous Cape Bunker. This deep and boarded sand hazard extends very like the full width of the fairway, more than eighty yards. The forced carry over the "sleepers" is about 175 yards—we are now paralleling the beach and the Great Pebble Ridge, with the sea itself quite close—a not inconsiderable hit if the wind be strong into us or even on a left-to-right slant. But we clear this hurdle, so fearsome in days of old, our ball landing out of sight but safely, to leave us with a short iron, semiblind, to a green in a hollow, sand sealing off this putting surface.

The exquisite 5th, 136 yards, slightly rising and heavily bunkered, plays toward the sandhills. Then come a couple of superb par fours, both nearly 400 yards and generally fighting the wind. The views from the tee on the 6th—across Bideford Bay to the Isle of Lundy, down to the fairway tumbling along beside the beach on the left, and over so much of the splendid links—are exhilarating, and the uphill second shot to a narrow green set on the diagonal is a demanding one. It is a sharp turn to the left that makes the second shot on the 7th exacting, especially with a sandpit squarely in front of the green but, misleadingly, twenty yards short of it. The very good 8th, 182 yards long, is open across the front but presents sand right and left. As for 9, it is a short par five, only 467 yards, often played downwind. Nonetheless, it confounds us, maybe because of the immense fairway to roam around in along the way, or maybe because of a tiny, teasing bunker smack in front of the green daring us to carry it, and certainly because the green itself is a vague target, slightly raised, and entirely too shallow to hold a hot second shot. It all adds up to Herbert Fowler at his most ingenious.

And now we have reached the country of the Great Sea

James W. Finegan

Rushes, fierce growths probably unique to Westward Ho! This curious vegetation, some four to five feet high and rather akin to a spiky form of pampas grass, grows in huge clusters. A ball hit into them is either lost or unplayable or—and this you will probably have to see for yourself to believe, but it's true— impaled on one of these prickly killers. We have idly noted the rushes on the 7th, 8th, and 9th, but they are easily avoided on these holes. On the 349-yard 10th, however, which doglegs smartly left, we have no choice but to drive blindly over a vast expanse of these "porcupine quills," cutting off as much of this hazard in the elbow of the dogleg as we think we can. On 11 and 12 the rushes, now paralleling the line of play, imperil both the drive and the second shot. The 13th—no rushes here—is the shortest par five in my experience, all of 421 yards. There is no unusual configuration of land or hazard that would make it necessarily a par-five; it's just another quirky moment courtesy of Westward Ho! Then the rushes return to beset us on the fine 14th, 177 yards, as well as on the 15th, 408 yards and bending right, where making up our mind prudently as to our capabilities off the tee is key to any chance we may have on this great hole.

Over the years, the 16th, 141 yards, has been lauded by serious observers as everything from "one of the best short holes in England" to "the best short hole in the world." It has a crowned green and its share of sand. Forgive me for saying that I find it pleasant and unexceptional, no more and no less.

The 17th, by contrast, is a genuine tester, 554 yards long, complicated by a paved road and a watery ditch, both crossing right in front of the green. And then, squarely in front of the green on the 394-yard 18th, is another watery ditch, intimidat-

All Courses Great and Small

ing, bedeviling. We do not gain the clubhouse at Westward Ho! without a struggle.

And what a treat it is to spend some time in this convivial place that is now more than 115 years old. Its knotty-pine lockers must be the same age. The principal attraction here is the little museum of golfing antiquities, including wooden clubs dating to 1840, featheries, gutta-percha balls, the first rubber-core balls, a fine collection of the club's medals, some well-nigh priceless golf art, and, of course, happy reminders of Westward Ho!'s favorite son, J. H. Taylor.

Born within sight of the links, John Henry caddied for Horace Hutchinson, whose attacking style of play probably rubbed off on the boy. A member of the famous triumvirate (Vardon, Braid, Taylor), he was the first great English professional, winning the Open Championship five times, between 1894 (he was only twenty-three) and 1913. He also played a central role in the formation of the British PGA. Yet over the long years of his extraordinary career he never forgot Westward Ho!, returning whenever he could to the place where his love for the game was born. In 1957 Royal North Devon paid this warmhearted man what he judged to be the highest honor of his life by electing him president of the club. He died in his cottage overlooking the links—"the finest view in Christendom," he called it—in 1963, at the age of ninety-two.

Yes, here on the Northam Burrows beside Bideford Bay is a great and historic club, a great and historic and unique links. With its grazing livestock, its often ill-defined holes, its occasional boarded bunkers, and its Great Sea Rushes, this links may not be everyone's cup of tea—in fact, it is *sui generis,* a law unto itself. But to those with an appreciation for the roots of the game, Westward Ho! is to be sought out, to be savored, and, in the end, to be treasured.

North on the coast some forty miles lies Ilfracombe Golf Club. Its clifftop layout measures 5,893 yards against a par of 69. I recall it from a round twenty-five years ago as treeless, hilly, full of mountain-goat stances, very lightly bunkered, possessing a couple of crisscross holes, and on balance, in no sense to be taken seriously. Still, it is not easily forgotten, because every moment of every hole discloses stupendous views over the Bristol Channel to South Wales.

If there was for J. H. Taylor a course he thought of as his second favorite, it might well have been Burnham & Berrow, located in Burnham-on-Sea, Somerset, an hour and a half north of both Saunton and Westward Ho! The club was founded in 1890, and in 1892 engaged the young man, all of nineteen, as its first professional. Taylor would later say, "I was fortunate in that I was afforded a splendid opportunity of developing my mashie [5-iron] play at Burnham, for everybody who is familiar with it knows it to be one of the most sporting courses conceivable, with its large sandhills and small greens, necessitating very accurate approach play."

There is no record of who planned the golf holes when the club was formed but Hugh Alison and J. S. F. Morrison revised them substantively. Against a par of 71, the regular markers add up to 6,393 yards, with the championship tees at 6,760. Strikingly set amid massive sandhills on the Bristol Channel, with South Wales's Royal Porthcawl to be spotted across the water on a sunny day (Chapter 17), Burnham & Berrow has played host to the English Amateur, the English Stroke Play, the British Ladies, the British Boys, and the PGA Seniors.

All Courses Great and Small

Played directly toward the sea and into the prevailing wind, the 370-yard opening hole snakes its way along a sequestered valley formed by high, grass-cloaked dunes, the fairway rising gently as it tapers, hollows to the right and left of the green and a steep sandhill immediately behind it all the defense this sloping putting surface needs. We promptly find ourselves wondering whether the course can possibly live up to the promise of this stirring start. Well, the 2nd is an altogether splendid two-shotter: high tee, down into a dip, then edging left and climbing through the dunes to a long, narrow green with sand at the left and an abrupt little falloff at the right. The 3rd, an invigorating 350-yarder that sees us on a dune-top tee where our falling drive must search out a scrap of fairway far below and then our shortish iron must search out an evasive green deep in a dell of dunes. The 4th is a short par five where buckthorn raises its implacable head for the first time. The superlative 146-yard 5th presents a tightly bunkered green cocked up mockingly in the sandhills. And at the 390-yard 6th a lagoon along the left endangers the drive, low dunes and buckthorn awaiting the errant second shot.

It has been a marvelous run, these first six holes, classic links golf of the highest standard. However, the 7th and 8th, routed over flat, featureless, and sometimes marshy ground, are a letdown. So is the 410-yard 11th. These holes are pedestrian. But since every other hole on the course is a worthy companion to the opening six, we cannot let these three detract from our delight in Burnham.

The 13th, 506 yards, rumbles energetically along over ridges and swales to a narrow, dune-encased green. The 14th, 168 yards, rises over broken ground to a green set starkly high above us on a ridge. On the great 15th, 416 yards, we drive blindly from a high tee, then work our dipsy-doodle way along a narrow fairway to a green in a dell. Fun is what we get on 16, a two-shotter of only 326 yards: another high tee, a cluster of low dunes and two pot bunkers in the middle of the fairway to be cleared on our pitch to a two-tier green.

Fun is not the word that comes to mind on the last two holes. Both are severely testing. Low mounds, sand, and steep falloffs ring the green on the magnificent 17th, a 180-yard knob-to-knob shot across a junglelike wasteland. And the heroic 18th, 441 yards, is certainly among the half-dozen finest finishing holes in the UK. First it doglegs left over low ridges in the sandhills. Then the dauntingly long second shot must clear another dune ridge, one that has broken the fairway into two parts, and go on to pinpoint a narrow opening squeezed by deep greenside pot bunkers.

With its heaving, tumbling terrain, its giant dunes, its forced carries from the tees and exacting shots to the greens—these putting surfaces are among the very best in England—Burnham & Berrow provides great natural golf in a setting of great beauty. Worth keeping in mind: it also provides simple but comfortable accommodations for as many as eight in the dormy house. An overnight stay lets you play this terrific course at least twice and perhaps also fit in a game on the worthy relief nine (3,166 yards, par 36) laid out near the sea by Fred W. Hawtree.

The sparkling 92-room Saunton Sands, only a par five from the East and West Courses, is a full-facilities hotel: indoor and outdoor pools, squash and tennis courts, spa, room service, hair dressing salon, musical entertainment most nights, and, per-

haps most important, panoramic views revealing a sweep of tawny sand beach backdropped by the mighty sandhills.

There are plenty of reasons for North Devon and Somerset to serve as such a powerful lure for vacationers. The countryside is unfailingly pretty (green meadows billowing away to the horizon), the coastal scenery is often ravishing (as the golf clearly proves), and there are countless specific attractions. Like Exmoor, stark and brooding, the red deer and the ponies running free. (Stop at Rugglestone Inn, Widecombe in the Moor, for a pint.) And Arlington Court, a richly furnished Regency manor house on the edge of Exmoor. And betting-Billy's Lynton and Lynmouth. And Clovelly, a fishing village whose main street, far too steep for wheeled vehicles of any kind, descends in steps some 400 feet to the tiny cove. And Coleridge Cottage, where the poet wrote "The Rime of the Ancient Mariner," and we are suddenly carried back in time, willy nilly, to sophomore English class in high school.

CHAPTER FOURTEEN

Three Courses at The Belfry, Plus Six You've Never Heard of

BIRMINGHAM IS WHERE we're going now, leaving the sea behind at Burnham & Berrow and heading northeast to the Midlands. The M5 is our road, and a much-traveled highway it is (think of it as I-95 between New York and Philadelphia, with even more trucks). This drive from Somerset to The Belfry, ten miles north of Birmingham, in Wishaw, should take about two and a half hours.

As Nick Edmund put it in *LINKS* magazine, "To paraphrase Shakespeare: Some courses are born great, some achieve greatness, and others—like The Belfry's Brabazon Course—have greatness thrust upon them." The Ryder Cup has now been played here four times. Would this course ever have been the venue for the match if The Belfry were not the headquarters of the British PGA? No. And yet this eighteen, which has witnessed rather more than its share of high drama—Europe shocking the U.S., 16½–11½, in 1985; a stomach-churning tie in

James W. Finegan

1989; America squeaking by, 15–13, in 1993; and losing embarrassingly, 15½–12½, in 2002—is not dismissable. Now, thanks to revisions by one of its co-authors, Dave Thomas (Peter Alliss was his partner on the original design, 1977), this is a very good American-style parkland course.

I have tackled the Brabazon only once, in mid-July of 2001 with Bevan Tattersall, head greenkeeper at The Belfry. Bevan was then twenty-eight. He is six feet seven inches tall, trim and solid, red-haired, even-featured.

The Brabazon is flat; overall elevation change does not exceed fifteen feet. Because of mature trees that separate most of the holes from each other, the course is not open in aspect or feel; neither, however, is it claustrophobic. Bunkering is moderate—seventy-eight sand hazards of various shapes and sizes. The overriding feature of the course is water—streams, ponds, lagoons, lakes, you name it (I don't think there's a waterfall). It is quite possible to hit a shot into water on fifteen holes. And there are five holes where both the drive and the second shot can drown. Staying dry on this pleasant patch of England is not a matter of carrying an umbrella.

From the regular markers, the Brabazon measures 6,400 yards against a par of 72. The round over Bevan's perfect turf begins with a straightaway two-shotter of 369 yards, followed by an intriguing 321-yarder that bends left around the trees to reveal a narrow green blockaded first by a stream, then by sand. The 501-yard 3rd (538 from the championship tees), also doglegging left, was the big news. The hole used to be a long, dull, straight par four; now it's a very tempting risk/reward par five, with a lake at the left front of the green daring the big hitter to try getting home in two. There may not be anything original

All Courses Great and Small

about Dave Thomas's concept here, but the design is skillfully executed. After a long drive, Bevan, whose swing has tremendous arc, failed to get up on his 3-wood shot, the ball splashing short by ten feet.

The next six holes have little in the way of risk/reward options. It's just risk, with water persistently giving pause, hole after hole after hole, and having to be hurdled at the green on the 4th, 8th, and 9th.

The 10th is unique, one of the world's great short two-shotters. We played it at 284 yards. Running along the right side of the fairway is a lagoon, which tapers into a stream abutting this very shallow green. Trees along the water tend to complicate matters (a) on the drive for those courageous players going for the green from the tee, and (b) for the rest of us having to pitch our little wedges over the water to this curiously angled target with three bunkers behind it. In the Ryder Cup the hole has usually measured a mere 262 yards. You may want to try the same tee shot that the pros are encouraged to attempt; it's about as much pure thrill as the game affords. This wonderful match-play hole is fraught with strategic considerations. In a 1993 Ryder Cup foursomes (alternate stroke), Ballesteros and Olazabal were 1 down to Kite and Love as the match came to the 10th tee. Ballesteros had the honor and, after noodling the options for what seemed an eternity, decided to lay up with a 4-iron. Then Kite, batting for the visitors, pulled out his 3-wood and fired a lifetime shot over the water to within four feet of the cup. Love holed the putt for an eagle and a 2-up lead, and the Americans went on to win the match, 2 and 1.

The 11th, 365 yards from the regular markers, reminded me that I had asked Bevan whether there was any hole that he thought was weak or humdrum or both. He said there was just one. The 11th is straight; bunkers pinch the landing area of the drive as well as the front of the green. After we putted out, I asked him, "Is that it?" "That's it," he conceded. "One of these days Dave Thomas will do something here, something to give the hole a bit of a spark, but what that might be I don't know."

I was particularly struck by the 14th, 166 yards, with its narrow green and very natural-looking eighty-yard-long bunker on the left that threatens to swallow even the slightest pull. It was also in the 1993 Ryder Cup that Faldo, all square with Azinger, here unfurled a perfect 6-iron—literally perfect—the ball landing about fifteen feet short of the flagstick and disappearing into the hole. Their match ended even.

The 18th is a terror, one of the game's most dramatic finishing holes, with the opportunity for disaster accompanying us every foot of the way. Measuring 418 yards from the regular markers, 473 from the tips, it doglegs boldly left. Water imperils the drive and, even more harshly, the long second shot. There is no bailout area. Trees on the left bordering the lagoon are a serious consideration on the drive for the hitter hoping to cut the hole down to size. A large, flat bunker tight at the right of the tee shot landing area shuts the door there. The drive must be stung and it must be straight. The same applies to the second shot, which has to clear the lake and gain a narrow green, this one flanked by sand, triple-tiered, and nearly 200 feet deep. Some of the best shots in Ryder Cup history—for instance, Christy O'Connor Jr.'s 2-iron to three feet to beat Fred Couples in 1989—have been hit on this hole, a selection for *The 500 World's Greatest Golf Holes* book.

The Belfry's two other eighteens, also designed by Dave

All Courses Great and Small

Thomas and Peter Alliss, are enjoyable if unexceptional. Like the Brabazon, both are routed over essentially level ground and both benefit aesthetically from the numerous beautiful trees (oak, silver birch, holly). Water threatens the shot five times on the Derby, four times on the PGA National. The Derby measures 6,009 yards against a par of 69. Most of us will find the PGA National to our liking at either 6,150 or 6,640 yards.

A full-fledged golf resort, The Belfry is big (324 accommodations) and bustling (twenty-one meeting rooms, eight bars, five restaurants, a nightclub, and more). The staff is knowledgeable and obliging, golf is accorded its proper spot in the overall scheme of things (the top spot), and the handsome period decor of The French Restaurant is actually surpassed by the outstanding cuisine, presentation, and service.

Roughly twenty minutes from The Belfry, in Sutton Coldfield, is Little Aston Golf Club. If The Belfry's Brabazon was rather more than I had expected, Little Aston turned out to be somewhat less. And this I deeply regretted. Knowing how highly it has been regarded by British golf writers and course architects, I had long looked forward to playing it.

The club was founded in 1908. For a fee of ten guineas (about $60), Harry Vardon laid out the course in what is a beautiful woodland setting. His teasing crossbunkers—one thinks of the 3rd, 10th, 16th, and 18th—are an appealing feature of the design. The terrain is rolling, with an overall elevation change of about fifty-five feet. From the regular markers, the course measures 6,397 yards; par is 72. Over the years, Little Aston has hosted many important tournaments, including the English Amateur, the British Ladies, the English Ladies, and on a number of occasions, the Dunlop Masters.

James W. Finegan

When I played here in late summer of 2001, the secretary paired me with a stocky chap in his late sixties from the north of England. A 9 handicapper, he drove with a Callaway ERC II. He also used—and to good effect—a scandalously expensive putter, the first time I'd ever seen this weapon in the flesh. His golf bag was a very sturdy one and it rode on an even sturdier battery-powered trolley, which could probably have transported the owner himself in a pinch.

The 1st hole is a lovely opener, 382 yards long, steadily downhill, sand framing the tee-shot landing area, sand right and left at the green. The 2nd, 411 yards, comes right back up the hill, seven bunkers along the way, two more greenside, right and left. It plays at least 440 yards. It is sand that gives Little Aston much of its character. There are 101 pits by actual count, some of them deep, many of them with high, swoopingly contoured lips.

The 3rd is an irresistible down-and-up shortish par five, with one of those patented Vardon crossbunkers lurking on the hill-side a hundred yards short of the green to snare the underhit second. Four is a level 312-yarder that must yield a lot of birdies, followed by a 150-yarder almost completely ringed by sand, the green perhaps a little too spacious, all things considered. And the 6th is a hard-nosed cousin of the 1st, also downhill, but more heavily bunkered, thirty yards longer, and altogether excellent.

The twelve remaining holes include a number of pretty medium-length par fours that drift gently down or up, that bend naturally right or left, but that rarely find the way to our memory bank. Little Aston occupies an ideal setting for the game, secluded, peaceful, beautiful old trees on the periphery

All Courses Great and Small

of the property utterly shutting out the world; the graceful one-story clubhouse, with its gables and chimneys and generous windows, a sanctuary of calm and comfort, suggesting, in the warm simplicity of its appointments, the clubhouse at Swinley Forest. We are happy to be here, but it must be said there is a sameness to some of the golf holes and, equally to the point, a lack of distinction to some of them as well. We would welcome additional pulse-quickening moments, even an occasion or two when failure to execute the shot will find us face to face with a double or triple bogey. Little Aston is perhaps too considerate of our goodwill, too well-behaved.

A dozen or so miles northwest of Little Aston, in Stafford-shire, lies Beau Desert Golf Club, on land that until the 1930s was part of the estate of the Marquess of Anglesey. The first Marquess, Henry William, earned his title and this land for services to England in the war against the French, specifically in the final defeat of Napoleon, at Waterloo, in 1815. The story has it that when Henry William's leg was shattered by gunfire he cried out to the Duke of Wellington, "My God! I've lost my leg!" Glancing down, the Duke replied, "My God! So you have!", then turned back to his telescope to observe the battle.

In 1912 the sixth Marquess retained Herbert Fowler to lay out a course here. It was intended for local golfers as much as for the Anglesey family. By early 1920 the Marquess was starting to divest himself of his Staffordshire properties. When he suggested that the local golfers take over the course, the Beau Desert Golf Club was formed. Ten years later, however, the ground on which the course was laid out was to be sold at auction. Two of the club's directors were delegated to attend the sale with the aim of submitting the winning bid. But prior to the

199

auction, both got a bit tipsy at lunch. When no one else was interested in buying the land, the pair, clearly intoxicated, wound up bidding *against* each other and thus boosting the knockdown price to £4,000. This was far more than the club could afford. Fortunately, the Marquess took pity and gave £2,000 back to the club.

Beau Desert is an admirably natural heathland course. Bunkering is light—there are only forty-two sand hazards, the majority of them small. Crossbunkers are common. Overall elevation change is more than 100 feet, and sometimes the ups and downs are steep. The green complexes are fascinating. In a 1974 report to the Committee, Fred Hawtree wrote: "There are a great many eccentric contours which lead to . . . approaches and putts that go beyond a spirit of adventure." Today the greens still have plenty of interest, but they are no longer unruly.

Par is 70 on this 6,300-yard layout. On the opening hole, 304 yards long, we can pretty much take a 4 for granted but still get a kick out of launching our drive over a nineteenth-century gravel pit that is 100 yards wide and thirty feet deep. We take nothing for granted on the 2nd, one of seven long two-shotters. Starting from an elevated tee in the trees, it measures 458 yards, plays most of the way over level ground, and features a wicked crossbunker sixty-five yards short of the green. A couple of other par fours on the way out are also quite good—the 418-yard 5th, where we drive over a ravine into a hollow only to be faced now with a sternly uphill second shot that must clear a crossbunker fifty yards short of the green; and the 263-yard 9th, deliciously old-fashioned, plunging from a high tee, then climbing to a high green—unless you can play it knob to knob and drive the green!

All Courses Great and Small

The incoming nine also has its quota of good holes, beginning with the 10th, 142 yards, gently rising through the trees to traverse a deep semicircle of sand tight to the plateau green. The level 12th is another of the hefty par fours, 426 yards and a double dogleg, first curving right, then curving left, the green defended by a couple of pot bunkers at the left front, plus a low, rough-cloaked mound at the right front.

Like the opening hole, the closing hole offers a good birdie chance. A par five of only 480 yards, it runs downhill through the trees, encouraging us to go for the green lying below with our second shot. However, blockading the green, perhaps twenty-five yards out, is an impenetrable belt of gorse, effectively a wall of thorns. Still, we may well succumb to the temptation, if for no other reason than that the green is vast, more than 14,000 square feet. In fact, it is somewhat smaller than in the past, when it was thought to be the largest green in England, so immense that the man cutting it with a single-width hand-mower would walk 6,000 yards in the process, roughly the overall length of the course then.

New Hall, a luxury country house hotel not fifteen minutes from Little Aston and about forty minutes from Beau Desert, is superlative. Surrounded by a lily-filled moat and twenty-six acres of open parkland (a nine-hole pitch-and-putt course here), this is reputedly the oldest moated manor house in England, dating to 1200. Its sixty beautifully furnished accommodations include a number of suites. Cooking is of the highest standard, and it is Caroline Parkes, the proprietor, who personally places the dishes before the guests.

Queen Victoria, one story has it, so disliked gritty Birmingham that she had the blinds drawn when her train passed through. And if, even today, England's second largest city is not noted for its aesthetic appeal, there are still a number of attractions in the metropolitan area that are well worth seeking out: the Victorian shopping arcades; the canals, a large network of artificial waterways that astonish us; the medieval town of Lichfield, with its ancient cathedral; the Museum of the Black Country, actually a restored village, including a coal mine; and, of course, not twenty miles south of the city, Stratford-upon-Avon.

About an hour's drive northeast of Birmingham, in Leicestershire, outside Melton Mowbray, lies Stapleford Park, one of the finest country house hotels in the world. The handsome Victorian stables are a reminder that the Cottesmore Hunt used to assemble here. It is said that the Prince of Wales (later the Duke of Windsor) wished to buy Stapleford Park, but his mother vetoed it because of "the danger to his morals if he were freely exposed to the hunting set."

The Stapleford Park estate encompasses 800 acres, more than enough room for a new course by Donald Steel and his partner Tom Mackenzie. This is the fourth course they have designed for the entrepreneurial golf club and golf resort developer Peter de Savary, best known for the Carnegie Club at Skibo Castle, Dornoch.

Woodlands, ponds, and streams all feature in this eighteen. There is a very natural feel and flow to the golf holes, in large measure because of the Steel/Mackenzie minimalist approach. They accepted the land as they found it.

The regular markers add up to 6,400 yards; par is 73. A six-hole stretch beginning at the par-four 7th—a lagoon on the right and a bunker on the left frame the tee shot landing area—puts pressure on the swing. On the 272-yard 8th, the snaking river Eye sets up options with varying degrees of drama: an open-the-shoulders driver over the water, aimed at the center of the green and having to carry 245 yards for sweet safety's sake; the left-hand route, crossing the river twice, the second shot a very short pitch along the length of the green; and the third option, timidly driving right, which leaves a longer approach shot over a pair of bunkers to a shallow green. Great fun whichever way you go at it! The 168-yard 9th, its green sited on the diagonal and sloping from high right to low left, is followed by a 314-yarder played from an elevated tee down to a fairway flanked by beautiful old chestnut trees. A pond lurks at the left side of the angled green here. The 497-yard 11th is pure confrontation: out-of-bounds tight on the left the entire length of the hole, sand and a pond on the right at the landing area for our drive, and a stream across the front of the green eliminating any chance of a runup. As for the rising 410-yard 12th, the crossbunker twenty-five yards short of the green calls to mind Vardon at Little Aston and Fowler at Beau Desert. Despite the water hazards that pop up with some frequency, we play to our handicap at Stapleford Park, enjoying the round on a course designed to please rather than to punish, a course for gratifying holiday golf.

Setting aside such amenities here as the spa, the equestrian center, clay target shooting, and falconry, to say nothing of the gardens and the terraces and the captivating Capability Brown park, where sheep graze freely, there is, at the core of it all, the stately great house, dating to the sixteenth century. The public spaces—saloon, drawing room, library, billiards room, dining room (seventeenth-century carved plaster and woodwork by Grinling Gibbons)—are splendid yet warm. And the fifty-one

James W. Finegan

spacious accommodations have each been fashioned by a different prominent figure in British interior design. As for the cooking, unfussy but imaginative, it measures up in every respect. In our experience, no luxury country house hotel in Britain and Ireland surpasses Stapleford Park, and only three or four are its peers.

The drive south, principally on the M1, to Woburn Golf & Country Club, in Bow Brickhill, at the northern end of Buckinghamshire, takes nearly two hours. In addition to golf, this American-style club offers tennis, squash, swimming, and skeet shooting. Three full-length eighteens—the Duke's, the Duchess, and the Marquess—are carved out of forests of hardwoods and evergreens on rolling terrain. The youngest of the three, the Marquess, which debuted in June of 2000, is now the site of the British Masters. This tournament, which had regularly been played over the Duke's, numbers among its winners Greg Norman, Lee Trevino, Seve Ballesteros, Nick Faldo, and Ian Woosnam.

Designed by Peter Alliss, Clive Clark, Ross McMurray, and Alex Hay, the par-72 Marquess measures 6,329 yards from the regular markers. It moves through deep valleys and across high ground affording magnificent vistas over Bedfordshire as well as Buckinghamshire. The opening half-dozen holes are solid, but there is a sameness about the approach shots. Regardless of the length, which can be anything from 120 to 210 yards, the shot to the green is a falling one.

Now we arrive at the 509-yard 7th (538 from the tips). Here the tee shot is fired over a valley to a broad fairway split by a spinney of tall pines. The player hoping to reach the green in two must drive right of the pines and then, with an intrepid sec-

All Courses Great and Small

ond shot, carry a wilderness valley and three deep pot bunkers in the slope leading up to the putting surface. Those of us taking the more cautious—and longer—route will drive left of the central trees. After a second shot along a narrow dipsy-doodle fairway, our third turns out to be an uphill pitch to a green sloping away to the right and with a steep falloff on that side. This 7th on the Marquess is a most uncommon hole: strategic, original, and great.

The 427-yard 9th is also marvelous stuff, one of the best holes on the course. The drive must be carefully positioned—neither left nor long. The second shot, perhaps a 5-metal, is struck from on high, across another deep valley, to a shelf green somewhat below us and carved out of the opposite slope. Oaks and rhododendrons create a beautiful backdrop for this putting surface, which is neatly angled to the line of flight and has a pair of deep bunkers under its right flank to snare the shot that just fails to get up.

Coming home there are many good holes, but it is the three shortest that we remember best. The thrilling 14th, 198 yards, is played from a very high tee down to a broad, two-tier green stoutly defended by sand, and the less thrilling but perhaps more demanding 17th, a level 155-yarder, requires the shot to be softly drawn around a large oak tree at the front of a richly contoured green if we are to have any chance of getting near a hole at the back or on the left. And then there is the 12th, at 270 yards the course's shortest par four. The drive must first carry a pond and then avoid a narrow stream skirting the left side of the fairway. The approach shot, admittedly a very short pitch, must now carry this stream and a second pond, at the right front. If you think it all adds up to a lot of water for such a short hole, keep this in mind: Here at Woburn, where there are fifty-four holes of serious golf, the 12th on the Marquess is the only water hole!

The Duke's Course, designed by Scottish-born Charles Lawrie, opened in 1976. In addition to serving as the site for the British Masters fourteen times, it was also used on nine occasions for the Women's British Open, whose winners here include Patty Sheehan, Liselotte Neumann, and Karrie Webb. The Duke's measures 6,554 yards from the regular markers against a par of 72. What gives this lightly bunkered layout character is the adroit use of trees in the tee-shot landing area and at the green. What detracts from the course's appeal is the "backing and forthing" on 7 and 8, 10 and 11, 14 and 15.

Three consecutive holes on the first nine are outstanding. Selected as one of *The 500 World's Greatest Golf Holes,* the 121-yard 3rd plummets 100 feet into a sea of rhododendron, bracken, and pine, with the green tilting so severely from back to front that too much bite on the shot will find the ball retreating into a deep swale of fairway. The 366-yard 4th rises all the way, curving left around a smooth shoulder of hill to a long, two-tier green, heavily bunkered, in a dell. Another dogleg left, the 5th is one of my favorite short par fives in Britain (and there are more than enough *short* par fives in Britain). To avoid a steep, rough-covered slope eating well into the line of play from the left, the drive must be kept right, into a constricted fairway. The second shot must also be shaded carefully right—but trees threaten here—if we are to carry a ravine that we have managed to skirt from the tee.

The Duchess, which opened in 1980, is also the handiwork of Charles Lawrie. From the regular tees it measures 6,442 yards; par is 72. Again, trees regularly prompt caution; sand only infrequently does. The agitated ground—dips and climbs and falloffs and cambers—lends test and pleasure to the round. We are struck by the challenging nature of three of the four short holes: the 2nd (182 yards, sand squeezing the narrow green, a high bank right and a falloff left); the unusual 7th (198 yards, big bunker right, a sharp ridge running diagonally across the hole from right to left and past the green on the left to ensure that any shot missing on that side kicks down into the trees); and the 13th (185 yards, a falloff on the left into the trees, and one lonely greenside bunker, short right).

There is a lot of good golf at Woburn, indeed, some of it very good, and all of it routed through beautiful woodlands with ideal elevation changes

Not ten minutes from the golf and country club is Woburn Abbey ("showplace of England" is how the Duke of Bedford immodestly advertises his home), a treasure trove of antiques, silver, porcelain, and paintings. Also on the estate are the Antiques Center, with more than fifty dealers, and the Woburn Safari Park, where many kinds of wild animals can be approached closely by car. I am not kidding when I say that a baboon would snatch the 6-iron out of your golf bag and test his swing if you were careless enough to leave the bag in the luggage rack on the roof of your car.

CHAPTER FIFTEEN

Lancashire: Three Royals, Five Uncommon Commoners

OUR LAST CHAPTER on England is a cornucopia. Each of the eight courses here, along the Irish Sea, is a pure links. Three are royal—Royal Birkdale, Royal Lytham & St. Annes, Royal Liverpool; they are also British Open venues. The other five on this forty-mile stretch of Lancashire coast are either very good or excellent.

So let's take the M6 north out of Birmingham, bypassing Liverpool, to Preston, then head east to St. Annes-on-Sea, home of Royal Lytham & St. Annes Golf Club, founded in 1886. Here there is no sight, nor sound, nor salty scent of the sea. It is, in fact, a full mile away. Still, what with the sand-based turf and the occasional ancient mounding and the fierce fescue rough, this is obviously links golf.

We come to Lytham with some awareness of the outstanding golf architects who have had a hand in shaping its holes (Tom Simpson, Herbert Fowler, Harry Colt, Hugh Alison, Frank Pennink, Donald Steel, et al.) and of the great doings here that began in 1926, when the club initially hosted the Open Championship and Bob Jones claimed the first of his three British Open crowns. Over the next seventy-five years, eight players would capture the claret jug here: Bobby Locke, Peter Thomson, Bob Charles (the only left-hander to win this title), Tony Jacklin, Gary Player, Seve Ballesteros (1979 and 1988), Tom Lehman, and David Duval.

If you've got a long memory, you may recall that the Ryder Cup Match was played here twice, in 1961, when Arnold Palmer and Billy Casper led the U.S. side to victory, 14½–9½, and then in 1977, with Jack Nicklaus, Tom Watson, and Raymond Floyd (Tom Weiskopf elected to stay home and go hunting) as the marquee attractions for the visitors, who won, 12½–7½.

Nonetheless, though Lytham has often been the scene of great events, it does not strike me as a great course. A worthy venue for major competitions, yes; a layout that can make the best players in the world sweat, yes; but, paradoxically, not a great course.

Put quite simply, Lytham St. Annes has poor terrain. It is too often flattish and featureless and charmless. Oh, there is an attractive stretch from the 6th through the 10th, where the ground tumbles and pitches and climbs and dips and we relish the very feel of the links. But this is short-lived, and as we start the long trek home we find ourselves on dull ground once again.

Since the terrain itself could provide little in the way of interest or challenge, the only thing to do, apparently, was to dig holes, man-made excavations in such profusion as to trap the wary and unwary alike. At one time in its history, this links contained 360 sand bunkers, an average of twenty per hole. Today it has a mere 200. But take no comfort from the reduction: these 200 are everywhere. (The last three holes alone provide fifty-three separate opportunities to extricate ourselves from sand.) Bunkers threaten *every* swing on *every* hole: the drive, the fairway metal, the approach, the pitch, the chip. There is no surcease. They stare us down and they swallow us voraciously. Many of them are tiny, steep-faced pots, where the loss of at least one stroke is a foregone conclusion. Others, like the pair carved out of the massive, solitary dune at the 11th to snare the thinly hit tee shot, are large, sloping, menacing. Some are slyly disguised in tiny folds of rough along the edges of the fairways or cut cunningly out of sight in the lee of larger bunkers at the green. There is one such hidden hazard eating into the left edge of the 10th green and another into the right edge of the 18th.

Playing to a par of 71 and measuring almost 6,700 yards from the regular tees, Lytham is inordinately challenging for the club player. Notice of this is well served on the opening hole, a superb 206-yarder with a green all but swaddled in sand. It is one of the three holes on the course that were selected by the editors of *The 500 World's Greatest Golf Holes,* the other two being 17 and 18.

As you would expect of an Open Championship course, Lytham is full of mightily taxing two-shotters, like the 2nd, 420 yards, with a big bunker in the face of a mound 200 yards from the tee and precisely on the ideal driving line; the 3rd, 458 yards, with the railroad unnervingly tight on the right and equally unnerving bunkering tight on the left; the 15th, 468 yards, doglegging gently right, usually played into a headwind, the second shot often blind; the 17th, 413 yards, bending sharply left, with a Sahara down that side and across the middle so as to create two fairway islands; and the 386-yard final hole, a tiptoe past sand from beginning to end. These holes are hard, very hard. And Royal Lytham is on no account to be missed. It is a bona fide shrine, and a course that you may well find more appealing than I do.

Lunch or a beverage in the imposing red-brick Victorian clubhouse, full of intriguing memorabilia, is a treat. Bob Jones joined the club during World War II, when he was stationed in England with the Army Air Force. He used to come to Lytham on weekends and play with any members who happened to be on hand. It was on one of these visits that he gave the club the mashie he used for the fabled 175-yard bunker shot he played to the green on the 17th hole to overtake Al Watrous and win the 1926 Open. The mashie, which is on display in the Club Room, is competed for annually in a members' handicap tournament.

Some thirty minutes south on the coast lies the redoubtable Royal Birkdale Golf Club, in Southport. It dates to 1889 and offers almost as much lore as does Royal Lytham and, for this golfer, a significantly finer links. These days Birkdale is the top vote getter as the greatest course in England. Eight Opens have been played here, beginning in 1954. The winners were Peter Thomson (twice), Arnold Palmer, Lee Trevino, Johnny Miller, Tom Watson, the ill-starred Ian Baker-Finch, and Mark O'Meara.

Like Lytham, Birkdale has also hosted the Ryder Cup twice. In 1965 the U.S. squad—Palmer, Casper, Boros, Lema, and Venturi its most eminent members—won, 19½–12½. In 1969

James W. Finegan

the match was halved for the first time, 16–16, when Nicklaus, in an historic display of sportsmanship, conceded to Tony Jacklin a putt of nearly three feet on the last hole of the last match to assure a tie. Ten years later Nicklaus said to me, "I thought what I did was in the spirit of the Ryder Cup. My teammates didn't necessarily feel the same. Several of them were really upset with me. Several others thought it was fine."

The golf holes today are largely the work of Frederic George Hawtree and his son, Fred W. Play the course at 6,700 yards and par is 72 (three par fives in the last four holes); at 6,300 yards, par is 71. We are struck at once by, if you will, the course's modernity, an absence of the eccentricities so often inherent in the very naturalness of seaside golf. Here the flattish fairways—there is very little undulation—prompt neither freak bounces nor awkward lies. Blind shots are all but nonexistent. This is a remarkably fair and straightforward test.

And a remarkably majestic, challenging, and varied one. The routing plan is unpredictable, hole after marvelous hole striking off in a fresh direction, bringing the wind off the Irish Sea into play from a fresh angle. The fairways are secluded avenues, threading their sinuous paths between the lofty dunes. Controlled driving is essential, for the fairways are somewhat ungenerous and the tees are often exposed and windswept. On the other hand, putting is no bugbear: The silken greens, frequently sheltered in the sandhills, are not complex. There are 114 bunkers, but only rarely are they deep. Scrub willow is plentiful and even more punishing than the gorse. The sea is glimpsed only occasionally, from a dune-top tee, as at the short 4th and the lovely two-shotter 11th.

No hole at Birkdale is less than worthy, and five or six of

All Courses Great and Small

them are great. A couple of par fours on the outgoing nine are in this category, one of them the opener itself. It is 430 yards long, low dunes framing it all the way, a boundary close enough on the right to disconcert the player who would unleash a big swing straight off. A spur of dune juts into the fairway from the left, narrowing the tee shot landing area; yet the drive held safely right can leave a blind shot to a green guarded left and right by sand. The 9th is some forty yards shorter than the 1st. Here our drive must find an elusive fairway well above us that curves right, and our medium-iron must traverse a deep swale to gain a plateau green.

I last played Royal Birkdale in 1999, late on a Sunday afternoon in June. I was alone. As I approached my drive on the 10th, I found myself halted by a man on the green, perhaps 130 yards away, who was practicing his putting. Noting my presence down the fairway, he moved slowly to the edge of the green and waved me up. I managed to hit the green with my iron shot, and as I walked onto it he said, "Well played, well played, sir," and came toward me with a warm smile and an extended hand. His name was Bob Halsall.

Now I could see that he was quite elderly, and he would soon tell me that he was eighty-five. Of average height, he was slender—the blue cardigan sweater, buttoned halfway up from the waist, fit him loosely—but he was not stooped. I lagged to within two feet and he removed the flagstick so I could tap in. I told him I was an American and suggested that he must have been a member of Royal Birkdale for a number of years. This got him going.

As it turned out, Bob Halsall was not a member, but he enjoyed well-earned playing privileges. "I caddied here as a boy," he said. "Then I was the professional for more than forty years, from 1936 to 1979. I also got a winter job as teaching professional at Monte Carlo in 1948. Henry Cotton was the head professional, so I was working for him. He had just won his third Open—that was at Muirfield—and he was making the most of being Britain's top player. He was shrewd. I was teaching a rich Greek and Henry said he understood I was having real success. He asked me if I had been paid by my pupil. This was on a Friday, and I had just finished a session with the chap. I said I hadn't been paid, but was to receive the money on Monday, after the final lesson. 'No, no, no, Bob,' Cotton said to me, 'you should have gotten his money a few minutes ago, when the tears of gratitude for all you've done were welling up in his eyes. By Monday he may be socketing [shanking]!'"

The Cotton story had clearly jogged his memory, and as we stood there on the 10th green he began to talk about the occasion almost fifty years earlier when Frank Sinatra, who had a singing engagement in Liverpool, had come out to Birkdale to take a couple of lessons.

"This was in the very early 1950s," he said. "One night we went to a pub he knew in Southport, just the two of us, a lot of drinks and a lot of talk. We had hit it off well. There was a piano player. We bought him some drinks and he stayed on the job. I remember that Sinatra got up and went out to make a phone call, and when he came back he was smiling. This was when his career was at a low point—his voice was giving him trouble and Hollywood was not offering him much of anything. 'I got the part,' he said. 'In *From Here to Eternity*. I'm playing Maggio.' I congratulated him and then he asked me to come to America. He said the Sands Hotel in Las Vegas was going to build a golf course and he was one of the hotel's owners and he would see to it that I was made the head professional and that way I could go on giving him lessons. I thanked him but said I liked my jobs at Birkdale and at Monte Carlo and that I just couldn't give them up. He didn't like my answer. I guess he was not used to having a generous offer declined.

"We had a couple more drinks. It was getting late and there couldn't have been more than three other people in the place. Suddenly Sinatra said to me, 'OK, OK, maybe I'll never be in your class as a golfer, but I'm a helluva lot better singer than you are. You ever sing?' I said that as a boy I had sung in the church choir, but that was about it. I said that I could probably carry a tune as well as the next guy.

"'Well,' he said, 'I'm the next guy, so let's see about that. What d'you want to sing? Name the song and our friend over here will play and you sing. Then I'll sing. We'll ask the barmaid to judge who's the best.' He looked up at the barmaid—she was a heavy-set blond woman—and said, flashing that man-of-the-world smile we all knew, 'OK, doll?' She grinned and nodded.

"The piano player had passed out, dead drunk, and had to be propped up at the keyboard. I said I'd try 'How Deep Is the Ocean?' For some reason, I thought I could remember the words. And I did all right, even through the middle—you know, 'How many times a day / Do I think of you? / How many roses are sprinkled with dew?' It was an amateur's performance, of course, but I made it all the way and so did the piano player."

"How did Sinatra react?" I asked.

"Oh, he paid attention, he listened, and when I finished he had a little smile. But he didn't say anything."

"Then what?"

"Then he sang 'Night and Day.' And not just the main part, that we all know, but also the beginning, the verse—'Like the beat, beat, beat of the tom tom / When the jungle shadows fall'—and when you think of all we'd had to drink, he was pretty good. Then he turned to the barmaid to get her verdict. She never hesitated. She said, 'Oh, Mr. Sinatra, you're the winner.'

"I insisted that she'd been paid off, that she voted for him because he had given her a £10 note.

"'Oh, no,' she said. She was laughing. 'That's not true. Mr. Sinatra did not bribe me. You see, he gives me a tenner *every* night!'

"We all laughed and now it was time—it was past time—to close the pub and go home. Frank Sinatra and I parted friends. His singing engagement in Liverpool ended the next day, and I never saw him again."

I shook hands with Bob Halsall and wished him an even longer good life. Then I headed over to the tee of the par-four 11th, with its glimpse of the sea. Of two minds at that moment, I was sorry to be saying good-bye because I knew we would be unlikely ever to meet again, but I was also eager to continue my round on the great course.

The inbound nine has three holes—12, 15, 18—chosen for *The 500 World's Greatest* volume. Two of them, 12 and 18, also made the top 100. Secluded in the far sandhills out near the high ridge that shields the links from the sea is Birkdale's finest one-shotter, the 159-yard 12th. It is a picture-book hole. From the elevated yet sheltered tee we play across a valley of rough ground to a similarly sheltered target nestling in the dunes. The greenside pits right and left, together with the low dunes crowding in on the putting surface, make the target look even smaller than it is. The par-five 15th is grand and classic, essentially on the level, stretching away into the sea breeze, gorse and willow scrub right and left, bunkers (a total of thirteen) menacing every stroke, especially the phalanx that must be carried—or at least somehow avoided—on the second shot. On the 18th, a 452 yarder, the landing area for the drive is separated into two parts by a centrally-positioned—and gathering—kidney-shaped bunker. We must decide whether to go right or left. As for the green on this mighty two-shotter, so distant is it, and so inaccessible—bunkers, low dunes, high rough—that it might as well be in Cheshire.

Royal Birkdale is sublime. Of all the English courses, it may be the one most affectionately remembered by the traveling American golfer. And its sparkling white clubhouse, built in 1935, is a triumph of Art Deco architecture that was designed to suggest a luxury liner cresting the waves (in this instance, the sandhills). It is the most distinctive seaside clubhouse in Britain.

Royal Liverpool Golf Club, located at Hoylake, some ten miles west of Liverpool, is England's preeminent golf club. Founded in 1869, it is second in age among English seaside clubs only to Royal North Devon (Westward Ho!), which was formed five years earlier. The Hoylake links was laid out by George Morris, a brother of Old Tom Morris, but over the years substantive revisions have been effected by, successively, Harry Colt, Frank Pennink, and Fred W. Hawtree. It was here in 1885 that the British Amateur was inaugurated, and here it has been contested seventeen times. The club's two greatest players, John Ball (eight times Amateur champion as well as 1890 Open champion) and Harold Hilton (four times Amateur champion,

James W. Finegan

twice Open champion, and once winner of the U.S. Amateur), are generally felt to be the two greatest amateurs in the annals of British golf. A third Hoylake member, Jack Graham, never won the Amateur or the Open, but he reached the semifinals of the Amateur four times and was low amateur in the Open five times. He died in action on "Flanders fields" in 1915.

The Open Championship has been held at Hoylake ten times. Among the winners here were Hilton, J. H. Taylor, Walter Hagen, Bob Jones (1930—the second leg of the Grand Slam), Peter Thomson, and in 1967, Roberto de Vicenzo, when the last Open was played here. This decision by the R&A to drop Hoylake was prompted by the lack of space for car parking and the tented village.

For most golfers, the old links at Hoylake is not a case of love at first sight. From the windows of the dignified red-brick Victorian clubhouse, the links, with roads and houses hemming it in on three sides, looks flat and open and sere and, alas, dull. Distant dunes hiding the Dee estuary are backdropped by the far more distant hills of Wales. And though the terrain undulates in true links fashion, there is an overall absence of feature.

Still, the holes are scarcely defenseless. The bunkers—seventy-five of them, a mere handful compared to the 200 at Lytham—have steep revetted faces and are skillfully spotted to extract a heavy toll. The course is almost always firm and fast, shortening it, yes, but playing hob with the tricky little shots around the green. Then there is the wind, which sweeps in from the sea uninterruptedly across this level tract, where there simply is no shelter from it. And finally, here at Hoylake we must face up to a circumstance that is without parallel on the great championship courses: *interior* boundaries. Signaled by the

218

"cops," very low artificial embankments of turf, they pop up only three times, but when they do they strike terror into the hearts of the timid and can prove ruinous to the player tainted with hubris.

The course—6,909 yards, par 72—wastes no time in introducing us to this unusual danger. The 427-yard 1st hole is one of two here named among *The 500 World's Greatest Golf Holes.* It doglegs right, around the practice ground. Tight on the right—which is to say, *immediately* on the right—for the full length of the hole runs a cop. Over it is out of bounds, the harshest summary judgment. A sudden-death match on the 19th hole in the British Amateur once saw Horace Hutchinson and Bernard Darwin, between them, knock five balls out of bounds here!

For decades, the 7th struck most players as even more fearsome. A 200-yarder, it presented a narrow green crowded on the left by another out-of-bounds cop. It was entirely possible to hit a well-nigh perfect 5-wood or 2-iron into the heart of the green only to watch in dismay as the ball bounced left, over the cop and out of bounds, coming to rest no more than seven or eight paces from the hole.

I am unlikely to forget the first time I played the 7th, more than twenty years ago. Hosting me was one of the highly respected English golf writers of the day, Leslie Edwards. Two other Hoylake members, a schoolteacher and a ship's chandler, rounded out the fourball.

Leslie, a smallish, outgoing, and articulate man then in his early seventies, was in charge. He had a twinkle in his eye and a ready fund of Hoylake stories, generally with an American slant: Hagen, following his 1924 Open win, rode away from the club in the backseat of a convertible, top down, throwing golf balls to the cheering crowds; Leslie's father set up the first transatlantic radio broadcast of a golf tournament, the 1930 Open Championship, which Jones won en route to the Grand Slam; Masters champion Gay Brewer, having arrived too late to play a practice round for the 1967 Open, reacted intemperately as he found himself standing on the 6th tee in the opening round and staring at the high, man-eating jungle of briars and gorse to be cleared against the prevailing wind: "Jesus Christ, look at this!"

Whenever Leslie hit a weak shot, he would say, "Ah, that's a poor thing." His putting grip was eccentric. The hands were well separated, with the right hand holding the shaft as if it were a pen and the putter head were the pen point and he were writing on the green with it. A forerunner of the Calcavecchia claw.

Of my unconventional pass at the ball, he pronounced with his characteristic warm smile, "Jim Finegan, you've a lilt in your swing." Over the first six holes I had lived up to my modest reputation for accurate hitting, so that when I took my stance at the ball on the chilling one-shotter 7th Leslie announced: "There's only one man among us who can be counted on to hit the ball straight and that man is on the tee now." I promptly yanked the shot out of bounds. My host called the 7th "the most controversial hole in British golf." Reviled far more often than it was admired, this card-wrecker was altered in recent years by a vote of the Committee that did away with the boundary. Now it can be faced without fear and trembling.

The 8th is the other Hoylake hole named as one of *The 500 World's Greatest.* This straightaway 493-yarder looks eminently manageable—in truth, it looks eminently birdieable—as it moves over crumpled ground to a mildly raised green, a small deep pot bunker at the right front its lone hazard. In the final round of the 1930 Open, Bob Jones, after two excellent wood shots had left him fifteen yards short of the putting surface, twice hit his chip shot squarely but too softly and then missed a 12-inch putt to accumulate a double-bogey 7.

The next five holes all have the character and charm of great links golf, curving through the modest sandhills, the Dee estuary on our left. The punchbowl green on the 390-yard 9th inclines to embrace our second shot, but expect no such affection at the intransigent 10th, 411 yards, bending left, a partially hidden bunker to snare the pulled drive, an elevated green to defy the long second shot. The raised green on the 193-yard 11th, beside the beach, boasts only one bunker, but it is sited precisely where it can do the most damage, at the right front. The 12th, 412 yards and arguably the finest hole on the course, turns smartly left, a trio of malevolent pots in the crook of the dogleg daring us to clear them on the drive in order to shorten what will otherwise be a long second shot into the prevailing wind. The elevated green, with a large sandhill snugly left and a deep hollow immediately right, is a fiercely elusive target. In sum, a great hole.

The final five holes are stern, bringing with them the menacing cops and attendant interior out of bounds on 15 and 16. In both instances, a slice will find us beyond the pale and, as at the 1st hole, on the forbidden practice ground. This is a course that takes a little getting used to and more than a little heart.

Visitors are made to feel at home in the many-gabled clubhouse, with its portraits of Bob Jones, John Ball, Harold Hilton, and Jack Graham. On display is fascinating memorabilia—clubs and medals and cups from bygone days. Particularly fine, up on the second floor, its many windows giving on the links, is the Club Room, oak-paneled and high-ceilinged, with deep leather chairs. At each end of the room is a marble fireplace. Until the last weeks of his life, the nonagenarian Leslie Edwards could be found most days sitting at the fire, comforted by a glass of claret. He had vowed to live long enough to see the Open Championship return to Hoylake, and the club had acquired ten acres of nearby land and had guaranteed to build a new practice ground. In 2002, not many months after his death, the R&A announced its intention to bring the Open back to Hoylake in 2006.

So much for the three royals. It is time now to look at the commoners, five of them. They may not have the pedigree, but they certainly have the golf.

It was none other than Old Tom Morris himself who in 1891 laid out the links at Wallasey Golf Club, no distance from Hoylake. Among those who had a hand in revising the course were three Open champions, Harold Hilton, James Braid, and Sandy Herd. They made greens of an attractive naturalness, and propped a number of the bunkers, all of which have stacked-sod faces, boldly up out of the ground, like some at Carnoustie. Today Wallasey is a beautifully-conditioned jewel, with a rolling 370-yard opener that we ought to make a 4 on, followed by holes that range from good to outstanding, most of them over classically undulating linksland in the shadow of high, grass-covered dunes, with occasional magnificent views over the Irish Sea.

The last four holes at Wallasey constitute one of my favorite

All Courses Great and Small

finishing runs in the world. The 370-yard 15th features a plateau green perched high in the sandhills. At the 200-yard 16th, the tabletop green is crowded on the right by a massive sandhill and on the left by a long and steep falloff. The splendid 17th, a taxingly long two-shotter at 464 yards, begins on a lofty tee, plays exuberantly downhill, then uphill and blindly over a crest to a green in a dell of dunes. The great 18th, another bear at 441 yards, also starts with a big elevation change on the drive, which finishes in a tumbling, dune-framed fairway. This time the target for our long second shot—the fairway shrinks to almost nothing, then, just as surprisingly, bulges—is in view, right beneath the windows of the stolid hundred-year-old clubhouse. Prominent inside is a portrait of Frank Stableford, a Wallasey captain who in 1931 devised the scoring system that bears his name.

Less than ten miles north of Wallasey, in Blundellsands and adjacent to the Liverpool/Southport railway line (beware a slice on 11 and a hook on 15) is another exceptional links that, like Wallasey, has hosted final qualifying for the Open. West Lancashire Golf Club, founded in 1873, offers a course that is very gently rolling, its holes often framed by sandhills. Whether played at 6,200 yards or 6,760, this is a taxing par 72—long forced carries off the tee, tall fescue rough throttling any attempt at recovery, greens often teasingly sited on plateaus or in dells. We are indebted to Fred W. Hawtree and Ken Cotton for this course, which is laid out on 200 acres of prime linksland.

A pair of par fours on the second nine nicely illustrate the character of West Lancs, as it is commonly called. On the 355-yard 13th, we fire away from an elevated tee, the fairway curving left along a dune-framed valley to a green on a cunning low

223

plateau. The next hole, 412 yards, also begins on a high tee in the sandhills, but this time the downhill drive is blind, over a ridge, and the fairway bends sweepingly right, around a thick stand of pines, finally disclosing a raised green tucked in the lee of a wooded hillside.

Like most old clubs, West Lancs has its fund of anecdote. One story is extraordinary. In 1972 an assistant professional at the club by the name of Peter Parkinson took full advantage of the sharp dogleg on the 370-yard 7th. The hole has a high tee with panoramic views of the city of Liverpool, the Wirral Peninsula, North Wales, and Liverpool Bay north toward Blackpool, where, on a clear day, the landmark Tower can be seen. Young Parkinson was not distracted from the business at hand. Taking the most daring line over the inside of the dogleg, where await a couple of fierce sandpits and plenty of rough country, he launched his drive straight at the green and, as luck would have it, straight into the cup.

The clubhouse terrace at West Lancs is an idyllic spot, overlooking the 9th and 18th greens, the vista of the links stretching away to the shipping in the estuary and beyond toward the Welsh hills. There are few more beguiling places in British golf for lunch or a drink.

A five-mile drive north from West Lancs along the Liverpool/Southport Road, A565, brings us to Formby Golf Club, founded in 1884. When I played there in 1999, the receptionist took my green fee, showed me around the very attractive clubhouse, and got me a cup of drinking water from the kitchen. I volunteered that the club might want to install a water cooler, and he responded, "Excellent idea, excellent. I must put it in the suggestion book."

All Courses Great and Small

You are not likely to confuse either the course or the club here with the others in this chapter. The course is bordered on three sides by hearty evergreens that cut it off from the world. A number of holes are also individually isolated by trees. Still, this is neither a parkland nor heathland course, but rather one with links terrain that is never less than undulating, at times marvelously tumbling, and punctuated by high sandhills. If the opening three holes and the closing three holes are routed over somewhat dull ground, be assured that the stretch from 4 through 15 is excellent, blessed as it is with demanding shots (the drive on 9 from a high tee to a curving plateau fairway where danger lurks over the edge both left and right) and memorable holes (12, 13, and 15, all between 375 and 400 yards, all on rumpled and billowing ground, all presenting exquisitely sited greens that shrug off the iron shot that is anything less than precise). Heather makes the rough formidable. The original design was by Willie Park, Jr., with revisions by Harry Colt in the 1920s and Frank Pennink in 1984. From the regular markers, the course measures 6,500 yards; par is 72.

Formby might fairly be considered an "establishment club"—people of means who value the status that membership here imparts, not to mention people of influence, particularly with the R&A. Among the numerous important events that the club has hosted are final qualifying for the Open, three British Amateurs (Jose Maria Olazabal defeated Colin Montgomerie here in the 1984 final), three English Amateurs, and in 1965 the World Seniors, which Sam Snead won.

The clubhouse—100 years old, white walls and red tile roof, a tall clocktower, the timepiece itself in full view from the 1st tee and the 18th green—is attractive and spacious. Within its walls are four single and three twin-bedded rooms for traveling male golfers. This is not to suggest that women aren't well provided for. Indeed they are, perhaps uniquely so. Standing side by side with the Formby Golf Club is the Formby Ladies Golf Club, which, founded in 1896, is completely independent: its own clubhouse, its own course, its own greenkeeping staff. The ladies' eighteen—5,374 yards, par 71, varied and picturesque and testing—is enclosed within the men's course. Men are welcome, as are ladies on the Formby Golf Club course.

The town of Southport lies three or four miles north of Formby. Here, cheek by jowl among the most majestic sandhills of all on this stretch of coastline lie Hillside, Southport & Ainsdale, and Royal Birkdale. It was at Hillside, founded in 1911, that Jay Sigel beat Scott Hoch in the final of the 1979 British Amateur. A venue for Open qualifying, Hillside has also hosted the British PGA (Tony Jacklin's last win of consequence came here in 1982) and the British Ladies Championship. Fred W. Hawtree was chiefly responsible for the course we play today.

The dichotomy between Hillside's two nines could scarcely be more striking. The outbound half is routed over low and relatively level land. The railway line, close along the left on the 1st and 2nd, and the stream that defends the green on the 386-yard 3rd, give pause. But it is the inbound nine, brilliantly carved out of the huge sandhills near the sea, that is the glory of Hillside. Here are consistently strong holes, beginning with the 140-yard 10th, which rises modestly to a crowned green in the dunes. The lofty tee on the par-five 11th sets the stage for a superb hole that doglegs left along a dune-framed valley to a plateau green with a very large and deep bunker under its right edge. This 493-yarder was selected as one of *The 500 World's*

All Courses Great and Small

Greatest Golf Holes, perhaps in some small measure because the tee looks down not only on Hillside holes, but, flanking them, holes at Royal Birkdale and at Southport & Ainsdale, to produce one of the truly arresting moments in golf. The nine concludes with two rousing tests, the steeply down dale then sternly uphill 532-yard 17th and the 428-yard closing hole, where the falling drive, often wind-aided, gives us a chance to reach in two a green rather close to the dreaded white stakes.

Possibly taking its cue from its ampersand mate Royal Lytham & St. Annes, Southport & Ainsdale opens with a par three, a 180-yard carry over thigh-high rough to a fiercely bunkered (nine deep pots) and fiercely undulating green. This links, laid out by James Braid in 1923, is endearingly old-fashioned, with its blind and semiblind shots, low mounding sometimes serving as a welcome backstop at the green, and an occasional crossbunker deceptively short of the putting surface. At the S&A, as the locals call it, we drive through narrow gaps in the sandhills, steer our way along winding valleys between some ridges, and aggressively sail high over others. It is exhilarating golf from start to finish. Like the 1st, the 153-yard 8th is another superior one-shotter, but in this instance the green, set above eye level on a plateau, has no bunkers. The sharply sloping ground is all the defense needed on a hole that was chosen as one of *The 500 World's Greatest.* So was the 16th, which claimed a spot among the top 100. Playing into the prevailing wind, this par five measures just over 500 yards. A massive sandhill must be surmounted on the second shot. Glowering down from the face of this pyramidal grass-covered dune is a wall of railroad ties, which serves to prevent erosion and, at the same time, to dispatch a thinly hit shot to the perdition of the pits below.

The fourth Ryder Cup Match, in 1933, took place at South-port & Ainsdale. Great Britain and Ireland, whose luminaries (Abe Mitchell, Alf Padgham, and Perry Alliss) were all but unknown in the United States, won, 6½–5½, downing a visiting team led by Gene Sarazen, Walter Hagen, Craig Wood, Paul Runyan, and Horton Smith. The American squad's Denny Shute three-putted from twenty-three feet on the home green to hand the cup to the host team. Four years later, the Americans—Sarazen, Snead, Nelson, Guldahl, and company—returned to the S&A; this time they won, 8–4, the first victory in the Match by a visiting team.

The Liverpool/Southport area is not noted for quality hotels or gourmet dining. Convenient to Hoylake and Wallasey is the moderately priced Bowler Hat Hotel, in Birkenhead, a thirty-two-room inn dating to the nineteenth century. Guest rooms are a mixed bag, some cramped, others roomy enough. It will do for a one- or two-night stay. In Southport the most comfortable hotel is the Prince of Wales, on Lord Street. Public spaces are pleasant, but when we stayed here in 1999 the guest rooms needed refreshing. The Woolton Redbourne Hotel, in South Liverpool, is a comfortable and captivating inn set in a lovely garden. Guest rooms as well as public spaces are a bow to Victorian clutter. But the only golf course within a thirty-minute drive is Wallasey.

Several restaurants should be mentioned. On the Wirral Peninsula, Tony's Leisure Club and Restaurant—yes, that is its name—provides good cooking and attentive, friendly service. In Southport, the moderately priced Forge Brasserie is a seafood and steak restaurant with a rustic feeling and a highly convivial atmosphere. And at Giovana, also in Southport, the

Italian cooking is delicious, the service is impeccable, and the ambience—attractive furnishings, soft lighting—is relaxed. Including a bottle of chianti, the bill in 1999 for two people having a three-course dinner was under $50.

Tourists do not flock to Liverpool, but it does offer the largest Anglican cathedral in Britain and the lively Albert Dock (cafes and restaurants, shops, the Maritime Museum, an exhibit called "The Beatles Story," and more). Roughly thirty minutes south is Chester, full of tourists. With its ancient city walls, timber-framed houses, arcades forming covered passages, and a celebrated cathedral dating to the twelfth century, it is one of England's most medieval-looking towns. It is also compact.

As for Southport itself, it is a winner, and Lord Street is one of England's beguiling avenues—early nineteenth-century villas as well as gardens and shops, most of the latter with glass marquees that permit window-shopping in foul weather. Even the seafront, with its rides and bingo games, has a charm of its own. And speaking of seafronts, Blackpool, fifteen minutes up the coast from Royal Lytham, is a triumph of honky-tonk—garish, gaudy, and great fun, its promenade along the beach jammed with vacationers and concession stands and thrill rides, including what was for years the world's biggest roller coaster.

CHAPTER SIXTEEN

North Wales: Seven at the Sea

 WALES, which is about the size of Massachusetts, is no mere western extension of England. The English are Anglo-Saxons; the Welsh, by and large, are Celts. This may help to explain their stubborn individuality and the warmth of the welcome they extend to travelers (not to mention such tongue-twisting place names as Ysbytty Cynfyn and Llanwmaddwy). For travelers coming from Greater Liverpool, it is a very short run indeed—south on the M63, then west on the A55 to Llandudno, home of the North Wales Golf Club.

The club was founded in 1894 by a Manchester businessman who laid out the holes with help from Hoylake's John Ball. The course is routed over a confined tract of linksland along Penmorfa Beach. The panoramic coastal and mountain views are splendid, and never more so than on the 9th, 10th, and 11th holes, a trio of invigorating par fours beside the beach. Against a par of 71, the course measures only 6,247 yards from all the way back. Bunkering is light, as is gorse. Water comes into play on four holes. Blind shots pop up on occasion. But it is wind and the lay of the land that are our true opponents.

On our most recent visit, in late summer of 1999, I played with the newly appointed caterer, who had belonged to the club for ten years but was about to forfeit his membership because he was now an employee. Only mildly annoyed at this turn of events, he had pretty well decided to join Conwy Golf Club, in view across the bay. Though the fairways that day at North Wales were sometimes scruffy and weed-infested, the greens were excellent putting surfaces, fast and true.

There is a patch of meadowy golf early on, holes 3 through 7, but the rest of the course is authentic linksland, with the last seven holes full of bold sandhills. The jottings on my scorecard tell the story: "Green cloistered in a dell of dunes. . . . Classic short par four along and above Llandudno Bay. . . . Blind drive over dune ridge rising abruptly in front of tee. . . . Forbidding broken ground smothered in long fescues. . . . Forced carry from elevated tee in sandhills beside beach, sea at my back. . . . Dunes thirty to thirty-five feet high ringing tiny green with only the flag visible—wild!" That last entry refers to the 151-yard 16th, where from a high tee we look out over a wilderness of sandhills backdropped in the distance by the sea. The only sign that a putting surface must be in there somewhere is a small white square of wind-whipped cotton. This is an indelible moment, perhaps because we have no idea what lies in wait.

Though Conwy (Caernarvonshire) Golf Club is just across the water, I managed to have trouble finding it on our first foray into North Wales many years ago. I decided to get both gas and directions. At the service station, I was uncertain whether I should pump first or pay first, so I asked the woman who was filling her tank a few feet away. She told me to pump first, then, moments later, asked whether I was in Wales on holiday.

"Yes," I said, though strictly speaking that was probably not the truth. "And it's so beautiful I'm sorry we're going to be here only a week."

"Maybe then you won't be collecting your coupons," she said.

"I'm not sure I understand," I replied.

"Coupons," she repeated. "The coupons they give you when you pay for your petrol. Save up enough of them and you get a gift from the catalog."

She was a woman in her mid-fifties, and by now I had noticed that her car looked to have plenty of mileage on it and the coat she wore was neither new nor stylish.

"Oh, no," I said hurriedly, finally comprehending. "No, no, you're right, of course, they're no value to me. If you'd like, I'll be pleased to give them to you. By all means. They used to do this back home, with Green Stamps, but not anymore." Then I added, "We always saved Green Stamps."

I hung up the nozzle and started across the paving. She fell into step beside me.

"I won't tell you what it is I'm saving for," she said. "You'd think me silly."

"I'm sure I wouldn't."

"Still, I'm not going to tell you. I will say it's taken a long time, but I'm getting near the end now."

I paid for the gas—it must have been the one time in my life I wished I had needed more—and handed the coupons over to her. She thanked me and left. Then I got the directions. As I drove away, I wondered whether it had been easy for her to approach a stranger with this request. She had not appeared

All Courses Great and Small

diffident. I found myself admiring her forwardness—her cheekiness, some might say. She had spotted the opportunity and seized it. And the net of it was that we were both glad she had.

Conwy is also spectacularly set between the sea and the mountains. The game has been played here since 1869, making this one of the oldest courses in Wales. Over the years it has hosted the important Welsh championships, plus the British Ladies and, in 1970, the touring professionals' Martini International. George Duncan, who would win the 1920 Open Championship, ran the golf shop here in 1914 but was fired because of his inclination to slip away on Saturday afternoons in order to play football (soccer) for Conwy.

The course has been revised several times, most recently by Frank Pennink. Bunkering is moderate. The wind off the sea lashes this treeless and level tract full of hummocks and hollows, ripples and ridges. Tackled at either 6,400 or 6,650 yards, this par 72 is all most of us can handle.

The 375-yard opener gets us easily away from the clubhouse, to be followed by a couple of classic links holes, a 147-yarder over the corner of an old garden wall to a green set naturally in the dunes, then a superb shortish two-shotter where the drive is blind and the approach is to a slightly elevated plateau green by the shore with two deep bunkers in the face of the slope (reminiscent of the 10th at Portmarnock).

Beginning at the 5th, there is a seven-hole stretch of big golf containing three solid par fives (523, 537, and 503 yards), a strong par three (177 yards into the prevailing wind to a narrow green), and three very rigorous par fours (442, 441, and 435 yards), also into the prevailing wind. The last six holes are played along corridors framed by impenetrable gorse, some-

233

times reinforced by thorny berry vines (as if reinforcement were needed!). Conwy is stern. And if it does not make the heart sing, you will be at least respectful—and, I think, honestly glad to have played here. It is second in North Wales only to Royal St. David's for pure golfing challenge.

As your headquarters for playing at Conwy and North Wales, consider the Old Rectory, in Llansanfraid Glan Conwy. Views over the estuary to Conwy Castle and the mountains of Snowdonia are magical. A couple of the six guest rooms are small, but all six are furnished chiefly with antiques and heirlooms. Michael and Wendy Vaughan (she is an outstanding cook) own and run the inn. The last time we were there, a harpist entertained in the pine-paneled drawing room during cocktails.

Conwy is perhaps the best preserved medieval fortress/town in Britain, with its circuit of high town walls incorporating twenty-one towers. Nearby are seaside Llandudno, a winning combination of Victorian refinement and contemporary tacky; Llandudno Junction, famous for Collinge Antiques (impressive collection of grandfather clocks); and seventy-acre Bodnant Garden, with both formal and informal plantings.

We head west now on the A55, soon crossing the Menai Straits to the Isle of Anglesey on the bridge near Bangor and following the A5 out to Holyhead, the port for the Ireland ferries. It was James Braid who laid out the links of the Holyhead Golf Club, in 1912, at Trearddur Bay. This course has plenty of ups and downs. It also has some blind shots. There are fewer than fifty bunkers, but some of them are deep. Gorse, heather, and bracken menace the off-line shot from time to time. And prominent rock outcroppings determine the flow of several holes, giving them a nice sense of definition.

All Courses Great and Small

Holyhead does not play along the sea, but the sea is in view at a distance. We begin by heading for it on a straight line from the 1st hole through the 4th, where a plateau green on this short one-shotter perches above the strand. But we never again come that close to Trearddur Bay. There are some exceptional holes: the 2nd, a par three played from a platform tee over a gorse-infested swale to an elevated green with falloffs on both sides; the 3rd, a short par five where the changes in elevation keep us guessing—we start high and we finish high and in between drop into valleys twice, one of them on our blind second shot; the 9th, a punishingly long two-shotter, 454 yards, steadily uphill and into the prevailing wind, with high mounding in the middle of the fairway to deflect the underhit second shot and four bunkers at the green to swallow the off-line second shot.

Picture Holyhead as a true holiday course—short (6,058 yards, par 70), attractively varied, occasionally demanding, downright fun.

On the road now and back over the Menai Straits, then west on the A55, picking up A499 at the entrance to the Lleyn Peninsula and following southwest through Nefyn and, on the B4417, out to Nefyn & District Golf Club, proud possessor of one of the most dramatically sited courses in my experience. Call it the poor man's Old Head of Kinsale or Pebble Beach. But let me hasten to add that the golf holes at these two celebrated venues are notably finer than those at Nefyn. Still, when it comes to stupendous views and the sheer exhilaration of playing shots in a clifftop setting high above the sea, neither of them can put this remote Welsh course in the shade.

The club was founded in 1907. The original course architect

James W. Finegan

is unknown; some revisions were made by Fred W. Hawtree and A. H. F. Jiggens. In 1919 an invitation was extended to Prime Minister David Lloyd George, of Welsh parentage, to preside over the reopening of the eighteen after its temporary closure during the World War. As the club history amusingly notes, ". . . it says a lot for that gentleman's public spiritedness that instead of coming to Nefyn he attended the Peace Conference at Versailles."

Lightly bunkered and short, Nefyn cannot be stretched to 6,300 yards. Par is 71. The Irish Sea is in view from every hole, and eleven holes skirt the cliff edge, at heights that range from sixty to 160 feet. The opener is robust, a 458-yard par four that finds us driving straight out to sea, and often straight into the wind, from an elevated tee, the fairway plunging to provide us some much needed assistance, then curving smoothly right as it rises to a green far above the beach.

The next three holes, a couple of medium-length par fours and a 466-yard par five that is our best birdie chance in the round, all commence on high tees and run their entire length disconcertingly close to the cliff edge. A slice is fatal. The six holes that follow are laid out at a remove from the waves, and then we come to the extremely narrow spit of land, jutting well out into the sea, over which the next seven holes are routed. What follows is sometimes hair-raising, with fairways merging (12 and 16, 13 and 15) and tee shots launched right over the green we've just left (14 over 13, 15 over 14). There is a shortage of available ground as we tightrope-walk above the roiling waters. The 415-yard 13th, calling up the marvelous 10th on Turnberry's Ailsa, is a great hole: a platform tee set thrillingly high above the sea, a dogleg left around an inlet daring you to bite off all you believe you can chew, a green sited on the edge of a promontory and defended not by sand but by rock outcroppings.

Not by any rational judgment is the par-five 12th, only 478 yards, a great hole. Nonetheless, it is just possible that no other hole in this book is quite so memorable. Its principal features are a public thoroughfare, a public house, a "pothole," a blind drive, and a blind second shot. The blind drive, from very high ground, appears to head straight off into the Irish Sea. Nothing else is in view on the line we must take. We keep reassuring ourselves that there has to be a fairway down there somewhere, but it is not easy to believe. So we swing. The ball soars away against a backcloth of sea and sky, then disappears, and, miracle of miracles, fetches up in a haven of mown grass far, far below. Our blind second shot must now surmount a hill and somehow avoid, on the other side of it, a concealed and monstrous sinkhole—a crater—in the middle of the fairway and about eighty yards short of the elevated shelf green. Implausible? No, unthinkable. Now when you have putted out, please do not forget to look over the cliff to the right of the green. Down at the water's edge lies a tiny fishing village, complete with a pub, Ty Coch, to which golfers with sturdy legs may—and often do—repair for some liquid reinforcement before continuing the struggle.

Eight holes (yes, eight) were added in 1993, so now there are 26 holes here. Ignore these newcomers. You want the original (Old) course. You will also want to have lunch here—smashing views of 1, 11, and 18, together with a tantalizing glimpse of that minuscule fishing village in its cove.

Perhaps thirty minutes away, down the one road that will

take us southeast from Nefyn, lies Pwllheli (pronounced Pool-thelly, and meaning "saltwater pool"), a very popular resort with a long beach, a promenade, a harbor, antiques shops, and a golf course, built in 1900. I'm afraid that the course is the least of the town's attractions.

For too much of the way, Pwllheli (6,108 yards, par 69) offers flat and forgettable parkland golf. Still, there are also half a dozen true links holes here, routed over hummocky ground and pocked with penal pits. What a welcome breath of sea air these six holes are! Old Tom Morris fashioned the original nine; James Braid revised it and extended the course to eighteen holes. But provenance notwithstanding, Pwllheli disappoints.

Nearby Plas Bodegroes does not. Like Padstow's Seafood Restaurant, Plas Bodegroes bills itself as a "restaurant with rooms." The rooms, some with four-poster beds, are sparkling and comfortable in this house that dates to 1780. The setting, totally isolated in the trees, has about it a hideaway quality. The cooking on our two-night stay was inspired (e.g., a scallops and crab terrine with curry mayonnaise, roast saddle of lamb with a flageolet bean casserole, and a cinnamon biscuit of apple and rhubarb with elderflower sauce).

Roughly forty minutes east of Pwllheli, on Tremadog Bay, is the most extraordinary tourist attraction in Wales. Portmeirion is a *faux* Italianate village, a multihued fantasy that includes lodgings, a campanile, colonnades, fountains, formal gardens, reflecting pools, a grand piazza and a couple of petite piazzas, to say nothing of the "Pantheon," with its gilded Burmese dancers atop Ionic columns and a giant Buddha left over from a film set. Noel Coward wrote *Blithe Spirit* while staying in one of the cottages for a week. And as you wander about, it may be with a sense of déjà vu—for Portmeirion is where *The Prisoner,* a television series starring Patrick McGoohan, was shot. This 1960s show has a cult following and is regularly rebroadcast. In fact, even as I write this it is being shown on PBS here in the Philadelphia area. The tentacles of North Wales are long.

Half an hour south on Tremadog Bay lies the links of Royal St. David's Golf Club (1894), at Harlech. The setting is romantically beautiful. In the distant background are the majestic peaks of Snowdonia. Brooding over the golf holes from its rocky precipice is four-square Harlech Castle, more than 700 years old, its outer walls still intact. At the opposite end of the links is a massive range of sandhills.

Patric Dickinson's account, in his classic *A Round of Golf Courses,* of how the golf holes came into being here is so beguiling that it must be quoted:

> One day in the nineties a Mr. W. H. More, from the heights, saw a figure far below engaged in some strange form of exercise. He investigated and found a young man hurling a boomerang about . . . the young man said that his name was Harold Finch-Hatton and that he had recently returned from Australia. A few days later, Mr. More observed him at some even stranger pursuit and perhaps a little gingerly went to investigate again. "Capital place for a golf links," said Finch-Hatton. "Come on, let's lay one out." And so they did.

Since More had never so much as held a golf club in his hands, the actual routing of the holes lay solely up to Finch-

Hatton. Over the years there have been changes to the original scheme, some of them by the Committee.

On our most recent visit to Harlech, in 2000, I spoke briefly with the professional, John Barnett, who proudly informed me that the course had just emerged in a poll of British Isles courses as the third toughest—Carnoustie was first and, he said, "An Irish course was second." Harlech is a very stiff examination, comparable in degree of difficulty to Rye. Par at Rye (one par five, five par threes) is 68. Par at Harlech (two par fives, five par threes) is 69. Not many of us are up to the task of breaking 80 at either of them in the wind. Harlech has hosted all the important Welsh championships, not to mention the British Ladies and the British Youths.

For most of the round, the course is open in aspect and elevation changes are minimal. There are more than 100 bunkers. Streams beset us on half a dozen holes. Fairways and greens are generous targets, but the rough is throttling and there is gorse. Playing the course at 6,400 yards, we face seven very long two-shotters—436 yards, 463, 430, 436, 450, 427, and 428—and a couple of par threes over 200 yards. Big hitting pays off handsomely at Harlech.

The first nine is a lot of "backing and forthing" over basically level and nondescript terrain. Oh, two of the first three holes are a couple of those indigestibly long par fours mentioned above, and the 4th is a very good one-shotter, 188 yards, a little swale short of the raised green and some low dunes behind it. But we find ourselves wondering how Harlech could be so highly regarded. The answer is the second nine. It is superlative.

At the exacting 11th hole, 153 yards, the narrow green is cloistered in the dunes. On 10, 12, and 13, however, the play is very much out in the open—the problems are in full view—as we tackle three long two-shotters, each with plenty of style and spirit. At the 430-yard 10th, a stream must be cleared on the long second shot. The 12th, 436 yards, finds us taking aim on the castle from an elevated tee, our drive coming down in a bunker-squeezed landing area. Then all that remains is to avoid greenside sand right and left on yet another of those full-blooded second shots. Curving left and drifting ever so slightly downhill, the 450-yard 13th is a beauty, its necklace of dunes easily carried on the second shot, but clusters of bunkers inter-mingled with low dunes defying us at the green.

And now, at last, we plunge into a tract of sandhills, tall and short ones, ridges and hillocks and hollows, rumpled fairways and hidden greens and long-legged rough (skylarks breed here, and twelve varieties of orchids flourish). The 14th, 220 yards, with only the flag itself in sight, demands a long forced carry over deep rough to a green on the far side of a swale and framed by dunes. Undeniably great, it calls to mind the 3rd at Sandwich.

The 432-yard 15th is the best hole at Harlech. Another long forced carry, this one from an elevated tee, must clear a phalanx of sandhills to gain an angled fairway flanked in the landing area by water ditches. Our second shot, semiblind, must follow the line of a narrow dune-framed valley to a smallish ledge green sequestered in a horseshoe of low sandhills. A great and heroic hole from start to finish, this one is routed over terrain so naturally perfect that no artificial hazards were needed.

If the 16th, 354 yards, is not great, it is certainly grand, and it offers us the rare treat of playing to the green on a par four with an iron. From the highest tee on the links—the only time a view of the sea presents itself—the drive is fired down into a joyously tumbling fairway lined by dunes. Seven small bunkers guard the long, narrow green, three of them out front, misleadingly far out front. But with a 7- or 8-iron in hand, we may dream of putting for a birdie.

The 17th is the last of the par fours and one of the finest, a 428-yarder. Sand awaits right and left to trap the off-line drive. Though the hole is straight, the green is slightly angled to the fairway, with sentinel sand on both sides. Real danger, however, is posed by a bold crossbunker twenty yards short of the green. Can we carry it? Into the breeze, maybe not. Still, as the joke has it, we didn't come 3,000 miles to lay up.

Now we bid farewell to the marvelous sandhills country— the marvelous *golfing* country—and turn to the anticlimactic home hole, a 201-yarder played over level ground to a green open across the front, well bunkered on the sides. It is not easy, but neither does it possess even a suggestion of sparkle. Perhaps one day Royal St. David's will find a way to build more golf holes in the duneland here that is yet untouched.

Midway between Harlech and Aberdovey are Bontddhu Hall Country House and Penmaenuchaf Hall. Bontddhu Hall was not as well maintained as we had expected, but this Victorian Gothic structure, strikingly set in fourteen acres high above the Mawddach estuary and with its creaking staircase, old oil paintings, beamed ceilings, and marble columns, does have distinction. With much the same views, Penmaenuchaf Hall, built in 1860, is in every sense—setting, architectural lines, gardens, public rooms, guest quarters, cuisine, service—a superior example of a country house hotel. Even a single night's stay here is to be remembered with affection.

All Courses Great and Small

A forty-minute drive south along the coast, through Barmouth and Tywyn, brings us to Aberdovey, which might appropriately be the spiritual home for golf writers, because it was here that Bernard Darwin grew to learn and love the game. In *The Golf Courses of the British Isles,* Darwin opens the chapter on Wales in forthright fashion: "There are several very excellent courses in Wales, but I am quite determined to put Aberdovey first—not that I make for it any claim that it is the best, not even on the strength of its alphabetical preeminence, but because it is the course my soul loves best of all the courses in the world. Every golfer has a course for which he feels such blind and unreasoning affection."

A grandson of the great naturalist Charles Darwin, Bernard came to Aberdovey first as a boy of twelve or thirteen, in the late 1880s. And over the years, which would see him twice gain the semifinals of the British Amateur and compete in the inaugural Walker Cup Match (1922), he also won the Aberdovey

Golf Club's stroke play championship seven times and its match-play handicap championship three times. In 1920 he reached the final of the handicap championship only to lose to a man of the cloth, ". . . to whom I had to give rather too many strokes. When he beat me on the 17th green my then-small son exclaimed passionnately, 'I shall pray for his damdedation!'"

Though he had studied law at Cambridge and had practiced as a solicitor for eight years, when the opportunity arose to earn his livelihood by writing about golf for *The Times* and *Country Life,* he seized it—and single-handedly transformed golf reporting from columnar names and numbers into literary journalism. His approach and style were highly personal, reflecting his conviction that golf is the most complex and wonderful of all games, and to immerse oneself in it must be, incomparably, the best thing a man can do. He was chosen president of Aberdovey in 1924, then again in 1944, the latter tenure ending only with his death in 1961.

The village of Aberdovey is shoehorned between the estuary of the Dovey River and the steep hills that mark the end of the Cambrian mountain range. We are fans of the tiny Maybank Hotel here: five guest rooms (on the small side), moderate tariffs, good food, sincere hospitality, and a commanding view of the world of the Dovey estuary, that enchanting watercolor of sailboats and white cottages, of salt marshes and sand dunes.

During the period 1910–1940, Harry Colt, James Braid, and Herbert Fowler took turns revising the links. The first nine measures only 2,919 yards, but into the prevailing brisk breezes off the sea, that 2,919 plays like 3,419, and the par of 34 more like 36. Happily, the reverse is true coming home, where the 3,520 yards feels like 3,200.

All Courses Great and Small

The golf holes are laid out over a long strip of all but treeless duneland characterized by irregular lies on hummocky ground. Sheep and cattle graze on this supremely natural links, where greens are usually fenced off by low-voltage electric wires. These putting surfaces are true and nicely paced, full of subtle burrows. Bunkering is moderate. But the long rough is a place to be shunned, whether it is framing the generous fairways or serving as shaggy surrounds for the greens and giving the links its almost primitive aspect that is so appealing.

If Aberdovey has its share of distractions—beachgoers parading back and forth, kite fliers atop the very highest dunes, children tumbling down the sandhills in great hilarity—it also has its share of good and testing golf holes. Most vivid in memory are the one-shotters. Cradled in the dunes and totally blind, the 173-yard 3rd is suspenseful, the hidden green somewhere on the far side of a sandy rise, in a deep hollow where bunkers and steep falloffs promise disaster for the misdirected shot. The 5th, nearly 200 yards from its elevated tee in the sandhills, and the 160-yard 9th, where a broad bunker appears to be sealing off the front of the green but, deceitfully, is a good fifteen paces short of it—both are also first-rate. Which brings us to the last of the short holes, the 149-yard 12th—and what a joy it is to arrive there! When we climb to the large plateau green atop the dunes, we gaze down upon the estuary, the beaches, the village, the dark green hills both near and distant, and the vast sweep of Cardigan Bay, that foam-flecked arm of the Irish Sea.

I particularly remember when Harriet and I first came to Aberdovey, in August of 1989. Our daughter, Megwin, then twenty-four, was with us. She relishes the game and can hit the ball. On the second day, we did not tee off till five o'clock that afternoon. Now, in the gloaming, the three of us approached the green on the 18th. Lights had begun to blink on in the hillside cottages, and what had been a long, lazy twilight was suddenly fast fading. The flagstick was a necessary guidepost as Meg and I struck our lag putts. Then, in moments, the round was over. We would be leaving Aberdovey in the morning, but not without regret. I am compelled to let Darwin have the last word about this magical place, a passage from a book of reminiscences called *Life Is Sweet, Brother:* "The spell is strong. Stand at sunset on the little promontory by the old croquet lawn at Pantlludw [his grandmother's home], deep in moss, with a long slope of treetops below you, looking down on the Dovey as it runs to the sea, and it is very strong indeed. I even wonder sometimes if it will ever catch me by the throat. I hardly think so, but it is a bewitching spot, the blood is in me, and I used once to play rather well at Aberdovey. So you never can tell."

CHAPTER SEVENTEEN

South Wales: One of the World's Great Golf Destinations

 LET IT NOT BE SAID that I neglected to outline the route for the last leg of this odyssey, which began up in Berwick-upon-Tweed sixteen chapters and 2,000 miles ago. The drive from Aberdovey down to Newport takes us south to Aberystwyth, east to Leominster, then south to Hereford and farther south on the A4642 to Coldra Woods, home of Celtic Manor Resort, just outside Newport.

Wales has no other golf venue even remotely like Celtic Manor, which will host the 2010 Ryder Cup Match. Indeed, there is little that can fairly be compared to it, if only from the standpoint of scale, anywhere in Britain and Ireland. On 1,400 acres of hills and valleys have been created three outstanding eighteens, a 72,000 square-foot clubhouse, a 400-room five-star hotel, a golf academy with twenty-eight bays and the latest computerized video equipment, and a health club that includes a truly sybaritic Roman-style heated indoor swimming pool, plus a

James W. Finegan

sauna, steam room, Jacuzzi, gym, aerobics studio, and beauty salon. Wales has come a long way from *How Green Was My Valley*.

The first two courses were designed by the late Robert Trent
Jones, who seized this opportunity to celebrate his Welsh heritage. The third course, which is where the Ryder Cup will be
played, was designed by Robert Trent Jones, Jr. In keeping with
the American look and feel of it all, the turfgrass—tees, fairways, greens—is an American bent.

The first of the three eighteens to open, in 1995, was Trent
Jones's Roman Road Course. The landscape—and very distant
seascapes—are knockouts, over the lovely Gwent countryside
of meadows and wooded valleys to the mountains in the north
and across the Bristol Channel to Somerset in the south. Par is
69. Playing from the white markers, 6,495 yards, calls for vigorous hitting (seven par fours ranging from 413 to 448 yards,
three of the one-shotters at about 200 yards). This is a hilly
course, hilly and exhilarating, with fanciful bunkering and fes-
tive greens, both characteristic of the patriarch's best work.

On a course studded with exacting holes, the 420-yard 10th
is among the finest. It plunges dramatically, then doglegs
sharply right over a stream to a raised, narrow, triple-tier green
defended by steep falloffs on three sides. Only a perfectly
struck iron will hit and hold this target.

Very nearly forty years ago, Trent Jones laid out a superb exec-
utive-length course at the Williamsburg Inn. Well, here at Celtic
Manor, in the twilight of his long and brilliant career, he did it
again. Called Coldra Woods, this 4,000-yard eighteen opened in
1996. Par is 59. The thirteen par threes, which range from 114 to
243 yards, are unfailingly first-rate. With its abundance of high
tees, natural ravines, complex greens, and demanding shots, Col-

dra Woods just may provide more pure pleasure than any other course in the world of this modest length.

In May of 1999, Wentwood Hills, laid out by the elder of Jones's two talented sons, was unveiled. A year later it became the site for the Wales Open, a European Tour event. And in 2001 it was chosen over Gleneagles, Turnberry, Carnoustie, and Loch Lomond for the 2010 Ryder Cup. Routed over 210 acres, this is very big golf—7,403 yards, par 72, from the tips, broad fairways, generous greens, large water hazards, bold elevation changes, vast panoramas. You will probably choose to play it at 6,660 yards.

A four-hole stretch, 5 through 8, is especially memorable. In fact, if you can complete it with one ball, you will leave the 8th green in a highly self-congratulatory mood. Water is the peril that must be faced again and again and again—on eight consecutive swings, believe it or not. It is tight on the right and the left on the par-five 5th. It is tight on the left for the drive on the par-four 6th, followed by a 175-yard second shot over a lagoon to gain the green. On the 150-yard 7th, another lagoon must be carried to reach the putting surface. And on the two-shotter 8th, water skirts the right side most of the way. We stumble toward the 9th tee with a case of water on the brain. Still, it must be conceded that water then comes into play on only two of the last ten holes of this mighty and very beautiful championship course.

The luxurious five-star hotel has a total of 400 rooms and suites, many with balconies. One restaurant offers "Celtic Fusion Cuisine." Whatever that means, it's terrific.

Not half an hour from Celtic Manor is St. Pierre Hotel, Golf & Country Club, in Chepstow. It, too, is a golf resort, though on a lesser scale. Here there are two eighteens, plus subsidiary amusements ranging from billiards to lawn bowling and including squash and tennis courts, a hotel headquartered in a handsome gray stone manor house dating to the sixteenth century, and in the middle of the complex, a functioning parish church, St. Pierre, that goes back to Norman times.

The resort goes back only to 1960. The Old Course, designed by Ken Cotton during a two-hour stroll through the frost-covered deer park on a winter's morning in 1961, opened in 1962. It has been the scene of numerous amateur (Curtis Cup in 1980) and professional events, including the Dunlop Masters and the Epson Grand Prix. Among the winners here were Tony Jacklin, Bernhard Langer, Greg Norman (he drove the 362-yard 10th with a 3-wood en route to victory in 1982), Seve Ballesteros, Ian Woosnam, and Jose Maria Olazabal.

We play this rolling par 71 at 6,492 yards. Trees give the layout its bite, often dictating the line of play, a circumstance that is proclaimed on the 564-yard opening hole. Here, grand old hardwoods edging out over the fairway on the right prompt us to head left, only to find trees encroaching from that side and all but blocking the path to the green. On at least a dozen holes, it is trees that require us to hit the ball dead straight or, failing that, draw it or fade it. Curiously, however, the most famous hole on the course is one that has no trees, the 230-yard 18th. From a high tee we play across a shallow valley containing a lake to a closely bunkered shelf green on the opposite slope. It is a tremendous finishing hole.

The second eighteen, called the Mathern Course, opened in 1975. At 5,762 yards, par 68, it is considerably shorter than the Old. But thanks to a meandering stream, which seems to pop up every time we turn around, there is no shortage of challenge. And the distant views of the graceful new bridge spanning the Severn River are captivating.

The hotel has more than a hundred accommodations, most of them in lodges. Among the amenities are a heated indoor pool and a health and beauty salon.

Now we head to the sea and with immense pleasure embrace Royal Porthcawl, by common consent the premier golf club of Wales, its course viewed by many as the very best in the principality (you'll meet my selection at the end of this chapter). Founded in 1891, the club is situated on the Bristol Channel fifteen miles west of Cardiff and twenty miles east of Swansea. Numerous professional events have been held here, including the 1961 Dunlop Masters, won by Peter Thomson. Porthcawl is alone among Welsh clubs in having hosted the British Amateur, which has been contested here five times, with Americans (Dick Chapman in 1951, Dick Siderowf in 1973) carrying the cup back across the Atlantic twice.

Ramsey Hunter, a greenkeeper, laid out eighteen holes here in 1895. Over the next fifty years, Harry Colt, Tom Simpson, Fred G. Hawtree, J. H. Taylor, Ken Cotton, and Donald Steel all took turns remodeling or adding holes. Despite its seaside setting, Porthcawl cannot, strictly speaking, be called a links since it is not routed over land recovered from the sea. The ground does not undulate. Nevertheless, with its sand-based turf, it has much the feel and playability of a links. There is plenty of gorse and heather, not to mention carnivorous bunkers (nearly a hundred) and thick rough. Blind shots are no rarity. Neither are sea views: The water is in sight on every hole. The course measures 6,400 yards from the whites. Par is 72.

James W. Finegan

With neither trees nor sandhills to blunt its impact, wind is a powerful force here. (One night in 1990 the pro shop was blown off its foundation and wound up in smithereens all over the car park!) And because the routing plan is imaginative, the holes move toward every point of the compass and our blustery battle is a constantly shifting one.

I played here in 1993 and 1997, on both occasions with John Sanders, club captain in 1994. He looked to be about sixty when I met him. Partly balding and of medium height, he played off 12 and used his husky build to hit for distance. A successful real estate salesman, he was a congenial companion, full of stories about the club. "I think you'll enjoy reading the club history," he said. "It has some good stuff. One member, a Dr. J. B. Siegirt, who was neither an officer nor a leading player, is named. Why? He invented pink gin!"

The round at Porthcawl starts with three par fours running close beside the beach and into the prevailing wind, the opener mild (326 yards), the second both astringent and great (416 yards, with a stiff forced carry over rough country from the tee), and the 3rd a charmer (378 yards, semiblind uphill second shot). Next comes the first of the one-shotters, a long iron gently falling to a large green defended by half a dozen cruel pits, followed by a 476-yard par five, which climbs abruptly to a steeply sloping troughlike green with a boundary at the left.

The next six or seven holes offer more of this varied and enormously satisfying golf. On the 13th, 413 yards, we drive out to sea. The panorama from the tee shot landing area is sublime: all around us golfers heading in every conceivable direction; beyond the green that lies far below, waves breaking on the rocky foreshore as a backdrop to our long iron; the splendor of

252

Swansea Bay and the dark outline of the distant Devon and Somerset coasts completing this breathtaking canvas.

After the short, sand-guarded 14th comes a pair of 420-yarders, similar and equally strong but running in opposite directions: downhill drives to constricted landing areas, the long second shots rising to greens where only the flag is visible. The round concludes with a par five and a par four, both of which, thanks to Tiger Woods, are now firmly entrenched in club lore.

Tiger headed the American squad when the 1995 Walker Cup Match was played here, and John Sanders was eager to tell me a couple of Tiger stories in 1997. The 511-yard 17th moves gently uphill at the start, then doglegs left toward the green on rather level ground. "I was following Tiger on Thursday during a practice round," John said as we arrived at the tee of the three-shotter. "He smashed one of those colossal drives of his here, and when we finally got out to the ball it had traveled 360 yards. Three hundred and sixty yards! Which left him 150 yards. So he took out his pitching wedge and hit it dead straight and exactly 150 yards, into the hole for a 2, a double eagle. I know it was the best-played hole I will ever see."

The downhill 18th, however, turned out to be an entirely different kettle of fish. It measured 413 yards for the Match. The strand is not many paces behind the tri-level green and the club-house is not many paces left of it. "Tiger was playing Gary Wolstenholme in the final match of the first day," John said, "and they were level as they teed off here. The U.S. was down by a point. So if Tiger could win the hole, the day would end in a tie. But he made a hash of it. First he pulled his drive well into the rough, then he pull-hooked an 8-iron up against the foundation of the clubhouse, which is out of bounds. That settled that, and we wound up leading at the end of the first day, 7 to 5." And winning the Cup, 14 to 10, at the end of the second day.

A further word about the clubhouse, which is as irresistible as the golf holes. An old, low, dark-stained wooden structure, it was built more than a century ago in London, to house laborers at Queen Victoria's Diamond Jubilee Exhibition. After the great event, it was dismantled and hauled to Porthcawl, where it was reassembled, a pavilion on the sands with an airy seaside charm. Stretches of wood decking emphasize the clubhouse's kinship with the beach and the sometimes cataclysmic waves. Here at Porthcawl, where the Atlantic Ocean clashes with the Bristol Channel, there is a forty-foot tide, one of the highest tides in the world.

It is not every day that the traveling golfer has an opportunity to spend the night at one of the world's great clubs unaccompanied by a member. The dormy house at Royal Porthcawl can accommodate a total of twelve, women as well as men, in six single and three twin-bedded rooms, each with private bath. At the end of a day of great golf, you can enjoy a tasty dinner in the clubhouse and a good night's sleep by the sea.

Just a couple of miles down the road is Pyle & Kenfig Golf Club. The course was laid out by Harry Colt and Hugh Alison in 1922 and extensively revised by Philip Mackenzie Ross in 1951. P&K, as it is known, measures 6,122 yards from the regular tees; par is 71. This course has a split personality. A public road runs through the links, separating the front nine, on the road's inland side, from the back nine on its seaward side. The first nine is open, plain, fully exposed to the wind. And if it has none of the grandeur of the second nine, it is still stimulating, full of ticklish little dips and knobs, not to mention quirky bounces and unsettling lies.

The 10th is a good medium-length two shotter. And now we tackle a five-hole stretch of the most magnificent seaside golf—as exhilarating and demanding as comparable stretches at, say, Brancaster or Sandwich. The 500-yard 11th runs gently downhill as it edges left, then gently uphill over uneven ground to a green exquisitely sited in the dunes. If it is not a great hole, it is surely a perfect one. The next hole *is* great—particularly when played at its full 186 yards—carrying us into the heart of the giant sandhills as we aim out to sea and into the prevailing wind, the big, sloping green cocked up tauntingly in the dunes, bunkers short, left, and right.

Thirteen and 14 are two more great holes, both par fours, both commencing on platforms high in the sandhills, both with stunning sea views, each bending vigorously right through a dune-framed valley to a green beckoning from a dell of dunes. On the 416-yard 14th, there is a chance to shorten the second shot by unleashing a death-or-glory drive over the corner of the dogleg, where the thick marram grass that mantles the mounds renders the sliced tee shot unfindable or, perhaps worse, unhittable.

On the last hole of this remarkable quintet, another high tee is the launching pad, this time for a 200-yard shot to a green well below, where sand defending the entrance and gorse behind the putting surface give us plenty to ponder.

As its name suggests, Southerndown is a downlands course. In fact, it may be the most notable example of the category. A downs—in this instance, Ogmore Downs—can best be thought of as an expanse of open, high, grassy land, generally treeless and rolling. The turf is more cushiony than on a links and provides less run on the ball. The terrain may or may not undulate. At Southerndown it emphatically does. Here, too, high on this exposed headland roughly halfway between Cardiff and Swansea, we are constantly warring with the wind, which teams with the gorse and bracken framing the fairways and the sand patrolling the greens for a sturdy defense of the strict par of 70. At 6,615 yards, Southerndown is almost too severe, and at 6,105 yards it is still as much as many of us can handle.

Dating to 1905, when the club was founded, the course is the cumulative handiwork of Willie Fernie, Willie Park, Jr., Herbert Fowler, and Harry Colt. My introduction to it took place in May of 1993 on an uncomfortably cool day marked by an off-and-on drizzle and a light breeze. I went out with two members, Clive, a fifty-year-old with a 16 handicap, and Richard, a twenty-year-old with a 3. The younger man—six feet three inches, 210 pounds, fit and powerful, blond, still a hint of baby fat on his face—confided to me that he played every day, for money if at all possible. A long but sometimes wild hitter, he had a very deft short game. He inveigled Clive into an eighteen-hole match for £10—no nassaus—and gave him three quarters of the difference in their handicaps, which worked out to ten strokes.

The early going at Southerndown is fierce. The 373-yard opener, climbing some seventy feet and into the prevailing wind, played fully 430 yards that day. Next comes one of the great holes in Wales, a rolling 448-yard par four, also against the wind, which will require three shots for most of us, to say nothing of some luck if we are to avoid a diabolical scattering of bunkers in the fairway forty to ninety yards short of the green. Mercifully, the breeze is our ally on the 412-yard 3rd: blind drive, semiblind second, uphill from tee to green. The muscular Richard handled the three holes with aplomb. Clive, abruptly 2 down, struggled. So did I.

The rest of the nine is somewhat more manageable, yet every bit as stimulating. Included are a shortish par five that, despite the climb, is reachable in two by the big hitter (Richard did it, then two-putted for birdie), and a couple of top-class one-shotters, the medium-iron 5th across a valley to a plateau green, and the long 7th, 231 yards downhill.

It is at the turn that we reach the highest point of the course, with the 10th tee 300 feet above the sea, providing glorious views to Newton Bay, the Gower Peninsula, and Porthcawl, and across the Bristol Channel to the Somerset and Devon coasts, where we can envision Burnham & Berrow, Westward Ho!, and Saunton awaiting our return. Two very demanding par fours, both lightly uphill, follow the par-three 10th, and on the green of the 12th the £10 match ended. Here Richard coaxed in a curling twenty-four-footer for birdie, plucked his ball out of the cup, and without breaking stride, reached over in a smugly peremptory fashion to shake Clive's hand. But Clive, not believing he had lost the match, instinctively backed away, insisting that he was six down with six holes to play.

"Not so," said the younger man. "You were four down at the turn and I just won 10, 11, and 12." There was no further protestation and, in fact there was no further conversation between the two of them.

The three-hole finish at Southerndown is nearly as intimidating as the three-hole start. The long second shot on the uphill 16th, 412 yards, seems ineluctably drawn to the bunker at the right front of the green, and the drive on the 410-yard 17th must be held up well to the right in order to avoid running down into the left-hand rough. The 18th, 437 yards, is splendid. We drive from an elevated tee to a bi-level fairway (two parallel stretches separated by a band of rough) that sweeps down to the largest green on the course, the last in an unbroken skein, beginning on the 1st, of marvelously contoured and individualistic putting surfaces. We have at last come down from the heights, though nowhere near to sea level. It is a great and testing finale. But then, these two adjectives can fairly be applied to the entire course.

There are two country-house hotels in southeastern Wales that I can recommend: Egerton Grey, dating from the seventeenth century, sits in seven acres of gardens in a secluded valley ten miles from Cardiff. Expect antiques, Edwardian bathrooms, open fireplaces, old paintings. Not all ten guest rooms are spacious. Dinner by candlelight in the mahogany-paneled dining room is a treat. In Coychurch and high on a hillside in seventeen wooded acres is Coed-y-Mwstwr ("Whispering Trees"), a Victorian manor with twenty-three guest rooms (decor tasteful but not distinctive). Count on solid comfort, a hospitable staff, and top-notch cuisine in the Eliot Room (high ceiling, oak paneling, candlelight). Worth noting: Both hotels often host wedding receptions on weekends.

Realistically, you can take in only a small fraction of the sightseeing opportunities in South Wales. But certainly compact Cardiff is not to be ignored: the astonishing castle, every square foot of its interior covered with fanciful decorations; the adjacent Roman wall with its carvings; the National Museum (notable collection of modern European art); and Bute Park and the Sophia Gardens, both on the river Taff.

All Courses Great and Small

We head west on the M4 now to go about twenty-five miles out to Pembrey, near Burry Port, on Carmarthenshire Bay, where Ashburnham Golf Club, founded in 1894, is located. The Welsh Amateur has been held here numerous times over the years, to say nothing of important professional tournaments such as the British PGA. Dai Rees, Bernard Gallacher, and Sam Torrance all won here.

The course today is the result of revisions by J. H. Taylor, Fred G. Hawtree, and Ken Cotton, himself a member of the club. You'll probably choose to play this gently rolling links, with its low dunes, at either 6,627 or 6,212 yards. Par is 72. A boundary threatens the sliced shot on five of the first seven holes. Bunkering is moderate, but rough is penal. The narrow, sand-based fairways undulate mildly, producing almost no capricious bounces. Since the holes are clearly defined, we know what is required of us at all times on this eminently fair course.

I played here in 1993 with David Rees, who would become captain of the club in 1994, its centenary year. A sixty-five-year-old retired schoolmaster, he is less than average height but wiry and muscular. He claimed a handicap of 8, then shot 76, four over par, from markers adding up to more than 6,600 yards. He used to be a 2 or 3 and he won the club championship once.

"I was a rugby player," he said. "Never struck a golf ball. Then when I was about thirty I tried this game. Loved it right off. My wife took up golf much later than I did, and she actually plays more than I do. I'd come home from school in the late afternoon to find a note on the fridge: 'Dinner in oven. Gone to golf club.'" He laughed warmly at the thought of it.

The round begins at Ashburnham with a downhill 188-yarder, out of bounds unnervingly close to the right side of the green. I knocked a solid 5-wood shot about thirty-five feet from the hole and felt quite pleased with myself. David now proceeded to plant his 5-wood twelve inches past the cup, almost grazing the lip. "I've never holed in one here," he said.

"But?" I asked invitingly.

"But," he laughed, "I have made six aces, three on the 12th, three on the 16th. That ought to be enough for anybody."

The daunting 2nd, 440 yards and into the prevailing wind, delivers us to the long stretch of holes, 3 through 16, nearer the sea and with true linksland character. I remember several of them with particular pleasure: the 173-yard 6th, a great hole, played to a kidney-shaped green elevated in the dunes and defended by a pot bunker on the left and a steep falloff on the right; the fine 410-yard 9th, which calls for a solidly struck iron over a mound guarding the small plateau green; and the 509-yard 14th, where the second shot, blind over a high ridge, must be perfectly positioned in order to set up the pitch to a green fetchingly sited in a dell of dunes.

As we climbed the steep slope of the final fairway, David said, "The most extraordinary shot ever hit at Ashburnham was hit on this hole. It happened in the Home Internationals [an annual event among teams of the best amateurs from England, Scotland, Wales, and Ireland]. England's John Davis, with a powerful wind at his back—still, the hole measured 377 yards—hit a drive that landed on the clubhouse roof and caromed off it to finish pin high just left of the green." He pointed to the spot. I looked back down the long hill to the tee, then up at the clubhouse roof, and then over at the spot where the titanic drive had come to rest. It could not have been done, but it had been done, and by an amateur.

All Courses Great and Small

After the game, as we were enjoying a drink and the sea view, David said with pride, "Ashburnham is the most Welsh of all the golf clubs in South Wales. Many of our members as a matter of course speak Welsh here, not English." With that we both went silent for a moment, and sure enough, at the very next table the native tongue held sway.

About three-quarters of an hour due west of Ashburnham, on the opposite side of Carmarthen Bay, lies Tenby Golf Club, founded in 1888. The old reliables Braid and Ken Cotton, plus one Ernest Fitchett, fashioned this wonderful links, which has it all: worthy holes routed cleverly through the sandhills, imaginatively contoured greens (some members believe, without hard evidence, that Alister Mackenzie shaped several of them) sited on teasing plateaus or in dune-ringed dells; antic fairways that toss and tumble; a goodly share of blind shots and hidden bunkers; an old railway line separating three holes from the rest of the course; a crisscross circumstance (the drive on 14 is fired squarely over the 15th green); and intoxicating views of Carmarthen Bay.

Understand, Tenby is not a great course. There are three holes—the short 6th and the par-four 7th and 15th—that are pedestrian. And the fairways often call for preferred lies. But so much here is rewarding and grand that we overlook the shortcomings.

The course at its longest measures only 6,232 yards. But since par is 69, our work is cut out for us. And if there were any doubt of it, the first four holes, all two-shotters, resolve it. The 1st, 2nd, and 4th measure 463, 429, and 415 yards, respectively. They are superb—the vigorously rippling fairways, the perfectly placed greens—and, played into the prevailing wind, they are dauntingly long. Less than a week before we made our first visit to Tenby, in mid-May of 1993, the club championship was held. Bob Storey, then club captain, said to me, "The weather was so vile—a cold rain driven along on winds of thirty miles an hour—that of the seventy-three who started only twenty-four finished. One fellow, who had the honor on the 4th, ran up a 10 on the hole but still had the honor on the 5th!"

The 3rd hole, at 382 yards and, for a welcome change, with the wind at our back, should give us a break. Instead, it is the #1 stroke hole, doglegging softly right through the dunes. The landing area for the drive seems generous enough, but it is actually quite confined if we are to have a level stance, a clear line of sight, and a decent angle of approach. The second shot is played to a plateau green that slopes sharply from back to front and is defended at the left by a small pot bunker and at the right by a deep hollow. This is a great and classic links hole, and you will sense it at once.

Among the last half-dozen holes are a couple of legitimate birdie chances (the short par-four 13th and the short par-five 14th), together with the falling 174-yard 17th (enthralling view of the links, the bay, and Caldey Island), and the unique 18th. Immediately beneath the high tee on this 419-yarder sits Black Rock Cottage. Our drive must clear the roof and find the narrow fairway with a boundary at the left and bunkers at the right. The cottage has long been a source of contention between its owners and the club. Once, a topped drive just missed the lady of the house as she puttered in her garden. When her husband forcefully protested, the captain's response was a model of political incorrectness: "She shouldn't have been there in the first place."

All Courses Great and Small

In five acres of gardens and woodlands at the far end of the course is Pennally Abbey. The lounge, dining room, and conservatory of this small hotel all look out to the links, the sea, and distant Tenby itself. So do Rooms 5, 6, 7, and 8. This view is enchanting, and never more so than in the lingering twilight of spring and summer, with the shadows slowly stealing over the wrinkled countenance of the old links, and the lights winking on in Tenby. The guest rooms, good-sized, are furnished with antiques and chintzes. (Spouses who find a traditional double bed too confining should specify twin beds.) The very good cooking is contemporary and creative.

The principal attraction here in the western part of South Wales is the town of Tenby, perched on a promontory high above the sea. It is a beguiling melange of medieval town walls, narrow cobblestone passages, broad beaches, and boats bobbing at anchor in the harbor. Try also to find time for a visit to St. Davids, the smallest cathedral city in Britain; Pembroke Castle, where the panoramas from the wall-walks are inspiring; and the Dylan Thomas Boathouse Museum, in quaint Laugharne, where the poet wrote *Under Milk Wood*.

Only two or three times in a lifelong pursuit of the best golf this world has to offer will an unknown course surface that is so superlative it would compel us not simply to cross an ocean but, if necessary, to circumnavigate the globe. Such a course is Pennard.

Golf has been played here, on the heights above Three Cliffs Bay, since 1896, but the Pennard Golf Club was not formed until 1908. James Braid was hired to design the course. Judging some holes to be too difficult, the Committee asked Braid to alter his plan. The Scot refused, declaring, "The links were laid out to the best advantage and the ground was of such an excellent nature that I am confident that at Pennard you have a golf course to rank with the best in the kingdom." Nonetheless, in years to come Braid himself and then Ken Cotton did effect certain revisions.

On my first visit to Pennard, in May of 1993, I went around with Peter Robbins, sixty-two years old and a 12-handicapper. When he asked me what courses I'd played in South Wales, I mentioned Ashburnham and my round with David Rees.

"What a remarkable coincidence," Peter said. "He and I were on the faculty at the same school. I taught English. It's a miracle that when we retired we were still friends." Now he was smiling.

"Why do you say that?"

"Because it was he who persuaded me to give up rugby, shooting, fishing, gardening, and heaven knows what all for this obsession with golf!"

In the course of the round, Peter introduced me as an American golf writer to perhaps half a dozen members, including, on the 14th tee, a player who said, "I just last night finished reading a wonderful book by an American colleague of yours, that fellow who caddied on the European Tour for a while, then played in Scotland."

"To the Linksland," I said. "Michael Bamberger. He's a good friend of mine."

"I hated to see it end," he said.

"Perhaps you noticed the references to me," I suggested. "Michael Bamberger mentioned me in connection with both Cruden Bay and Machrihanish in his book. I was the one who told him about those courses."

"Ah, yes," he said, obligingly but unconvincingly. "I'll have to go back and check those chapters when I get home." Then, not sure what else might be expected of him in this exchange, he added brightly, "I do hope you'll tell him about Pennard. Maybe he'll want to visit us one day and write about the course."

I'm pleased to report that when I got back to Pennard four years later, in 1997, no such deflating encounter took place. I did meet Vicky Thomas. The nine-time Welsh Women's Amateur champion and six-time Curtis Cupper was playing in some kind of an interclub match and, as she confided to me, "giving plenty of strokes." I suppose I should not have been surprised to find the internationalist competing in an event of such modest consequence, because Pennard is a very egalitarian club. This was a Monday, a Bank Holiday as it happened. That morning, at ten o'clock, a shotgun start had kicked off a mixed scramble. That afternoon, at three o'clock, a tea dance commenced, complete with live music. You've got to love this club.

In a very real sense, Pennard may be the most unusual of the world's greatest courses. The holes are routed over classic linksland—sand-based, tumbling, full of hummocks and hillocks and hollows, pocked with dunes large and small, blessed with all manner of plateaus and dells that make ideal green sites. In sum, precisely what we might dream of beside the shore. But this spirited terrain is not beside the shore—it is 200 feet *above* it! And so Pennard is called "The Links in the Sky."

Gorse and heather are encountered on some holes. There are daisies in the fairways from time to time, bluebells and buttercups in the long rough. Forced carries are uncommon. Blind shots are not uncommon: Depending on the length of your drive, you may not be able to see where you are going—on it or on the second shot—half a dozen times. Earth was not moved to smooth off the rough edges of this masterpiece and make the going easier.

The course has a total of only forty bunkers. It is the topography itself that provides the first line of defense on this admirably natural links. Bear in mind that this is a hilly tract, not merely rolling but shot through with dramatic elevation changes. Then add to this the eccentric cant and camber of many fairways, not to mention the concealed falloffs and hollows at greenside. Awkward lies are part of the order of things at Pennard, as attested to by a local joke: "How to confound a Pennard player? Give him a perfectly flat lie."

The ponies are only a minor distraction. Owned by a local farmer who has grazing rights on the links and who eventually sells them for horsemeat, they roam at will—well, almost at will. Low electric wires surround the greens to ward the animals off. The greens, it should be noted, are excellent: consistently smooth and fast, sometimes audaciously sloped and contoured, as on 7 and 16.

This par-71 course is short, only 6,265 yards from the tips. Length notwithstanding, the holes are wonderful, from 1 through 18. There is not a weak or prosaic hole on the course, and at least eight are great. From the outset, the game is on. The 1st hole is a 447-yard par four. An elevated and fully exposed tee is our launching pad for a drive across a valley to a facing slope. The uphill second shot is played over a soft rise to a hidden punchbowl green.

The delightful 2nd, 145 yards, offers a gently falling and

semiblind shot to a green cloistered in the dunes—we see only the flag. And the 3rd just may be a perfect two-shotter of medium length: 371 yards, the drive into a slightly rising and dune-framed fairway, where the wind will probably be in our face, a broad green awaiting with a single bunker at three of the four corners.

The 4th is a fine par five doglegging left over cranky ground, and the 5th is a 171-yarder from a pulpit tee down to a triple-tier plateau green with steep falloffs all around. Both are historic golf holes, at least in the annals of Welsh jurisprudence. Some seven or eight years ago, the greens on both holes had to be shifted well to the left. The holes had run very close to a boundary, beyond which were cottage gardens. Occasionally a pushed or sliced shot would plunk into the petunias. One cottage owner took the club to court in order to prevent further incursions. Determined to understand at firsthand the grounds for the suit, the Welsh High Court actually sat here, in session on the spot at Pennard. Having weighed the evidence, the justices ruled in favor of the plaintiff and the club was forced to move the two greens.

Now comes one of the best and most stimulating stretches of four consecutive two-shotters in my experience. The 6th, 400 yards, runs from an elevated tee across a valley to a fairway (landing area bunkered right and left) that turns easily left on the opposite slope and climbs steeply to a green corseted by dunes. Playing into or across the prevailing wind this is a great hole, offering, in the bargain, our first view of the beach and the cliffs and the Pennard Pill River snaking its way to the sea far below us. The 7th, 351 yards, heads out to sea from yet another high tee. The line of flight between the sparse ruins of a

James W. Finegan

thirteenth-century church on the left and the more imposing ruins of twelfth-century Pennard Castle on the right presents one of the unforgettable prospects in golf, our drive winging away over a deep chasm to come to rest in a turbulent patch of fairway, with the Bristol Channel shimmering pewter in the distance. The rough country on both sides of the fairway is inhumane, and the green, concealed above us in a cluster of sandhills, slopes sharply away from the approach to conclude this adventure.

The 8th, 357 yards, doubles back, tending to rise where the 7th falls. It is splendid, testing, and less daunting than its predecessor. It is called "The Church," and every few years the local vicar will come out to these evocative remnants on a Sunday to hold Evensong here, during which the members are asked to refrain from playing 7 and 8. Also, if you should hit into the ruined church, itself an integral part of the course, you are requested not to swear.

The 9th, a magnificent 441-yarder, turns abruptly left—five bunkers in the crook of the dogleg—then climbs gently to a sand-free green tucked left. It brings the first nine to a triumphant close.

The second nine is routed over more severe terrain, with the valleys deeper and the walking tougher. Three holes are superb: the 180-yard 11th, knob to knob across a deep valley; the 368-yard 14th, with its dune-encased landing area and its second shot that must carry a sharp bank rising immediately in front of the putting surface; and the 400-yard 18th, where the drive from a high tee must find a landing area constricted by a gorse-covered slope on the right and heather on the much lower ground to the left. One hole is merely marvelous: the

12th, just under 300 yards, with a blind short pitch—devilish, ticklish—to a narrow green with a steep drop on the right. One hole is classic: the 165-yard 15th, gently rising to a tri-level green in the sandhills. And four holes are great: the 13th, 196 yards, another of those delectable knob-to-knob shots, this one to a plateau green with a high mound at the left and an acute falloff right ending in a sandpit; and the three par fives, all short and any one of which would be welcome on any seaside course, however eminent. The 492-yard 10th, menaced by gorse right and left, plunges from a high tee to the valley floor, edging left along the way, then climbs at least as vertically to a shelf green, this one with three bunkers in front, two in back. The 16th, 493 yards, begins high in the dunes—a heartstopping panorama of cliffs and beach and Channel—the drive falling to a typically heaving Pennard fairway. Following a blind second shot over a ridge, the approach rises steeply to a clifftop green that slopes perilously down from back to front, sending many a lag from above the hole, when the greens are skittish, down into the fairway. And the 17th is a 488-yarder that may well find us cracking our drive over a herd of ponies fifty or sixty yards in front of the tee (a favorite grazing spot). We must guard against the fairway's sloping to the right in the landing area—very rough country down there. The hole now bends markedly left as it climbs steadily up a narrowing draw to finish at a green framed by grassy mounds. The strategic considerations—for instance, how much of the dogleg's angle dare we cut off on a gambling second shot that is blind and must carry even rougher country?—are very real. The possibility of a 4 is seductive. But the probability of 6 if we are too greedy cannot be ignored.

James W. Finegan

The shot values at Pennard are consistently of the highest order. Sometimes power—especially in the face of the stiff breezes that rake this aerie—is a requisite. More often, however, the need is for finesse on the uneven terrain, with its uncertain bounces. Always is keen judgment called for—what is doable, what is not? Shotmaking options pop up again and again—should the shot be played all the way through the air or much of the way on the ground?

I see no reason to back away from an unflinching conclusion: Pennard is a very great course, in my experience one of the twenty greatest in the world. How many well-informed American golfers are aware of this? Very few indeed. But it is true. And if this is the least heralded great course, it is also the least visited. Even the Welsh rarely bother. Admittedly, the fairway turf may be a notch or two below standard. The occasional blind shot may nag. The design can strike us a couple of times as too sporty, even a shade unfair. The demands on our swing may be strict. The hills and the winds may beleaguer us. But this is a golf course, towering above the sea, that embodies, hole after hole and to the highest degree, the pleasurable excitement that is the one indispensable ingredient of truly satisfying golf. Equally important, it consistently calls for solid swinging and sound thinking. And it does so in a setting of rare beauty and splendor. I would as soon play Pennard as any course in the world.

But then, looking back over this long journey you and I have made together, might I not say the same of such shrines as Royal St. George's and Royal Birkdale, of Sunningdale Old and Rye and Wentworth West, to say nothing of such lesser-known treasures as St. Enodoc and Alwoodley, Silloth-on-Solway and

All Courses Great and Small

Southerndown and The Addington? Yes, I believe I would. For sheer joy in the game—and excellence in the test—the outstanding courses of England and Wales rival the outstanding and better-known courses of Scotland and Ireland.

Go and be surprised and be delighted.

Golf Clubs, Golf Courses

In telephoning England or Wales, the country code is 44.

ABERDOVEY GOLF CLUB
Aberdovey LL35 ORT
North Wales
Tel: 01654 767493
Fax: 01654 767027

THE ADDINGTON
GOLF CLUB
205 Shirley Church Road
Croydon CRO 5AB
England
Tel: 01817 771055
No Fax

ALWOODLEY GOLF CLUB
Alwoodley, Leeds
West Yorkshire LS17 8SA
England
Tel: 01132 681680
Fax: 01132 939458

ASHBURNHAM GOLF CLUB
Burry Port SA16 OHN
South Wales
Tel: 01554 833846
Fax: 01554 832269

BARTON-ON-SEA GOLF CLUB
New Milton
Hampshire BH25 5PP
England
Tel: 01425 611210
Fax: 01425 621457

BEAU DESERT GOLF CLUB
Hazel Slade, Cannock
Staffordshire WS12 5PJ
England
Tel: 01543 422626
Fax: 01543 451137

THE BELFRY
Wishaw
Warwickshire B76 9PR
England
Tel: 01675 470301
Fax: 01675 470256

BERKSHIRE GOLF CLUB
Ascot
Berkshire SL5 8AY
England
Tel: 01344 621496
Fax: 01344 623328

BERWICK-UPON-TWEED
GOLF CLUB
Berwick-upon-Tweed,
Goswick
Northumberland YD15 2RW
England
Tel: 01289 387256
Fax: 01289 387334

BROKENHURST MANOR
GOLF CLUB
Brockenhurst
Hampshire SO42 7SG
England
Tel: 01590 623092
Fax: 01590 624140

BUCKINGHAMSHIRE
GOLF CLUB
Denham
Buckinghamshire UB9 5BG
England
Tel: 01895 835777
Fax: 01895 835210

BUDE AND NORTH CORNWALL
GOLF CLUB
Bude
North Cornwall EX23 8DA
England
Tel: 01288 352006
Fax: 01288 356855

BURNHAM & BERROW
GOLF CLUB
Burnham-on-Sea
Somerset TA8 2PE
England
Tel: 01278 785760
Fax: 01278 795440

CELTIC MANOR RESORT
Coldra Woods
Newport NP6 2YA
South Wales
Tel: 01633 413000
Fax: 01633 412910

CHART HILLS GOLF CLUB
Biddenden
Kent TN27 8JX
England
Tel: 01580 292222
Fax: 01580 292233

CONWY GOLF CLUB
Morfa LL32 8ER
North Wales
Tel: 01492 592423
Fax: 01492 593363

COOMBE HILL GOLF CLUB
Kingston Hill
Surrey KT2 TDF
England
Tel: 01819 422284
Fax: 01819 495815

All Courses Great and Small

East Sussex National
Golf Club
Little Horsted
Uckfield
East Sussex TN22 5ES
England
Tel: 01825 880088
Fax: 01825 880066

Formby Golf Club
Formby
Merseyside L37 1LQ
England
Tel: 01704 872164
Fax: 01704 833028

Ganton Golf Club
Ganton
North Yorkshire YO12 4PA
England
Tel: 01944 710329
Fax: 01944 710922

Gog Magog Golf Club
Shelford Bottom,
Cambridge
Cambridgeshire CB2 4AB
England
Tel: 01223 247626
Fax: 01223 414990

Hayling Golf Club
Hayling Island
Hampshire PO11 OBX
England
Tel: 02392 464446
Fax: same as phone

Hillside Golf Club
Southport
Merseyside PR8 2LU
England
Tel: 01704 567169
Fax: 01704 563192

Hindhead Golf Club
Hindhead
Surrey GU26 6HX
England
Tel: 01428 604614
Fax: 01428 608508

Holyhead Golf Club
Trearddur Bay LL65 2YG
North Wales
Tel: 01407 763279
Fax: same as phone

Hunstanton Golf Club
Old Hunstanton
Norfolk PE36 6JQ
England
Tel: 01485 532811
Fax: 01485 532319

James W. Finegan

HUNTERCOMBE GOLF CLUB
Nuffield
Oxfordshire RG9 5SL
England
Tel: 01491 641207
Fax: 01491 642060

ILFRACOMBE GOLF CLUB
Ilfracombe, Hele Bay
Devon EX34 9RT
England
Tel: 01271 862176
Fax: 01271 867731

LA MOYE GOLF CLUB
La Moye JE3 8GQ
Jersey
Channel Islands
Tel: 01534 743401
Fax: 01534 747289

LINDRICK GOLF CLUB
Lindrick
Nottinghamshire S81 8BH
England
Tel: 01909 475282
Fax: 01909 488685

LITTLE ASTON GOLF CLUB
Streetly, Sutton Coldfield
West Midlands B74 3AN
England
Tel: 01213 532942
Fax: 01213 808387

LITTLESTONE GOLF CLUB
Littlestone
Kent TN28 8RB
England
Tel: 01797 363355
Fax: 01797 362740

THE LONDON CLUB
South Ash Manor Estate
Kent TN15 7EN
England
Tel: 01474 879899
Fax: 01474 879912

MOOR ALLERTON GOLF CLUB
Coal Road, Leeds
West Yorkshire LS17 9NH
England
Tel: 01132 665209
Fax: 01132 661413

MOOR PARK GOLF CLUB
Rickmansworth
Hertfordshire WD3 1QN
England
Tel: 01923 773146
Fax: 01923 777109

MOORTOWN GOLF CLUB
Alwoodley, Leeds
West Yorkshire LS17 7DB
England
Tel: 01132 683636
Fax: 01132 680986

NEFYN & DISTRICT
GOLF CLUB
Morfa Nefyn LL53 6DA
North Wales
Tel: 01758 720966
Fax: 01758 720476

NORTH WALES GOLF CLUB
Llandudno LL30 2DZ
North Wales
Tel: 01492 876878
Fax: 01492 872420

NOTTS GOLF CLUB
Kirkby in Ashfield
Nottinghamshire NG17 7QR
England
Tel: 01623 753225
Fax: 01623 753655

THE OXFORDSHIRE
GOLF CLUB
Milton Common
Oxfordshire OX9 2PU
England
Tel: 01844 278300
Fax: 01844 278003

PENNARD GOLF CLUB
Southgate, Swansea SA3 2BT
South Wales
Tel: 01792 233451
Fax: 01792 234886

PRINCE'S GOLF CLUB
Sandwich Bay
Kent CT13 9QB
England
Tel: 01304 611118
Fax: 01304 612000

PWLLHELI GOLF CLUB
Pwllheli LL53 5PS
North Wales
Tel: 01758 701644
Fax: same as phone

PYLE & KENFIG GOLF CLUB
Kenfig, near Bridgend
CF33 4PU
South Wales
Tel: 01656 783093
Fax: 01656 772822

QUEENWOOD GOLF CLUB
Ottershaw
Surrey KT16 OAQ
England
Tel: 01932 872178
Fax: 01932 874363

ROYAL ASHDOWN FOREST
GOLF CLUB
Forest Row
East Sussex RH18 5LR
England
Tel: 01342 822247
Fax: 01342 825211

James W. Finegan

ROYAL BIRKDALE GOLF CLUB
Southport
Merseyside PR8 2LX
England
Tel: 01704 567920
Fax: 01704 562327

ROYAL BLACKHEATH
GOLF CLUB
Eltham
London SE9 5AF
England
Tel: 0208 850 1763
Fax: 0208 859 0150

ROYAL CINQUE PORTS GOLF CLUB
Deal
Kent CT14 6RF
England
Tel: 01304 374007
Fax: 01304 379530

ROYAL CROMER GOLF CLUB
Cromer
Norfolk NR27 0JH
England
Tel: 01263 512884
Fax: same as phone

ROYAL GUERNSEY GOLF CLUB
L'Ancresse Vale GY3 5BY
Guernsey
Channel Islands
Tel: 01481 245070
Fax: 01481 243960

ROYAL JERSEY GOLF CLUB
Grouville JE3 9BD
Jersey
Channel Islands
Tel: 01534 854416
Fax: 01534 854684

ROYAL LIVERPOOL GOLF CLUB
Hoylake
Merseyside L47 4AL
England
Tel: 01516 323101
Fax: 01516 326737

ROYAL LYTHAM & ST. ANNES
GOLF CLUB
Lytham St. Annes
Lancashire FY8 3LO
England
Tel: 01253 724206
Fax: 01253 789275

ROYAL NORTH DEVON GOLF CLUB
Westward Ho!, Bideford
Devon EX39 1HD
England
Tel: 01237 477598
Fax: 01237 423456

ROYAL PORTHCAWL GOLF CLUB
Porthcawl CF36 3UW
South Wales
Tel: 01656 782251
Fax: 01656 771687

All Courses Great and Small

ROYAL ST. DAVID'S GOLF CLUB
Harlech LL46 2UB
North Wales
Tel: 01766 780361
Fax: 01766 781110

ROYAL ST. GEORGE'S GOLF CLUB
Sandwich
Kent CT13 9PB
England
Tel: 01304 613090
Fax: 01304 611245

ROYAL WEST NORFOLK
GOLF CLUB
Brancaster
Norfolk PE31 8AX
England
Tel: 01485 210616
Fax: 01485 210087

ROYAL WORLINGTON AND
NEWMARKET GOLF CLUB
Worlington
Suffolk IP28 8SD
England
Tel: 01638 712216
Fax: 01638 717787

RYE GOLF CLUB
Camber
East Sussex TN31 7QS
England
Tel: 01797 225241
Fax: 01797 225460

ST. ENODOC GOLF CLUB
Rock, Wadebridge
Cornwall PL27 8LD
England
Tel: 01208 863216
Fax: 01208 862976

ST. GEORGE'S HILL GOLF CLUB
Weybridge
Surrey KT13 0NL
England
Tel: 01932 847758
Fax: 01932 821564

ST. PIERRE HOTEL, GOLF &
COUNTRY CLUB
St. Pierre Park
Chepstow NP6 6YA
South Wales
Tel: 01291 625261
Fax: 01291 629975

SAND MOOR GOLF CLUB
Alwoodley, Leeds
West Yorkshire LS17 7DJ
England
Tel: 01132 685180
Fax: 01132 661105

SAUNTON GOLF CLUB
Braunton
North Devon EX33 1LG
England
Tel: 01271 812436
Fax: 01271 814241

SEASCALE GOLF CLUB
Seascale
Cumbria CA20 1QL
England
Tel: 01946 728202
Fax: same as phone

SEATON CAREW GOLF CLUB
Seaton Carew
County Durham TS25 1DE
England
Tel: 01429 890660
Fax: 01429 279114

SHERINGHAM GOLF CLUB
Sheringham
Norfolk NR26 8HG
England
Tel: 01263 823488
Fax: 01263 825189

SILLOTH-ON-SOLWAY
GOLF CLUB
Silloth-on-Solway
Cumbria CA5 4BL
England
Tel: 01697 331304
Fax: 01697 331782

SOUTHERNDOWN GOLF CLUB
Ewenny, near Bridgend
SA3 2BT
South Wales
Tel: 01656 880476
Fax: 01656 880317

SOUTHPORT & AINSDALE
GOLF CLUB
Southport
Merseyside PR8 3LG
England
Tel: 01704 578000
Fax: 01704 570896

STAPLEFORD PARK GOLF CLUB
near Melton Mowbray
Leicestershire LE14 2EF
England
Tel: 01572 787522
Fax: 01572 787651

STOKE POGES GOLF CLUB
Stoke Park
Buckinghamshire SL2 4PG
England
Tel: 01753 717171
Fax: 01753 717181

SUNNINGDALE GOLF CLUB
Sunningdale, Ascot
Berkshire SL5 9PR
England
Tel: 01344 621681
Fax: 01344 624154

SWINLEY FOREST GOLF CLUB
Ascot
Berkshire SL5 9LE
England
Tel: 01344 874979
Fax: 01344 874733

All Courses Great and Small

TENBY GOLF CLUB
Tenby SA70 7NP
South Wales
Tel: 01834 844447
Fax: 01834 842978

THETFORD GOLF CLUB
Thetford
Norfolk IP24 3NE
England
Tel: 01842 752169
Fax: 01842 766212

TREVOSE GOLF & COUNTRY
CLUB
Padstow
North Cornwall PL28 8JB
England
Tel: 01841 520208
Fax: 01841 521057

WALLASEY GOLF CLUB
Wallasey
Merseyside L45 8LA
England
Tel: 01516 911024
Fax: 01516 388988

WALTON HEATH GOLF CLUB
Walton-on-the-Hill, Tadworth
Surrey KT20 7TP
England
Tel: 01737 812380
Fax: 01737 814225

WENTWORTH CLUB
Virginia Water
Surrey GU25 4LS
England
Tel: 01344 842201
Fax: 01344 842804

WEST CORNWALL GOLF CLUB
Levant
West Cornwall TR26 3DZ
England
Tel: 01736 753177
No Fax

WEST HILL GOLF CLUB
Brookwood
Surrey GU24 0BH
England
Tel: 01483 474365
Fax: 01483 474252

WEST LANCASHIRE GOLF CLUB
Blundellsands, Liverpool
Merseyside L23 8SZ
England
Tel: 01519 245662
Fax: 01519 314448

WEST SUSSEX GOLF CLUB
Pulborough
West Sussex RH20 2EN
England
Tel: 01798 872563
Fax: 01798 872033

James W. Finegan

WOBURN GOLF &
COUNTRY CLUB
Bow Brickhill
Buckinghamshire MK17 9LJ
England
Tel: 01908 370756
Fax: 01908 378436

WOKING GOLF CLUB
Woking
Surrey GU22 0JZ
England
Tel: 01483 760053
Fax: 01483 772441

WOODHALL SPA GOLF CLUB
Woodhall Spa
Lincolnshire LN10 6PU
England
Tel: 01526 352511
Fax: 01526 354020

WORPLESDON GOLF CLUB
Woking
Surrey GU22 0RA
England
Tel: 01483 472277
Fax: 01483 473303

Hotels

In telephoning England or Wales, the country code is 44.

ATLANTIC HOTEL
St. Brelade
Jersey JE3 8HE
Channel Islands
Tel: 01534 744101
Fax: 01534 744102

THE BELFRY
Wishaw
Warwickshire B76 9PR
England
Tel: 01675 470301
Fax: 01675 470256

BELL HOTEL
Sandwich
Kent CT13 9EF
England
Tel: 01304 613388
Fax: 01304 615308

BERYSTEDE HOTEL
Bagshot Road, Sunninghill
Ascot, Berkshire SL5 9JH
England
Tel: 01344 623311
Fax: 01344 872301

BLACKBECK INN
near Egremont
Cumbria CA22 2NY
England
Tel: 01946 841661
Fax: 01946 841007

BONTDDHU HALL COUNTRY
HOUSE HOTEL
Bontddhu, near Dolgellau
LL40 2UF
North Wales
Tel: 01341 430661
Fax: 01341 430284

BOWLER HAT HOTEL
Prenton, near Birkenhead
Merseyside CH43 2HH
England
Tel: 01516 524931
Fax: 01516 538127

CELTIC MANOR RESORT
Coldra Woods, Newport
NP6 2YA
South Wales
Tel: 01633 413000
Fax: 01633 412910

James W. Finegan

CHARNWOOD HOTEL
Blyth, Worksop
Nottinghamshire S81 8HF
England
Tel: 01909 591610
Fax: 01909 591429

CHEWTON GLEN
New Milton
Hampshire BH25 6OS
England
Tel: 1 800 344 5087
Fax: 1 800 398 4534

COED-Y-MWSTWR HOTEL
Coychurch, Bridgend
CF35 6AF
South Wales
Tel: 01656 860621
Fax: 01656 863122

DANESFIELD HOUSE
Henley Road, Marlow-on-Thames
Buckinghamshire SL7 2EY
England
Tel: 01628 891010
Fax: 01628 890408

DEVONSHIRE ARMS COUNTRY
HOUSE HOTEL
Skipton
North Yorkshire BD23 6AJ
England
Tel: 01756 710441
Fax: 01756 710564

EGERTON GREY COUNTRY HOUSE
Porthkerry, near Cardiff
CF6 9BJ
South Wales
Tel: 01446 711666
Fax: 01446 711696

FEATHERS HOTEL
Woodstock
Oxfordshire OX20 1SX
England
Tel: 01993 812291
Fax: 01993 813158

THE GOLF HOTEL
Silloth-on-Solway
Cumbria CA7 4AB
England
Tel: 01697 331438
Fax: 01697 332582

GRIM'S DYKE HOTEL
Old Redding, Harrow Weald
London HA3 6SH
England
Tel: 02083 853100
Fax: 02089 544560

HALL GARTH GOLF & COUNTRY
CLUB HOTEL
Coatham Mundeville, Darlington
County Durham DL1 3LU
England
Tel: 01325 300400
Fax: 01325 310083

All Courses Great and Small

HILTON HOTEL
Maidstone
Kent ME14 5AA
England
Tel: 01622 734322
Fax: 01622 734600

HOLBECK HALL HOTEL
South Cliff, Scarborough
North Yorkshire YO11 2XX
England
Tel: 01723 374374
Fax: 01723 351114

HORSTED PLACE
Little Horsted, Uckfield
East Sussex TN22 5TS
England
Tel: 01825 750581
Fax: 01825 750459

HOSTE ARMS HOTEL
Burnham Market
Norfolk PE31 8HD
England
Tel: 01328 738777
Fax: 01328 730103

KINGS ARMS HOTEL
Askrigg-in-Wensleydale
Leyburn, North Yorkshire
DL8 3HQ
England
Tel: 01969 650258
Fax: 01969 650635

KINGS ARMS HOTEL
Hide Hill, Berwick-upon-Tweed
Northumberland TD15 1EJ
England
Tel: 01289 307454
Fax: 01289 308867

LA FREGATE HOTEL & RESTAURANT
Les Cotils, St. Peter Port
Guernsey GY1 1UT
Channel Islands
Tel: 01481 724624
Fax: 01481 720443

LANGAR HALL
Langar
Nottinghamshire NG13 9HG
England
Tel: 01949 860559
Fax: 01949 861045

LE STRANGE ARMS HOTEL
Old Hunstanton
Norfolk PE36 6JJ
England
Tel: 01485 534411
Fax: 01485 534724

LONDON OUTPOST OF
CARNEGIE CLUB
69 Cadogan Gardens
London SW3 2RB
England
Tel: 020 7589 7333
Fax: 020 7581 4958

James W. Finegan

Longueville Manor
St. Saviour
Jersey JE2 7WF
Channel Islands
Tel: 01534 725501
Fax: 01534 731613

Maybank Hotel
Aberdovey LL35 0PT
North Wales
Tel: 01654 767500
No Fax

Mermaid Inn
Rye
East Sussex TN31 7EU
England
Tel: 01797 223065
Fax: 01797 225069

Metropole Hotel
Padstow
Cornwall PL28 8DB
England
Tel: 01841 532486
Fax: 01841 532867

New Hall
Walmley Road,
Sutton Coldfield
West Midlands B76 1QX
England
Tel: 01213 782442
Fax: 01213 784637

Old Rectory
Llansanfraid Glan Conwy
LL28 5LF
North Wales
Tel: 01492 580611
Fax: 01492 584555

Oulton Hall Hotel
Oulton, Leeds
West Yorkshire
LS26 8HN
England
Tel: 01132 821000
Fax: 01132 828066

Penmaenuchaf Hall
Penmaenpool,
Dolgellau LL40 1YB
North Wales
Tel: 01341 422129
Fax: 01341 422787

Pennally Abbey
Pennally SA70 7PY
South Wales
Tel: 01834 843033
Fax: 01834 844714

Petwood Hotel
Woodhall Spa
Lincolnshire LN10 6QF
England
Tel: 01526 352411
Fax: 01526 353473

All Courses Great and Small

PLAS BODEGROES
Pwllheli LL53 5TH
North Wales
Tel: 01758 612363
Fax: 01758 701247

PORTMEIRION HOTEL
Portmeirion LL48 6ER
North Wales
Tel: 01766 770228
Fax: 01766 771331

PRINCE OF WALES HOTEL
Lord Street,
Southport
Merseyside PR8 1JS
England
Tel: 01704 536688
Fax: 01704 543488

RISING SUN HOTEL
Lynmouth
Devon EX35 6EG
England
Tel: 01598 753223
Fax: 01598 753480

ROYAL PORTHCAWL DORMY
HOUSE
Porthcawl CF36 3UW
South Wales
Tel: 01656 782251
Fax: 01656 771687

SAUNTON SANDS HOTEL
Saunton, near Braunton
North Devon EX33 1LQ
England
Tel: 01271 890212
Fax: 01271 890145

SEAFOOD RESTAURANT
Riverside, Padstow
Cornwall PL28 8BY
England
Tel: 01841 532700
Fax: 01841 532942

STAPLEFORD PARK
near Melton Mowbray
Leicestershire LE14 2EF
England
Tel: 01572 787522
Fax: 01572 787651

ST. PIERRE HOTEL, GOLF &
COUNTRY CLUB
St. Pierre Park, Chepstow
NP6 6YA
South Wales
Tel: 01291 625261
Fax: 01291 629975

STOKE PARK CLUB
Park Road, Stoke Poges
Buckinghamshire SL2 4PG
England
Tel: 01753 717171
Fax: 01753 717181

James W. Finegan

WHITE LION INN
Tenterden
Kent TN30 6BD
England
Tel: 01580 765077
Fax: 01580 764157

WOOLTON REDBOURNE HOTEL
Acrefield Road
Woolton, Liverpool L25 5JN
England
Tel: 01514 282152
Fax: 01514 211501

ABOUT THE AUTHOR

JAMES W. FINEGAN has made at least forty trips to the British Isles since 1971, always with his golf clubs in tow. He has written extensively about the pleasures of links golf for a variety of publications, including *Golf, Golf Journal,* and *The Philadelphia Inquirer.* He is the author of *Blasted Heaths and Blessed Greens* and *Emerald Fairways and Foam-Flecked Seas.* He lives in Villanova, Pennsylvania.

Printed in the United States
By Bookmasters